Going Native

going native

TOM HARMER

UNIVERSITY OF NEW MEXICO PRESS

ALBUQUERQUE

Library of Congress Cataloging-in-Publication Data:

Harmer, Tom, 1947–
Going native / by Tom Harmer.— 1st ed.
p. cm.
ISBN 0-8263-2317-0 (cloth : alk. paper)
1. Indians of North America—Religion. 2. Indians of North
America—Social life and customs. 3. Spiritual life. I. Title.
E98.R3 H24 2001
813'.6—dc21
00–011591

Design: *Mina Yamashita*

For Phil Bock

and

Beth Hadas

A Note on Language

I have invented my own orthography for representing the Salish Indian words used in this book. Rather than use the more accurate but inaccessible orthographies of linguists, I've tried to capture pronunciation in a way more familiar to English readers. In sounding out the Salish words, the usual English pronunciations apply, except for *x* which is a guttural "h" sound like *ach* in German, ' which is used to separate syllables usually run together in English or as a glottal stop, and *tl* which is one sound, similar to the "tl" in "bottle." Salish consonants are more complex than I've represented them here, and vowels without stress accent are usually barely sounded. The terms "Indian," "Salish," "Native," and *Skélux* are used interchangeably in this book, as they are on the ground where this story takes place. More comment on the writing of this book can be found in the Afterword.

1

Driving my old pickup truck south through the summer lush irrigated fields and orchards of southern British Columbia, I had the feeling something more than just another illegal border crossing was coming up. Something unseen lay across the divide, something besides the home of my Indian activist hitchhiker, Jim Woods, something that was going to make all the years of being on the run worth it. The certainty of how badly I needed something like that made me look around for some sign of what was coming.

What I noticed were the nighthawks, hundreds of them. Filling the opaque air of late afternoon, feasting on the rise of insects, they swooped and darted like giant crook-winged swallows, maneuvering in that erratic, wing-pumping, rakish way of theirs. The mountains are so close and so high on both sides of this narrow valley that the sun goes behind long before evening, cooling shadows fill with the release of moisture, alfalfa, and apple smells, and bugs drift over the highway. The windshield is so splattered with their colorful insides I can hardly see.

"Turn off here," said Jim, my passenger, my reason for coming this way. We were high on the south side of the valley where the paved highway turned away through the mountains, and I steered the truck onto a narrow dirt road over sagebrush hills.

"The border's not far, just a few miles," he said, bouncing in his seat as we went over rough spots. Still smelling of sweat from standing for hours in the merciless summer sun by the highway where I picked him up, he rode loosely in his seat like a cowboy, the thought of grabbing something to hold onto probably not even occurring to him. He was going home, and I was heading south by any road that went that way, back to the States, to Jimmy Carter America—home, too, though where exactly, I didn't know. We were out of sight of the main valley, winding through sandy hills, looking for a place to cross the border unnoticed because Jim was a wanted man, though the placid look on his wide brown face, his tank top and baggy chinos and tennies didn't fit my picture of a man on the run since Wounded Knee, wanting to slip home for some R&R before heading back to the trenches of Red Power activism.

Being an Okanogan meant his people's homeland was split by the invisible line of the international boundary that somewhere up ahead went down one mountain, across the sage hills and up the other mountain. He grew up knowing all the remote places where you could get a car across. What surprised me was how he turned out to be so gentle and funny on the ride down, nothing like the loud, bitter AIMster I expected once he told me where he was coming from and where he wanted to go. A big, big man who carried his weight like a rodeo star, he spoke in that Red English so soft and musical, that touch of rural border and a whole lot of Rez. His long glossy black unwashed ponytail fit perfectly through the opening at the back of his baseball cap. His only luggage was a carry-on flight bag.

Voices in my head were telling me, You got to slow down, stay awhile, stay in one place long enough so the land can start speaking to you. Migration fever. How I ever got into it, I don't know. On the move, never staying long enough in one place to know where I was, really. Make money where I could: Pump gas, trim trees, set chokers, feed cattle. But doing the rivers, the mountains, the forests, the canyons. Build a fire, hunt with a rifle, pick berries, fish. Some old European barbarian wanderlust transplanted into a pickup truck bashed-in on one side, crisscrossing the West.

Well, maybe I do remember how I came to this. They were opening my mail, watching me. I'd been a bad boy. Ran off to Canada in the middle of the war, helped buddies, even strangers, sneak the border. Even then I was like a Stone Age man, some kind of scout or throwback using ancient instinctive skills in urbanized modern North America. Watch the signs, sniff out the trail, look like something else, let the land tell you its story. Let the knowing how to do it bubble up from inside. Depend on my crocodile brain to shake them off my trail. Never stay long enough to let them catch up. It felt like I was born to escape Scot-free. Only I couldn't figure out how to land somewhere.

Always heading off to somewhere else started to bother me, when I wasn't enjoying it to the hilt. Something about knowing the trees and highways, the trails and the elk herds, better than I knew my own kind. Some I didn't want to know . . . the tie and white shirt who ran the little logging company but couldn't tell a loon cry from a thrush calling from deep forest. The rancher in his sixties whose cows roamed the public land like lords of the earth fouling the clear stream by my campsite with their immense droppings. But I had to eat and buy gas. So I went to work for them, cutting down big ponderosa pines with a chainsaw; even rode fence on a cow spread until the rancher shot a red tail hawk out of the sky with his .22.

They killed trees and hawks so easily because they weren't thinking about it. They were stuck on something else, like money in the bank, or what a lord of the wild they were to shoot hawks out of the sky. Scum of the earth, still gutting her for whatever she had to offer. But they were good men, too, decent and hard-working, and I worked for them, trying to stay out there, stay free. Then moved on.

Where could I go to ground? Take a stand? Be a local? It eluded me. I was too taken with what lay ahead, wondering what the next range of mountains glowing red in the sunset could offer. But as I migrated, I began to look with different eyes. Here? Is this the place? This particular valley, in this particular range, under this particular sky? I had lost the thread of my own life and had no way to tell. It was all so alive, so full of moods, smells, voices, and native languages.

And it was all mine. How could I stop moving and settle down?

Because it hurt. I was free, true. Scot-free. But who knew? Who cared? I was nobody, nothing, invisible. I needed to shake this solitude. Seek the company of my own kind. Talk to somebody, make contact. And in the infallible logic of right time and place, there's my hitchhiker Jim standing on the gravel, shiny with sweat. Like me, he's a border-runner, a son of nature, an escapee from the world of authority and deadly force. I don't think he would have told me anything about himself if I hadn't blurted out painful bits and pieces of my own story in the need to hear my own voice proclaim to someone who I was and what I was doing on earth. Most Indians I know wait quietly until they see what the relationship is going to be before they open up to a stranger. So I filled the void with myself, my passion, my words, giving him the full force of my desperate longing for a home. Long before I'm done venting, he's inserting his observations, his musical agreements, deftly blending our two journeys into one, "Yah, that's where I'm going, too. Home. We can run the border. Place I know," until the whole thing falls into place like it was meant to be, and we're raising a cloud of dust a mile high along the narrow dirt road.

Twenty-pound blocks of cedar wood left over from my job that summer splitting shakes on the Illecilliwaet River bounced around in the back of the truck as we crossed a dry wash and came to a fork in the road. Jim waved me to the right, so the truck ground up a cobblestone hillside in first gear, going slower and slower. At the top I looked in the rearview mirror at the dust rising like a marker of our run to the border lit by a sudden yellow shaft of sunlight shining through a gap in the mountains. Saw half my own face illuminated in the mirror, like someone familiar looking on, the Anglo cowboy sideburns, the mustache ever since the teenage car wreck left a web of scar on my upper lip. And that look in the eyes of burning concentration. No matter how many times I've run the border and nothing goes wrong, every time is the first time.

Jim looks at me, looks back at the shining pillar of yellow dust, back at me. "Nothin' to worry about. I've made this crossing hundreds of times. They don't even watch this area."

"Why not?"

"Free right to cross. And here, this is what you call a hot spot. The reserve on this side, allotments on the other. You don't think we're going to drive in a twenty-mile circle and cross at the border station just to visit family two miles away? No way. There's a barbed wire fence, but it's just to keep the cows apart. Besides, we're going to cross over and get to my mom's house okay. I called her last night. She had a dream that I came home on my uncle's birthday—today. Want to go to a birthday party, eh?"

"Sure," I said. The sense that there was something bigger, meant to be, that I was being let in on, bit by bit, grew stronger. The road came out on a rolling plateau covered with brush and cheatgrass, so dry it looked like no rain had fallen for months. We could see for miles in every direction. We passed an abandoned log cabin, door missing, rusted machinery lying in the weeds all around, and the droppings of cattle thick on the bare ground under the eaves. Mountains to the left glowed in the last light of afternoon. Then, abruptly, there was the barbed wire fence, freshly repaired across the double track leading into the United States. I stopped the truck and we got out. Nothing but the fence in the entire landscape indicated any kind of national transition.

"Hey! Anybody there?" I hollered. "I want in! You can't keep me out—I'm an American citizen! This is an American-made truck!" A cottontail rabbit darted away, his cover blown.

"They must of got wind that you were smuggling cedar into the States," Jim said, grinning. He headed off on foot down the fenceline to the east; I went west. A fresh breeze blew the dust away, and except for the rustle of sagebrush against my jeans and the primordial booms of nighthawks as they came out of dives overhead, the silence was deep, endless. Swatting at mosquitoes, I came over a rise that gave me a view down into the main valley on the American side. It took my breath away.

A mountain so steep few fir trees had found a foothold rose up six thousand feet from the flat valley floor to a summit still holding pockets of snow. The River of White Swans, Similkameen, meandered in loops and sloughs through a parkland of cottonwood and pine, hayfields and horse herds, around a distant spur of the mountain and out of sight. Beyond glimmered a lake that filled the valley. The wall of mountain was a palpable presence, something so massive and so near I could feel its naked brooding granitic power. It was the most beautiful place in the world.

The last rays of the sun lit up the topmost point, glowing deep gold, fading slowly to pink. Mountain goats moved like white phantoms with preposterous ease along the vertical, seemingly bare rock.

Jim came puffing up behind me, stopped, said "Ah."

"Man, that mountain is something," I said. "This whole place here . . . it's so beautiful!"

"Yeah, that's Chopaka, our sacred mountain. We're almost home." We lingered. The wind rose, blowing down the corridor of mountains with a damp coolness over arid brush, bringing the smell of fir forest and lichen-covered rock. A star appeared.

Jim turned back. "I found the new crossing," he said. At the truck he had me back up to a place where fresh tire tracks took off to the left through a grassy swale. We followed the trail to an opening recently cut in the five-strand fence at a low point between two hills, and drove through. Regaining the dirt track, we flew south trailing a cloud of U.S. dust now, lights on in the deepening twilight, passing ranch houses, cattle, wheeled sprinkler lines, beer bottles, our route becoming a well-traveled county road. Closer and closer to the foot of Chopaka looming higher and higher like a black monolith blocking out the sky to the west. Nighthawks darted right in front of the windshield, snatching flying insects before they collided. Even though this land had been forced into the mold of Indo-European thought, I'd been living on blind feeling for so long I could tell the mountain had eyes and ears in the vast gloom, watching the truck headlights search through this lower world, listening to the beating of our hearts drawing closer.

Cars and trucks passed us going the other way, just about every head covered with a cowboy hat. I sang cowboy tunes in my lamest country and western voice, including the one I made up as my migration theme song:

> As I go down this long, lonesome highway
> Lookin' for a place to call my own,
> I know that I will find it somewhere, someday,
> And then, I will no longer roam

all the way to a paved road, orchards, a broad lake, and in the dark we pulled into a place where I could see lights shining from a home back in the cottonwoods.

Always living there, where the Similkameen turns and slows in green-banked sloughs, in a narrow valley like a horseshoe around sagebrush slopes, under the steep cliff face of Chopaka Mountain, and living there still. But now instead of earth lodges there's a double-wide mobile home perched high above the flood level but close to the bank, so Jim's mother, Charlene, can look down on the greenish roil, the glacial meltwater flowing past as she washes, cooks, daydreams, staring at the clouds drifting off the peak above.

Her mother, Jim's grandmother, is boss here, a fragile unsmiling woman rarely moving from her cushioned kitchen chair, ruling with her silence and her way of ruffling her apron on her lap when the children get too loud. No introductions are made, I'm simply, pleasantly, handed a plate of food and room is made for me to sit down near Grandma. I can smell the river outside in the dark, carried on breezes rustling the curtains. I'm ravenous, and the fried chicken and gravy are delicious, but what's this black Jell-O stuff?

"It's *skwálip*, tree moss. You like it?" Charlene says. She seems to be everywhere at once, energetically supervising the other women and girls in making sure everybody gets plenty to eat. "Yes, it's like nothing I've ever tasted." When she brings more new foods, steaming camas and bitterroots, Indian ice cream, she makes a face just like I've seen Jim do: Puffs out her cheeks, bites her lip in concentration as she serves the food, then a bright smile but never looking me in the eye. In fact nobody looks me in the eye. Must be some kind of cultural thing. I instinctively like it. I can feel where they're coming from when there's no eye-searching going on. Must be twenty people in this large room, but nobody is awkward, nobody too loud except children, nobody showing any unease about the White man present. Where I see a lot of family resemblance between Jim and his mother, Charlene, I see none in Jim's grandmother. Everything about her is narrow, small, and wiry. But she has such a graceful presence. She starts to grill me in a barely audible voice about where I come from, each reply leading to another question, until she's got me talking about myself and relaxed, which was her intention. I tell her how I love that mountain out there.

"Yes, I been lookin' up at that mountain allllll my life. I was born here and here is where I will die. I neeeeever wanted to live anyplace else."

The birthday man, Jim's uncle, Clayton Tommy, sits in the male lineup along one table, no more a celebrity than anybody else, short and stocky, worn from a life of hard work outdoors. His short gray hair stubbles out over his ears, and he lifts his face, jutting out his chin to talk in an English dominated by the phonemes of his native Okanogan.

"That my nephew you smuggle across," he says with a big smile.

"My pleasure," I say. Come to think of it, I haven't seen Jim since we came in. Then I see him standing by the door, his hair loose and damp from taking a shower, clean clothes on, talking with another man. The other man seems drunk, weaving, eyes unfocussed. Short and muscular, very dark, with a faint mustache, he finally focuses on me and stares belligerently while he nods at what Jim is saying to him.

Then Clayton to me: "So you just passin' through?"

"I was. But then when I saw this country—that big mountain— from up there at the fence crossing, something really touched me. Maybe another White man showing up and settling down on your land isn't good news to you guys. But here I am . . ."

"They come and they go. We the only ones always here. Some Whites been here ranching a long time, couple of generations. They pretty good people. Now we see a lot more comin'. Apple orchards plantin' all over. That Chopaka, big mountain, eh?"

"Yeah, I saw snow up there, and mountain goats going across the cliffs, like walking on air."

"Them goats speak for that mountain, tell us how we gonna live. Always watchin' out for us."

Jim clumped over in shiny new cowboy boots and sat down, listening to the old man telling me stuff I really wasn't able to follow. Then he took it upon himself to educate me about the Native history of their homeland. How the mountain goats were to the Salish-speaking people of that interior mountain world like the bison were to the Lakota on the plains. Not so much that the goats were the food, clothing, shelter, and tools as the bison were, although they were eaten and their wool was woven into blankets. But that they were where you had to go if you wanted to approach the higher powers of this land, the highest and most difficult places looking down on the homes and lives of everyone. Those goats on Chopaka were the gatekeepers, guardians, messengers of the superpowers like Thunder and North Wind and Chopaka itself.

Jim told me how when gold was discovered and Whites flooded

in and the land was taken away, his people held fast to their homes and farms and ultimately were not forced to remove to the nearby Colville Reservation, itself reduced after further mineral discoveries and ultimately opened to White settlement. And how government agents came and drew lines around their tiny settlements like this one on the Similkameen River, calling them "allotments," and secured their future to live exactly where they always had.

Later, when I came out of the trailer's small bathroom and passed through an unlighted alcove, I saw a toddler in a crib beside an open window. The child was naked except for a disposable diaper and his little bottom jutted up in the chilly air. I pulled a blanket over him to keep him warm, and Jim's sister appeared at my side, a big, slow-mannered woman wearing jeans and a bright red velour blouse with beaded edging.

"He always just kicks it off. This is Brandon, Jim's nephew. You got any kids?" She closed the window and we stood talking about family things until the dark, mustachioed drunk came in. Turned out he was her husband, Jim's brother-in-law. He grabbed her arm and pulled her away, slurring, "C'mon, I don't want you talkin' to him!"

People were leaving. Some were outside the front door, smoking cigarettes in the porch light. I looked around outside for Jim. At the riverbank I suddenly realized I was standing by a group of men almost invisible to my eye. Hunter-gatherers in cowboy hats and baseball caps, standing around in the windy dark talking about the import of clouds building over Chopaka, the recent movements of deer, the slap of a beaver's tail in the river gleaming under stars. When their talk lagged, I told Jim what happened at the baby's crib. "What was that all about?" I asked.

One of the men laughed. Jim hemmed and hawed, then said, "Something we deal with, all the time, from your people." When I still didn't get it, he got impatient. "There's Indian people don't like White people, don't want nothin' to do with them, hate 'em. Like racism, you dig?" I felt naive and out of my element. I'd been operating by being in the moment, following the lead of events and circumstances, certain of something good for me unfolding in this new land. It was sobering to realize how open these people really were, considering what they'd been through for generations at the hands of my own people. Murder, conquest, forced to the bottom of a modern economy, children coerced into learning a foreign language and expected to live as my people did. It was actually kind of unfathomable how friendly they were to me. Would I be just another welcomed, privileged White visitor who smoothed it all over with a syrupy murmur at how "the natives were friendly"?

A sadness came over me that blocked any further thought. A grief that made no sense weighed on my shoulders. "So, well, guess I should go find a place to camp," I said, trying to throw off the mood. "Look around and see what I can do to make a living." But my words came out in a cracking voice. I felt like crying. It had nothing to do with Jim's revelation about his brother-in-law's hatred of Whites—it was more like everything crashing down around my ears, the rush of events coming to a halt in a moment of self-consciousness. I stood there not moving, not saying anything, tears coming down my cheeks, waiting for my unmanly seizure to pass. There was a rushing sound like wind in the trees that got louder and louder.

"*Aaaa,*" Clayton said, making a brushing motion with his hand over one of my shoulders. The man named Johnny, who wore a new cowboy hat with an eagle feather hanging loosely off the back of the brim, stepped forward and blew a cloud of cigarette smoke in my face. He weaved the cigarette's glowing tip around in front of my body. My mood instantly passed, my tears stopped. I looked around refreshed. Clayton looked so strange with his arm held high so he could reach above my shoulder.

"Tall son of a bitch, isn't he, eh?" Johnny said, stepping back. Clayton's hand dropped. He said in a high, singsong voice, like a ritual invocation, "You camp right here, *Skélux*, see what the morning bring." He spoke Salish to the others, and all but Jim strolled away. The cottonwood trees rustled in the breeze. I was suddenly so tired I could hardly stand.

"You got a sleeping bag or something?" he said.

I mumbled something about maybe I'd drive up into the mountains and camp, not quite comfortable with this show of concern for me, although I was exhausted. I had an urge to run off.

"Uncle Clayton knows what he's doing. He means camp right here, where the power came over you."

"I don't know about that. Well, it's a warm night. Mosquitoes aren't too bad here next to the river."

"You're a funny dude. You think all this was just an accident today? I thought you were looking for a place to call home. You just gonna drive away?"

I slumped down, too tired to argue. Jim went and got a flashlight, dug around in the truck for my bedroll and came back, the flashlight beam darting through leaves and branches.

"Look, I don't want to sound stupid, but I don't know what that was all about," I said as he dropped the bag. He looked around by the light of the beam: water, tree, sky, riverbank. In the west there was only the darkness of Chopaka lost in gathering clouds. Since he wasn't going to say anything, I asked, "What was that Clayton called me?"

"Skélux? That's our word for ourself in our language. Like 'Lakota' is for the Sioux. *Skélux* means like, 'person.' Him saying that to you is like he's calling you 'Indian.' The older people use that for White people who act like human beings, like natural people, none of that racist bullshit."

I rolled out the sleeping bag and sat on it. Jim continued to stand nearby, but he shut off the flashlight. As if reading my mind, he said, "You don't know anything about power, about spirits, do you?"

"What I read in books."

He laughed out loud. "Well, my uncle and Johnny Stemilt did just like they do when the spirit comes over a person in the dance house. Only this isn't the right time and place for that. So they wiped you off. Fed that spirit tobacco and stayed with you till the spirit backed off. You believe that?"

"I don't know. I don't know what I was grieving about."

"Me neither. You're a funny dude."

He walked away and I was alone with the wet murmur of river and wind in the trees. I stretched out and stared up at the stars. The Milky Way was a shimmering road cutting the sky almost in half, running from north to south. Where there was a noticeable gap in the star belt, the bright summer star Vega glimmered almost directly overhead. I felt as if I was lying on the beating heart of the earth. That I was for the first time ever exactly where I belonged. As I faded into sleep, I thought, how funny that nature has always been my refuge, and there I found the Indians, for whom it is life itself.

2

Time passed with the seasons on Chopaka Mountain. I got a job on a ranch where they let me live in an old trailer. From the front door, I could look up at the peak sitting off there to the northwest on the other side of Palmer Lake like a calendar photo, a silent witness to my new life going to ground in one place. The ranch was run by a clan of transplanted Montanans who had struck it rich when oil was discovered on their played-out high plains spread. Here in these narrow mountain valleys of Washington State they played at being cowboys, off on horseback with a passion every day, leaving the real work to me and the foreman, Stuart Bolster. We hauled hay to feed cattle, repaired miles of barbed wire fence, moved irrigation lines in alfalfa fields, drove the trucks, and did the other chores our gentleman ranchers disdained.

Stuart was about as local as you could get, having been born within sight of the ranch where we worked. He entertained me during our lunch breaks with stories of life in this region, called the "Okanogan" after the Indians and the main river running north-south in a wide valley to the east of us. How he would ride a calf to school in a one-room schoolhouse. How his dad taught him to ride a horse without holding the saddle horn: Seems the big mare bucked with the young Stuart aboard, so the eight-year-old "slapped leather" to keep from being thrown off. His dad leaned over from his own horse and struck his son's hand holding the saddle horn with the heavy handle of his quirt, breaking all four fingers. "Ride like a man, or get bucked off!" his dad told him.

Lean and rangy with his denim and his boots, his ever-present beatup straw hat, rolling foul cigarettes from a can of Prince Albert tobacco, Stuart nursed a chronic bad back with endless good humor. Wherever we were working, he'd drive us to some high viewpoint for our lunch break and his daily nap. On hot summer days he'd stretch out on the ground underneath the pickup truck; in winter he'd snore away leaning against the fogged-up window with the engine on, heater blasting. Then he'd scan the countryside with binoculars. "Them goats are moving back around to the shady side of Chopaka. Looks like Swenson is finally fixing his fence where the bull broke through. All that smoke—must be havin' another sweatlodge down at the Woods place."

Since we spent so much time together, Stuart became one of my teachers as I absorbed myself in the natural world of my adopted home. He knew every mountain, every creek, every trail, and he shared his love for this place with amusement at my inability to pronounce names he'd rolled off easily all his life. Sinlahekin Valley, Sarsapkin Creek, Ellameham Mountain; Conconully, Tonasket, Keremeos. Indian names, of course, and it wasn't until I started learning to speak the throat-cracking consonants of my neighbors' native Okanogan Salish tongue that the names came easier.

Each autumn I went deer hunting with Clayton Tommy and Johnny Stemilt on the open, grassy southern slopes of Chopaka. They'd take long gossipy breaks sipping sweet tea from a thermos at some vantage point and describe the ways of animals we saw. I learned how to say *stla'chínum* for mule deer, *too'k'toóps* for whitetail; *ch'kílhp* for Douglas fir tree, *mrílhp* for balsam fir.

One warm day we got separated and I came to a level place high on the mountain between the two summits, right at timberline. Above me it was only a short walk to the top, so I climbed up the bouldery slope and stood in the breeze looking out over the hazy, mountainous world all around me. I made out my tiny trailer beside an apple orchard on the shore of the lake below, and Jim's mother's bigger one on the bank of the river. I sat down to sketch the mountain slopes all around in my spiral notebook, and saw movement out of the corner of my eye. A peregrine falcon landed silently not ten feet away, feathers ruffling in the breeze. He eyed me, then scanned the horizon like I'd been doing. He stood long enough for me to be amazed, then took off in a long soaring dive into the steep nothingness. When I caught up with Johnny and Clayton at our camp near a spring in dense lodgepole pine, and told them about my ascent and the falcon landing by me, they both said, *"Aaaa."* This ah-ing I was always hearing turned out to be the way Indian people in that area let you know they're listening, they hear you, they feel strongly about what you're saying, or they agree with you.

"You son-of-a-bitch White man," Johnny said with his big smile, his face marked with burn scars from a car accident in his youth. "You don't sit down on the very top, eh?"

"No, off to one side."

"That's the way to do. That top place, that belong to the spirits, eh?" He lit a Salem, blew out a cloud of menthol smoke. "Bunch of shit, talk like that, eh?"

Then one bitter cold morning in late winter Stuart and I couldn't get the tractor started to haul hay out to the herd of cattle bawling for us on the flat below the highway. We tinkered and tried everything we could think of, but the tractor wouldn't start and we were running the battery down cranking the starter. Clayton's old Ford station wagon came creeping down the icy highway full of people on the way to town, Jim's mom Charlene at the wheel. It stopped and a window rolled down in back. Clayton leaned out, his breath a cloud of steam. "Take off the distributor cap," he yelled. "It's wet inside!" He rolled up the window and Charlene drove off. How did he even know we couldn't get the tractor started?

"He's always right, damn it!" Stuart said, unclipping the cap and turning it over. "Sure enough!" Beads of condensed moisture filled the inside of the cap. "I don't know how he knows, but he always does. And he won't say nothin' if you ask him." He carried the cap into his house and dried it off with the blast from his wife's hair dryer. The tractor started right up.

There was something different about Clayton Tommy, all right, something deep and authoritative and unlikely. I found excuses to be around him, just to listen to what he had to say. My own lifelong link with the natural world and my attitudes about ignorant White destruction of it lined up with something I sensed in the Native feeling for nature. Especially for the older people, like Clayton, there was something life-and-death about their respect for nature.

The Okanogan landscape was obviously suffering. A century of logging, mining, and cattle grazing had done its work. From the Woods place I could see the scars of uranium mining on a spur running north from Chopaka. Roads had been bulldozed through nearly every mountain valley and along every ridge, stopped only by the boundary of the Pasayten Wilderness. The conversion of thousands of acres into fruit orchards was eating up the traditional winter range of mule deer, and orchardists, fuming at the losses due to starving deer herds browsing their trees, were building tall wire-mesh fences all around their land to keep them out. The decline in deer numbers was dramatic, but instead of looking at actual causes, the state game department was going after poachers.

Clayton was going to testify at hearings about proposed new regulations that would undermine the traditional Native practice of hunting out of season. It was a right long since legally terminated but not strictly enforced. An escalation in the war on poachers was about all they could come up with to solve the problem. It was the same old story. The Indians had nothing to do with the decline of the deer, but they were the first to be attacked for seeming to have special privileges.

Clayton didn't want to go. He knew the point of view he represented was laughed at. He paced back and forth, muttering to himself, making tracks in the fresh snow that started falling as I helped Jim Woods change the oil in his ancient Ford.

Jim had been reading the new proclamations out loud. "See, they don't say nothing about what's really causing it. They can't do anything about the spread of orchards or new logging roads going into every nook and cranny, eh? They have to go after us!"

Clayton cleared off the snow gathering like dry fluff on a woodblock and sat down to drink the cup of coffee Charlene brought out for him.

"They don't see how the deer *know* they are our food," he said. "You treat 'em bad, they go away. Hide from us. Go under ground. They know what is in our hearts.

"This trophy hunter, that what hurt. The deer don't like that. Takin' the biggest rack, killin' off the fathers, the grandfathers. See, they got it backward. Poachers not ruining things for the legal hunter. They take just to feed their kids.

"It's the head-hunters that ruining things. For all of us. Legal, but wrong. The deer go away, punish us, if we not take what they offer and be thankful. Not the biggest, strongest buck. That some kind of sick in the mind, to do that."

He shook his head slowly. "But I go. Somebody got to speak for the deer."

3

The winter was hard—knee-deep snow and weeks with temperatures below zero. I left the cramped comfort of my trailer only to join Stuart in the daily chore of feeding cattle in valley-bottom pastures. We'd take turns, one driving the tractor, the other forking off hay from a stack pulled behind on a trailer. The cows waited for us swathed in the arctic smoke of their own breath, crowding and mooing anxiously as we moved slowly along, leaving a trail of fragrant green on the snow flats. In the relative warmth of the tractor cab I'd look up at sheer cliffs blown bare by wind where the off-white shapes of mountain goats moved. I wondered what they found to eat in their vertical world.

The only other thing I could do was go visiting. Sit in somebody else's heated home drinking coffee and listening to stories. Town was too far off to go more often than every other week. Clayton was gone for months, staying with relatives in the Nespelem area far to the east. He was involved with the Winter Dances, called *terr'kúm*, the spirit-partner ceremonials held in longhouses every winter. I was too busy with the startup of calving season to track him down. Out in the pastures where I patrolled in the ranch pickup, bald eagles sat in ponderosa pines, waiting to feast on afterbirth, or rose up off the carcass of a stillborn calf. The Chinook winds finally blew warm from the east, melting the snow, and I got a call from Clayton asking me to drive to Spokane and give him a ride home.

On the way back we stopped at a remote homestead on the Colville Reservation where he delivered some packages from town. Since we were west of the paved highway, on a whim I took the gravel road that passes Omak Lake to get to the Okanogan Valley. He slept most of the way, but sat up and looked around when we came to the eight-mile-long lake. He talked about the wake he had attended in Spokane, the recent deaths of elders who hardly spoke English, the drinking problems of relatives.

But his mood slowly gave way to the first signs of spring showing in the hills on every side. Meadowlarks sang their plinking songs from roadside perches, flocks of robins flew by, redwing blackbirds explored the drab remains of cattail marshes. We couldn't help feeling good.

Clayton pointed to the rolling mountains on the other side of the lake and told me that up there was where the legendary Bluejay had made his medicine and killed a herd of deer for his starving people. It was just the sort of thing that had drawn me to him in the first place, locating an ancient story in the landscape, bringing the old lore to life in the modern present, awakening something vivid and real inside me. I knew the story, of course, and many others like it. Since landing in the Okanogan, I'd been hearing Clayton and other elders telling the *chaptíkx*, the ancient stories about the Animal People who set this breathing world in place.

Omak Lake sits alone in a long valley between the high lava plateaus to the west and the rounded granite mountains to the east. The timber of the high country thins to grass and brush around the rocky shores of the lake. The road runs along the western shore, climbing higher and higher above waterline as the north end gets steeper and more rugged. Clayton called it a "sacred spot" and "a good place for the spirit." He told me that as a young man he stayed ten days on the shores of the lake, sweating each day in a tiny sweatlodge, swimming in the slightly alkaline waters, wandering on the steep slopes where he watched how deer and marmots and eagles lived.

Clayton wanted to stop, to park and walk down to the lakeshore, so I found a good spot and we got out. Oh, it was good to be on my feet and moving after hours of driving! As he made his steady descent to the lake, I took my time lingering on the brushy slopes, breathing in the springlike air.

Ponderosa pine and Douglas fir trees stood alone here and there. Brilliant green shoots were appearing from brown mats of snow-flattened grass. All over the hillsides the first buttercups bloomed, their tiny, porcelain-white flowers lying flush with the ground. The first arrowhead-shaped leaves of *shmucáhwin*, balsamroot sunflower, stood up from last year's shriveled remains. And in the shadows of a deep ravine that opened out to the lake I stepped over patches of rotten snow and rocks covered with the miniature antler piles called reindeer moss.

The lake's edge was littered with granite boulders, and more boulders were scattered out into the clear blue, some barely visible under deep water. I joined Clayton on a gravelly beach protected by a windblown fir leaning out over the water. He was gathering dry branches for a fire. I took over, snapping branches off a dead cottonwood and kindling a fire against the bank.

"How good to have a fire on the ground," Clayton said. He turned away, took off his clothes and waded into the frigid lake.

Cottonwood smoke billowed up damp, thick, surrounding me in its intoxicating perfume. I listened to the splash and pant of my old friend ducking in and out of the water, already familiar with the arduous purification rites of many older Indians. The flames blazed up, chirping and hissing on the damp gravel. Even though cottonwood burns fast and gives less heat than fir or pine, I always like the bright flame, the way it rarely pops with hot sparks, and the unique balsam scent. As the fire roared, I looked around for Clayton. He was down lake, hauled out on an offshore rock like a seal, gazing out on the water where returning Canada geese flew along inches above the water.

It was that time between winter and spring when neither held sway for more than a day or two. A day would come with springlike balm, then be swept with snow showers and bitter wind as if nothing was really changing. This day had been steadily warming to noon, and when the lone puffball clouds were not blocking the sun, I would begin to sweat under my heavy jacket. I sat down and stared at the fire, at "Indian television," feeling the damp chill of winter still seeping up from the earth.

Clayton came ashore shivering but grinning. He stood close to the fire, dripping, a placid look on his face. He looked younger, fit, renewed.

"Lots of bigfoots around here," he said, starting to dress. Instantly my reverie was broken and I instinctively looked around the hills. The Okanogan call them *schwanaítux*, bigfoot, or stick Indians: a legendary race of people who inhabit the wildest places and who appear part animal to those who glimpse them. Or so the stories about them say, I thought. Clayton warmed his hands close to the fire.

"Who are the bigfoots, Clayton?"

"Wild man of the timber. You know, stick Indians, like I been tellin' you in those stories. They get real frisky this time of year. Fire like this, they see, they come and take a look. Maybe some hairy woman drag you off into the bush!" I laughed with him. He turned around to warm his backside and looked around at the high country. Then that mischievous glint in his eye.

"You be some bush woman's man! She make you mate with her, hold you down 'till you please her! But she feed you good, they always got a lot of good stuff to eat." Clayton was always joking about getting me fixed up with some woman, but this was a new twist. Everybody has heard about bigfoot kidnappings, but I had a feeling there was more to these creatures than the lurid media accounts.

"Who are they really? What are they like?" I asked.

He glanced at me sideways and said nothing for a minute. I knew I was on shaky ground, asking direct questions of a traditional Indian about something not usually talked about with Whites. I should have said something like, "I wonder who they really are?" or "Sometimes I wonder what they're like?" That way I'd be expressing something deeply felt and he'd be free to talk about it or not, as he wished. Or bring it up at some later time after he'd had time to think about it.

Or just tell me an old story that answered my question at some later time when I'd already forgotten my question, which often happened.

A direct question was demanding, invasive, disrespectful in the eyes of these people who are careful to maintain each other's personal space and dignity. Jim Woods once told me that when he was a boy out riding horseback with his late father, if his father said something like "Somebody ought to close that gate," he took it as a command and jumped off to close it.

But it was too late. In the thoughtless way of my people I had already spoken. To my surprise, Clayton finally said, "Pretty good, you don't say 'Do bigfoots really be out there?' White man say that kinda thing don't exist. They got that sickness in the mind, White man's madness. They treat the world like it's something dead."

"Not me," I said. "*Schwanaítux stim xa'xá*." In my pigeon-Salish I was saying "Bigfoots something spiritually powerful."

"Yeah, Bigfoots are people, like Indian people. Only, see, way back before Coyote taught our people how to live, we were *psháya*, did not know anything. Not like to have culture and live in villages, like that. Then, see, the change came. The people came to be like, smarter how to do things. Coyote did that, he showed how.

"So, all these people came to be: Colvilles, Okanogans, Lakes, Sanpoils. Livin' together in big camps, fishing, dancing, having this way of life. But, see, some, they stayed that old way. They stayed out there, in the timber, like spirits. And they still around here. That's who they are."

I told him about a photo of a bigfoot I once saw in a magazine that looked like some kind of apelike man.

"See, they in the bush, they just like the bush. They are so old, from the before time, they are something else. Like us, but they the oldest ones, living like the animals do. That's why we give 'em matches. They don't have it easy, but they got the old power. They are *xa'xá*. They got that spirit way. But they're like us. They whistle, and we know they're around, they're watching, but they hide real good, maybe inside the rocks. Some go live with 'em, turn into bigfoots."

"You mean like Indian doctors, medicine people, that sort of thing?"

"No. Maybe a man goes way off, he live out in the bush alone, that his way. Like that guy, Indian Mike, way back in the timber. He talked some Indian language nobody could understand, maybe from the coast. He live all alone up there in those high mountains by Lake Chelan, eat deer meat, bear meat. Hardly ever talk, see people. Then don't ever see him again.

"Those that go off, live that way, maybe never return. After while they something else, maybe what other people see, a hairy shape in the woods. Can go that way, even today.

"But now, our Indian doctors, maybe not nowadays, but not long ago, some stayed out alone off in the bush, in the timber, for years at a time. They gain spirit, many of 'em, helpers. But they always come back, because what they got, they can use to help the people, cure the sick. They get married, raise families, sponsor Winter Dances . . . even get on the tribal council!"

Breaking more branches to keep the fire going, I said, "So the bigfoots are different from the helpers, the spirit partners for people, what you call *shumíx?*"

"Yeah, they not the same, but kinda. Bigfoots don't wait out in the timber for when people fast and come to ask for help. They not really caring about us, maybe take pity on somebody lost and starving, give 'em food or like that. But, then again, maybe a Indian doctor will have one to help, maybe he can find out things from bigfoots.

"It's hard to talk about. Say a man goes out to sit and fast, wander in the hills to gain spirit. Maybe he lonely or sad, not know what to do in life. Maybe he wander with that animal or that bird that show hisself to him, talk to 'em just like a person. You know, when you are there, *shumíx* appear just like a person. Man or woman. They are the most . . . the most . . ." Clayton scratched his chin, silent for a long time. "They are beautiful people, those ancient ones.

"So, maybe this man, he have no other desire but to wander the hills with his new partner. The one who appeared and now instruct him. Like twins, alone in the bush, till one day come, maybe he wake up with the sun, look around and he is alone. He have that song given to him, he remember his instruction, but he all alone out there now. Hungry. Thirsty. Miss his folks, his people. Time to go home. Maybe he so weak he can hardly walk, but now he feel different. He have that power now. They say, *wik'shumíx*, gain spirit. He got somethin'. He know he can call on that one, his partner, when he need help in life."

All that remained of the fire were some smoking embers in a bed of white ash. Clayton was fingering the mineral pattern on the rounded glacial boulder he sat on. I was immersed in the unceasing wash of waves, the huffing rise and fall of wind in the fir tree over-head, the soar of a circling eagle above the timbered summits across the lake. Fully awake to the breathing natural world around me and marveling at the unaccountable mystery of the richness of water, stone, tree, wind and sky. The very existence of nature with all its forces and manifestations, its ageless rhythms and solid yet ineffable beauty, had always held me spellbound. I wondered to myself if the Salish nature spirit quest that Clayton spoke about was a way to know the world better and find a place in it. He startled me when, out of the blue, he said, "Everything we have need to know is out there."

He gestured to the world around us with a slow wave of his open hand. "What the White people call Mother Nature, that our govern-ment. This time of year, North Wind, *iyoh'músh*, he turn things over to *stla'wálalt*, South Wind, like a change of government. All these pow-ers, these winds, the timber, the waters, the sun and moon, the animals and birds, they like a spiritual government. They watch over this world, they run things, just like always. We gotta live by their law.

"We live in a spiritual world. White people come here, they only see this lake, these mountains. But you different, you feel something,

something like pulling on you, to look deeper."

"That's true," I said.

"You not dormant like those others. I see you many times, kinda quiet, like you hear something way out in the hills, in the wind. See, the wind, the waters, they talkin' to us in a voice so beautiful, they showin' us how to live.

"*Awhá i xa'xá i ti'íkut,* this a power lake, this a dangerous place. Hard to bear, different voices makin' you listen. So nobody hangs around, except the White people who can't hear. Not my idea to come this way, you remember. Everybody go on the highway, over Disautel Pass. I not been this way for many years. But you choose this way to drive your truck. Maybe those ancient ones talkin' to you. They always wantin' us to come to them, to help us, to give us gifts of their power.

"I have lived a long time," he said, standing up and squinting as he scanned the open hills down the lake on the far side. "Over there, only a boy, they give me what I got to live by. This place my heart knows," he added in a low, affectionate voice. He started to walk away, along the shore of the lake, and I followed.

Nimble for a man in his sixties, he climbed bowlegged over the headlands of bare granite where the wave-cut beach disappeared. Rounded and smoothed boulders of every size and shape typical of glaciated landscapes stood here and there. Pebbles glittered in the wash of waves, and house-size boulders towered above us, covered with shaggy manes of lichen, moss and creeping shrubs.

Clayton paused to look at faint red ochre picture symbols painted on a cliff face, then moved on. I followed him up a scramble through thickets of coyoteberry bushes, called *yárr'kin,* which were just beginning to leaf out with tiny, bright green eruptions along scratchy branches. High above the lake we came to a break in the cliff, a level, earthy terrace covered with a pure stand of sagebrush. I breathed in the minty spring odor, brushed against the shaggy trunks, noticing rounded clumps of moss shining in the sun like frogs sunning in the bare dirt.

We sat on the ground at a spot overhung by sagebrush forming a natural arbor, our backs resting against the smooth granite wall. Rabbit pellets lay all around, mixed with tell-tale piles of snipped-off and chewed-on sagebrush stems. Above us the mountain rose up into timber and a flock of magpies dived and flapped from tree to tree. Below us, the expanse of lake shimmered and washed against the rocks, fully dominating everything else from this sheltered spot.

"Those rock pictures down below us, do they say something about this place?" I asked him, thinking this place could be an old questing spot.

"Yeah, in the old days, they put up something about what they got here. Tell what they see, who talk to 'em. Indian doctors, mainly. Out here them *shumíx* waitin' to take pity on us, give us something to call on in life. Something to live by, like a power."

"What is power, really, Clayton?" I asked, perplexed by his use of the word, and hopeful that his willingness to indulge my questions would keep up. But he said nothing, sitting at my side in silence as I gazed out over the lake, watching the way gusts of wind spread shimmering patterns gliding across the surface. Then he stood up and said, "This how it go."

I got up, too, thinking he meant it was time to go, but he stood there with his face turned to the sky, taking slow, deep breaths. He started to hum a tune, his weight shifting from foot to foot, like he was dancing in place, completely absorbed in what he was doing. I could hear a few Salish phrases, but his voice was so low and rhythmic I didn't listen closely. He gestured with his hands to the sky at certain repetitions of his song, then came to a stop. Eyes closed, rubbing his hands together, he said, *"Wai i hwi"* (something like "So be it").

When he sat back down, I followed suit. Both of us leaned back against the stone.

"Now it gonna rain a little," he said, looking at his fingernails. He yawned, folded his arms over his chest and closed his eyes like he was going to nap for awhile.

Looking overhead I saw there was little hope for rain since the few widely scattered clouds moving slowly across the sky from west to east were the kind that indicated fair weather. But as I watched, a cloud moved in front of the sun, our side of the lake darkened under the slow-moving shadow, and big raindrops fell diagonally on the breeze, splatting on rocks, bushes and our clothing. One hit me on the crown of the head and the water felt icy on my scalp. It was one of those freaky spring showers that last only seconds, the wet spots drying quickly in the sunshine that returned as the cloud moved on. Not all that unusual, but startling after what Clayton had just done and said.

For a long time I just sat there with a deep sense of wonder and humbleness in the presence of real mystery. I felt an intuitive certainty that the myth stories of Native peoples that told of powers to do things like causing it to rain were true ways to know and live in the world. At that moment I was living in the mythical now. I was grateful that this lore was not completely extinguished, stamped out by missionary and scientist alike, that it was still alive in my own day. That I could witness it—that Clayton would give me such a gift.

Instead of talking about power, Clayton had showed me. I'd heard about certain people having "weather power." Stuart had told a story about desperate wheat farmers down in the Palouse country during a drought in the thirties who called on a blind old Nez Perce who had such a reputation. Rain broke the drought the next day, according to Stuart. Was I seeing this power firsthand?

I sighed. Being a product of modern times, I had a hard time resisting the urge to explain away what had happened. Could it have been a coincidence? Did Clayton's lifelong observation of nature and weather give him the skill to anticipate a rain shower when I couldn't see the signs myself? Where do such doubts come from? The modern world has opted for measurable verification, calls belief in unseen powers childish and those who claim such powers fakes.

I sighed again. None of that applied to me, the border sneak, the man who would be free. My skepticism was nothing more than the universal human fear of being tricked, a healthy survival trait that kicks in at moments like this. I knew that the "there's got to be a logical explanation" way of thinking was just a way of living on the other side of the mind from where all our ancestors once lived in communication with nature. And where some still live today. Nobody wants to play the fool, but what could be more foolish than delving into the workings of unseen powers when you yourself don't believe they exist? That was it. Being skeptical was fine, but I had to guard against the urge modern culture promotes in us to seek validation for not believing.

"You can explain it away if you want to," Clayton said quietly, his eyes still closed. "It will go away. Then you have nothing. No power. All gone."

I was not surprised he could interpret my sighs.

"See, the White man waste his time trying to figure everything out. It don't come that way. It go like I show you. A power man do as his power show him."

A flock of song sparrows arrived, blew over us on the wind and settled in the bushes all around us, twittering and riding the swaying branches. Clayton made the soft sounds of their chirping talk, and one sparrow with his crest ruffling in the breeze eyed him from a high perch.

"Then it doesn't matter *how* you did that?" I asked.

"What matter is, Did it rain? Like the doctor, Is the person cured? Or like some see what comin', see into the future—did that thing they saw come to happen? Or the finder, like that Bluejay man over in Canada, found those lost girls just like his power show him. Or that one with the gift to hunt deer, he the best ain't he? So easy, like the deer give themself to him, he feed everybody.

"You know the power man have the power by what he do. He have the gift, so he of use to his people. They see, he cure the sick, he see danger comin' that happen like he say, he find what you lost, he have the rain come when it so dry your cows are dyin'.

"But see, English don't help. In Indian we say 'rain coming' or 'rain falling.' What this 'it' business? Rain doin' the raining! Rain a person, just like you and me, only more powerful. He don't look like us, he water from the sky. Only, say you got that gift from the one up there in the sky, how you say it in English? The bright one reaching out, like a light between the clouds, that one. With him, then you can see that rain like a man, real shimmery. So good lookin', *hus'ájits.*

"He hear that song, he have to come. That song is his. He give it to the one he choose, he take pity on, to sing, to call him. *Wai i hwi.*" He rubbed his hands together and the sparrows all took off in a flutter of tiny wings, as if of one mind.

"It's like love, like a blessing," I blurted out. He looked at me for a long time while I touched the leafy stems of sagebrush, felt the sturdy limbs so shaggy with loose, fibrous bark.

"Yeah, like love, like a blessing," he repeated. "You love our Mother, don't you?"

I nodded.

"For a long time now, I think you got something. Don't want to say, maybe crazy. We don't see this much in the White man. Some say the White man don't have no powers. This way only given to the Indian people. But there been some, just a few. I see you, hear what you say. Makes me wonder."

"Like a *shumíx,* a spirit partner? No, I don't think so," I said. But his words plunged me into childhood memories, strange encounters. Something came back to me, a conversation with a college professor when I was young, when I told her in a fit of adolescent boldness, "Only the wind is real."

"What that?" Clayton asked. I'd said it out loud.

"Only the wind is real." My heart fluttered at the words, my guts tightened. Why had this odd phrase stuck in my memory and come to me now? And why did I suddenly feel faint?

"*Aaaa . . . Aaaa,*" Clayton murmured. He was smiling broadly at me. "You not think so, but that how they talk. Now I know why you drive your truck this way. You got somethin'. What you got callin' to you, want you to wake up and remember. Do things when you not thinkin', draw you near a place like this, so powerful, so dangerous, *xa'xá.*

"Only the wind is real. Some kind of bird, maybe, love that wind, put that love in you. You love the wind?"

"Yes," I said without thinking. I remembered the terrific wind storm that hit Vancouver, B.C., one day in winter ten years before. The seaside park, usually thronged with people walking, sitting, beachcombing in any kind of weather, was completely deserted in the gale-force winds, the waves crashing over the seawall. I was the only person there, so immersed in the utter joy of standing at the outermost rocky point, simply at one with the power of the wind and the violence of salt waves on stone. I was oblivious to the city of a million people behind me. For hours I exulted in the blow, until I was so exhausted and chilled I barely made my way the four blocks to my room at a hostel to thaw out. But some newspaper photographer must have been driving by the busy avenue behind the park, because next morning on the front page of the *Province* there was a photo of a lone figure leaning into the wind at the point. "Only one person braved yesterday's gale-force winds to . . ."

"Clayton, I feel sick."

"Yeah, he tryin' to come on you now. Don't think about nothin'." He picked some sage and rubbed the fragrant leaves on my forehead, over my heart and midsection. I felt his hand on the back of my neck, thumb and fingers squeezing below my ears. Little by little my nausea passed. I felt better, I let go of any thoughts, I smelled the sage and felt his hand rubbing the sides of my neck. There was just the windy world around us, the lake washing below us.

"I'm okay now."

Clayton stood up and dusted off his pants. "Yeah, that good. He let go now. You not ready. Hard to remember sometimes. How it feel, how it go. Maybe don't come back so easy. I dunno, maybe with a White man, it go different. You can walk okay?"

I felt somehow more alive, more aware, more solid. "Yeah, sure." Walking away into the hills behind Clayton was pure pleasure. I followed him up faint deer trails, through thick stands of bitterbrush, out onto the open, rounded benches where the road wound along high above the lake. We got into my car and drove on until we came over the divide. Below us the modern world unfolded: the sawmill, apple orchards, the town of Omak along the river. As I drove, I thought about what he had said.

"What can I do to remember?"

Clayton didn't answer. Miles later, as we approached his house, he said, "I been thinkin'. You ever go in the sweatlodge?"

"No."

"Maybe what you got is waitin' for you to train yourself. Get clean and pure. Suffer for that gift. Maybe he want you to know the Indian way better. You ever fast, stay awake all night out in the hills?"

"Well, not intentionally," I said, laughing. "I've been stuck—stranded that way a couple of times."

"Well, you think about it. All that what happen will come back to you. That the old way. Come on you when you just little, just a boy, that *shumíx*. Then forget about it, grow up, go on in life. Only whispers, like. Some special way of knowin' things, not know how. See things, wonder about 'em. Not till later, it gets like you want to know something, lookin' for something. That the way it always go. That one, he lonesome now you don't remember him. You lookin' for him, not know it."

I stopped the car in front of his house.

"First the sweatlodge, the oldest way. Train-self, that how you could say it. *K'ulsht*. So you think about that. Maybe in your heart you want to do that. You let me know. I will help you."

What happened at Omak Lake sat uneasily on my mind as the relief of spring flooded the Okanogan. My days were filled with the heavy physical grunt of a ranch hand. The cattle still had to be fed hay until the grass grew in mountain pastures. Miles of fences weakened or broken by winter snows had to be repaired. After supper I'd sit out on the front step wearily smelling the fresh green, looking up at Chopaka, and wondering what it meant to "have something." Was there something I was supposed to be able to do like Clayton making it rain? My life had been unusual maybe, but nothing stood out as remarkably beyond human capacity as Clayton knowing we couldn't start the tractor and why, or that rain was about to fall on a cloudless day.

But he never said he made it rain. "The power man do as the power show him." He said the rain came when the man sang the song the rain gave him. The power was with the force of nature who granted it. The power man was like a conduit through which the spirit partner acted in the world of humans. Maybe that was it, maybe not. It was confusing when I tried to sort things out. Trying to understand just muddied the water.

All I knew was that something deep and compelling had been awakened inside me, something like becoming aware that the course and events of my life no longer seemed random, that they suspiciously hinted at some ongoing outside influence. Some conscious presence vaguely sensed somewhere by my heart, like knowing someone is watching you. And it had come at a point in my life when staying put for the first time in a decade was bringing to light the full force of what I had buried in years of wandering: I had no idea what I was here on earth for. All I'd ever done was react to what was put in front of me. Become expert at evading any constraint put on my freedom. Along the way I acquired a kind of sixth sense out in the hills, out on the road. Staying put was wrenching beyond belief.

Sure, I was powerful, but I thought of it as something to rein in and be careful about, so it didn't hurt other people. Ever since the military nightmare I would never think about, and the combat-mentality border crossings that I remembered mainly in the look of fear some people gave me, I had chosen my battlegrounds carefully, sparingly. I was a man, and I knew what throwing my own life away and surviving had unleashed. I wasn't one of those guys who'd become addicted to doing it over and over, and had to seek out ever more dangerous, violent proofs of their manhood. Taking a stand, staying put, was bad enough. I had settled down here in the Okanogan despite fears that I was only any good on the run.

A few days before, I was in a nearby town, standing in the corridor between the combined bar and general store. A heavy, bearded man in a faded campaign coat shouldered his way by me in a cloud of beer fumes, mumbling, "F——it . . . and f——you." He turned and I smiled, grateful for some kind of pure, unadulterated savagery to quell the muddle of confusing thoughts plaguing my mind. At least in a face-to-face fight there's absolute certainty about what to do. I was grinning when our eyes locked.

"What're you lookin' at?" he said in that voice that always made my blood race. I willed myself to that place inside where I threw away my life and heard only the voice that said kill or be killed. I became my body, absolutely without thoughts, and waited for the instinctive first move. His eyes wavered, then I saw fear creeping up in them. He softened.

"Vietnam dong hoa," he slurred, figuring me for a brother.

"101st Canadian Deserters," I said. He laughed as we slapped hands.

"Wish I'd had the guts."

"It all sucked."

"You from here?"

"No. Trying to make a life for myself here. Be the quiet little man off in the hills."

"F——ing hell-hole. I'm outta here. Gave it the best six months of my life. Seattle may suck, but at least they don't roll up the sidewalks at dark. Catch you later."

But Clayton wasn't talking about that kind of power. His power was an ability that went beyond human capacity, that defied logic, that came from the natural world around us and enhanced our lives. The truth was, I hadn't enhanced anybody's life, not even my own. I wasn't leaving a trail of destruction behind me, but I wasn't doing anybody any good either. I may have been free, but I was only surviving.

I sensed in what Clayton told me that something or someone mysteriously powerful in this world cared about me, wanted to help me, had already somehow touched my life when I was young, and was even now reaching out to me. Offering me something that would give me the ability to live a worthwhile life and be of some use to my fellows. It was a humbling thought.

As I sat on the doorstep listening to the hooting of an owl in the dusk, a question formed in my mind. If I delve into the old Indian ways, go "sweathousing" with Clayton, to unlock this secret of my life, what am I getting into? Surely even my *Skélux* neighbors did not take such a step without knowing what it was about?

I really didn't know what exactly it was I thought I needed to know before committing myself to what Clayton called "self-training," but such a simple, focused query brought quick results. Salish Indian Religion 101: The Origin of Sweatlodge and Spirit Partners came in the form of a story told by a strong, uncompromising woman of Clayton's generation the very next day.

Her name was Margaret Sisencha and she was visiting at the home of Larry and Elaine Dubois. Larry did seasonal work at ranches in the valley, sometimes with Stuart and me, and his wife was a teacher's aide at the school. With three children to feed and his per capita payment somehow fouled up, he needed cash to buy groceries at the store where we all ran up debts in the winter. I was there when the storekeeper refused to extend him more credit until he paid on his bill. He could have the groceries piled on the counter if he paid cash. I didn't have to think about it—he had young children—so I dug up what money I had and covered it. Larry insisted on taking me home for dinner.

His place was located in one of the coldest spots in the valley, under the north-facing slope of Aeneas Mountain. A snow-hushed forest of fir out the back door rose steeply up the mountain and disappeared into the low overcast that hung over the valley for days.

Margaret was Elaine's "auntie," great aunt, really, and there was tension between the old lady with gray braids and Larry with his rock 'n roll songs. Unlike the other Indians concentrated in extended families on allotments, Larry had moved his little nuclear family to this isolated spot in the midst of White orchardists and Mexican farmworkers. Larry was indifferent to his Native heritage and acted like he knew nothing about it. Margaret was one of those traditional elders who lament often and openly the younger generation's loss of interest in the tribal language and culture and ritualized relationships between humans and nature. The authoritative and respectful way she groomed and doted over the children while Elaine cooked dinner, her air of maintaining the sacredness of life, was displayed against Larry's shouting conversation over the boom box playing heavy metal rock songs all the way up to suppertime.

Margaret seemed familiar to me, but I didn't remember where I'd met her until after dinner when she handed a plate of cookies to one of the children and told her to "take this to the watermelon man." Then I remembered the day I was hauling watermelons in my pickup the summer before. I stopped at Split Rock beach on Palmer Lake, where three white women, wives of orchard workers I knew, were sunbathing and watching their kids swim in the shallow water. While we visited and teased, a family of Indians traveling from the Omak Stampede rodeo to their home just over the border in Canada made a rest stop on the beach. They strolled along the shore of the lake towards the outlet of Sinlahekin Creek where two boys tried their luck with fishing poles.

When they drifted back I had the tailgate down and was cutting up watermelon and passing out sweet, ripe slices to the women and sunburned children in bathing suits. As the Indian family passed by, I invited them to share with us. The three White mothers served them with the pieces I sliced and we all stood around smiling shyly, eating watermelon and spitting seeds.

There were the two boys with fishing poles, their mother and father, and two elders, who I thought were a married couple, the grandparents, but I later found out were brother and sister. This was Margaret Sisencha and her older brother, who everyone called Old Willie, and who I later learned was some kind of Indian doctor.

The old man stood apart behind the others, sucking slowly on the dripping red fruit, then said something in Salish. The younger Native couple laughed at what was obviously a good joke, then looked a little embarrassed. The rest of us smiled, wondering why we weren't let in on it, so I turned to the man about my age and said, "What did he say?"

He dropped his eyes and gave me a sheepish smile. "He wonders if maybe these three women are your wives."

Now Margaret Sisencha was looking across the room at me as I sampled Elaine's fresh-baked cookies.

"Where are your wives?"

"We got divorced."

"That's too bad! Nobody to cook for you."

Larry and Elaine looked at each other, but didn't ask. Margaret went on talking about divorce, as if talking only to the children, telling them how strange it was when the Catholic priests came to convert the Indian people and insisted that if you were married in the Christian church, you couldn't get divorced.

"These Indians don't know that isn't our way. Just some way brought in from somewhere else."

"Tell us a story, auntie."

"That's not our church. Something brought here."

"A story, a story."

"You know we have our own church."

"A story, auntie."

"Our church is older than time," she said in a high, deep voice. The children fell silent. Margaret glanced to see that the adults were listening. Elaine said, "*Aaaa.*"

"We call that *Kwílsten*, Sweatlodge. Sweatlodge is a person, a great person."

"*Aaaa.*"

K'saaaa'pi, long, long ago, what we call Sweatlodge, way back, he was *Xa'xá Iyilméhum*, chief of the spirits. This is the way it happened.

Spirit Chief called all the Animal People together, they had a big council, and he says to them, "A change is coming. A new kind of people is coming."

The Animal People were the original people of this land. People like us, but they were the spirits of all the animals and plants and nature powers we see now. And some that are gone. You can see they were people like us, but also like animals.

And they've been sensing this change coming for a long time. This council is called by the Oldest One, that chief. They are called together to decide what their names will be and how they will behave in the new time that's coming. He says, "Come back here at first light."

Some people there were angry. They didn't want this change that

was coming. They didn't want to help these weak humans that were going to people the earth. They went away, didn't want to have no part in it. Said, "They will be our food! We'll hunt and eat those new people." That's why we call them *en'ahlna'skéluxtin*, people-eaters.

To those that stayed, he said, "Come at first light and choose your names. The first to show up may choose any name. The next and the next, any name you want, until all are taken. And each one will have a power."

So they all went to where they are camping around the home of the Chief. Talking about what he said. Coyote, that Imitator, *Sin'kalíp*, he says, "I'm gonna be the first! I'm gonna get there first, before any-body. And choose first."

Coyote wants a powerful name. "I will be Grizzly Bear! or Eagle! or Salmon!" Everybody gets tired of him strutting around, bragging what name he will be.

Pretty soon he's the last one still awake, he's talkin' to himself. He's still awake, sitting at his fire, but he's getting drowsy. It's late and he plans to stay awake all night, so he can be sure to show up first. His wife is asleep, his kids are asleep, and he's talking to himself, trying to stay awake. Pretty soon he's falling to sleep anyway, he can't stay awake. Doesn't even know it.

Jerks awake! "Oh my! I'm gonna fall asleep if I don't do some-thing about it." So he feels around in his firewood, he finds two sticks just the size to prop open his eyelids. He sticks them in, they fit just fine to hold his eyes open. He's staring at the fire now.

"Now I won't fall asleep!" he says. But you know, soon he's sound asleep with his eyes still open. Propped open by those toothpicks! Snoring with his eyes wide open!

(We were all laughing as Margaret paused to sip from her glass of water. Even Larry and his youngest daughter, who had been drifting off like Coyote. The two older girls, twins with matching Minnie Mouse T-shirts and blue yarn ties on the end of their braids, had been listening with silent wonder, and I could see the growing curiosity and understanding in the wide gaze of their eyes.)

Well, so—morning came. The sun's already high in the sky. It's late morning and Coyote finally wakes up. He leaps up and runs to the Chief's camp. Nobody's there but the Spirit Chief, sitting there all alone.

And Coyote is so groggy, his eyes dried out, like sandpaper, from being held open all night with sticks. He blinks. Nobody else is there, so he laughs. He steps inside.

"I will be Grizzly Bear!" he says. "I will be the strongest of all the animals!"

And Spirit Chief says, "That name is taken."

"I will be Eagle. The new people to come will want my feathers to pray with."

"That name is also taken."

Coyote, he's faltering now. Knees buckling. He's beginning to see he's late. So, in a quieter voice, "I will be Salmon, the greatest of all the swimmers."

"All the names are taken, all but one. There is only one left. Nobody wanted your name, Coyote."

He drops down by the Chief's fire, just pitiful. His eyes so dry, he can't even cry.

"Coyote, you keep your name. That's the way it's supposed to be. I wanted you to be the last one here, so you slept late. Imitator is a good name for the work I have for you to do. You will have a special job to prepare the world for the new people coming, and they will remember you as a chief for what you do."

Iyilméhum put something in Coyote's eyes, make them heal up so he can see real good again. But they are still slant eyes from those sticks, like they are today. Slant eyes, knowing he got a big job to do.

"Your job, to stop those people-eaters killing the new people and make the world a good place for them to live in." And he gave him a power, like he gave all the Animal People who came before him. A medicine power.

When all those Animal People came for their names at first light, he pointed at their heart and put in them their power, what they got, what they can do and be. What they're going to help the new people with. And some of them, like Bear and Deer and Salmon, offered their bodies as food in return for respectful treatment.

He pointed to Coyote's heart, but Coyote thinks he's pointing at his guts. He thinks his power is in his guts! He'll have to grunt and poop out his power to make his medicine, to talk to his medicine power lying on the ground.

That Coyote, he got it wrong, but that's how he had to do it after that. So this special power he got, nobody else got. Just him.

Chief tells him, "This is to make your work go easy. If you need help, you can't figure out what to do, call on your power. You can change into just anything you want, be any shape. This is so you can rid the world of those monsters, and so you can make things good for the new people."

So that Chief, he's done. He tells all those Animal People, those *Chip'chaptík'xwul*, "These new people, they're pretty weak. They don't know anything, how to live. Can't hardly live. So now, when they send their kids out alone, send them to the bush, to the lonely places, you wait for them. You be there and talk to them. Maybe on a mountain top or on the shore of a lake, you be waiting when they come. Tell them what they're going to do when they grow up. Be ready for them so you can give them your power, give them your help in life.

"Tell them how they can find things easy. Like to be a good hunter, good fisherman, good gambler. The good root digger, good basket maker, good seamstress. Tell them how when they have trouble in life, they can call on you. That you will help them all their life."

He said all this to the Animal People. And it's still like that today.

And he says, "When the new time comes, I will take pity on the new people. I will turn myself into Sweatlodge. I will exist for the benefit of the new people. I'll have no body, no head, no hands or feet. I'll be who they set up with willows and covers, Sweatlodge. They can make me so they can sweat and purify. Clean off real good. Pray for what they want, what they need. When they build me and go in to pray, I'll take pity on them, whoever sets me up to do that. I'll give what they ask.

"This is how they can come to me in the world to come. Say maybe they're sick, or hurt bad, or things are going bad. They can come to me and I'll know it, I'll give what they ask for. Maybe they're going to die and they make me to help for what's going to happen. I'll help them. Show them what's coming, the next world. Maybe they'll be starting off to do something, go hunt for meat, or go off to war, or take a long trip, or take final exams. So they can make me and I will help them.

"That's what I'll be. Sweatlodge. *Kwílsten*, they'll call me. In the new time I'll be there for the good of the human people."

So that's how it all came to be. Coyote, because he changed things to the way they are, he said how people had to sweat. He made the rules. And to this day we make him, build him. And go inside to pray. Sing special songs to Sweatlodge, because he is *Xa'xá Iyilméhum* who did this for us. We know he hears us and he helps us.

That's how we know how to live. This was done for us. And so we have this good way to live. I went so far away telling this story, so now I come back.

5

Where do songs come from? Or the words that pop up and say themselves in tune until you sing them out loud? One came to me in the endless repetitive work of summer; came out of my mouth as I slogged through knee-deep dripping alfalfa wearing rubber boots to change the irrigation pipe. What I did was unfasten each twenty-foot length of aluminum pipe with a sprinkler head standing up from one end, carry it to the next unwatered swath, and fasten it into the end of the previous ones laid along in a line, until all had been moved and the end plugged, water pressure building. When all the spaced sprinklers rotated in rhythmic, clacking spray, I moved to the next field, and the next. It took all day to move the sprinklers twice. Start at dawn, finish the first change in late morning, sleep through the hottest part of the day, work through all the fields a second time till dusk, start over the next morning.

This was mindless work, meditative work, laying out evenly the cold, clear water into rich green growing food for cattle, this sweaty soggy labor under the burning sun. First a tune came to mind that matched my pace through the fields, balancing the springy lengths of pipe, a rhythmic series of notes that swung back to the beginning note at the end of each phrase. I'd been making up songs all my life, but this one came out of the blue, already word-for-word in its entirety, fitting perfectly to the melody:

> Listen to my song, oh mother
> As I dance alone here on you,
> Listen to my song, oh father
> As I dance alone before you.

It became my song of being alive here in this land, of being here doing this, of moving pipe without end as the weeks passed. I only sang it when I was out working alone.

The valley bottom was as humid as Georgia with all the ranches and orchards irrigating twenty-four hours a day and the lake evaporating in the stare of a tropical sun for eighteen hours each day. The lush bottomland was hemmed in by steep, semiarid slopes of grass and brush, long since dried to a tawny crisp. With so many outcrops of bare rock the hillside looked like a ratty old deerhide stretched over bones. Up above, timbered peaks faded into blue haze like islands in a glaring sea.

Relief from the heat was a dip in the cold lake or one of the creeks, followed by a nap in the shade of willows guarded by dragonflies. In the morning and evening the horses behind my trailer stood in clouds of mosquitoes. If I brushed my hand over their flanks, it came away bloody. They were losing so much weight we doubled their feed.

When the watering of fields was suspended for the first cutting, all I had to do was sit on a tractor going around in circles, pulling a swather through the standing alfalfa, leaving a row of tumbled hay for Stuart to stack with later. It was so hot now I sweated like a pig just sitting and steering under a wide-brimmed hat, enduring the hours of engine roar, vibration, and mow dust.

Johnny Stemilt showed up one day. I saw him in the shade of cottonwoods by the field I was mowing, walking slowly around my pickup truck, pausing to inspect the bashed-in side. Johnny was known as an authority on reading people by looking at their cars. After the terrible car wreck that he barely survived—walked away from with smoking clothes, so they say—some kind of power came to him that people said was uncanny. Nobody—not even Stuart, who could cuss with the best—could get used to the way Johnny routinely came to talk after that experience. You had to read between the expletives whatever it was he was really saying. Since the Native language had no swear words, no way of expressing profanity, and

Johnny rarely spoke English around his own people, this stream of irreverence was received mainly by White ears.

The same old eagle feather fluttering off the back of the same fading felt cowboy hat, looking like the gimpy old traditional he was, Johnny was giving my truck the third degree. From way off through the heat waves I could see him crouched motionless on his bootheels, staring meditatively at the vehicle's crumpled side.

He was still there half an hour later when I pulled into the shade for lunch, but his eyes were closed. When I shut off the motor and jumped down, Johnny looked up at me pulling lunch out of the truck window.

"Son of a bitch pickup tellin' me stories about you," he said, coming to see what I had to eat. He only wanted the warm can of pop, drank it all in a long series of gulps.

"How you doin' Johnny?"

"Why you wanna do that Indian bullshit? Nobody doin' that sweatlodge crap any more."

"What's my truck say?"

"She say you got nothin' to do with all that bumpin' into things." He was right.

"That's all?"

He closed his eyes, shook his head. Sweat poured down our faces like we were in a sauna. He fanned his face with his hat.

"You don't think high of your own people, what they doin' with the world," he said. I wasn't impressed. Anybody who knew me could say that. "So you wanna be a Indian."

"*Loot inchá* (Not me)," I said. He laughed, pointing a stubby finger at me, like that proved it.

"You wanna be a *real* Indian!"

"Look, Johnny. I don't want to be anything but what I am. I don't know what that is, but I'm workin' on it."

"You one of those antherpologists?"

"Do I look like one?" I brushed at my sweaty clothes covered with a fine, green dust. He shook his head again, like he couldn't figure me out.

"Why you wanna learn our religion?" he said finally, looking at me with what I thought was sincere curiosity. Johnny was always heading off the anticipated scoffing of Whites by his put-down of Native ways. I'd never heard him go this long without a cuss word.

"I don't think I do. It's not religion—I just have a feeling for what's going on: something older, something all people used to live by, before religion was invented. Even my people, way back, used to believe in stuff like you do. Like having reverence for where life really comes from—what's all around us.

"I don't know, it's just like real to me. I never could make sense of how I felt about life until I started talking to you guys, that's all."

He looked at the ground, listening.

"What I mean is, you guys still have that old way, you're still connected to all this, you're still talking with the earth and the wind and the animals. My people have been cut off from that for so long, they don't even think it's real. But I know it is."

"So you stole the land, you stole everything else, now you gonna steal our religion!"

He wouldn't look at me, but the square of his misshapen shoulders showed me how strongly he felt about this. I was suddenly tired of it. He wasn't talking to me. He was venting all his resentment against White people. No longer caring what he thought and having lost my appetite, I got up to go back to work. But I stood there watching him light up a Salem with his beaded lighter.

"Steal it? Who even cares about your religion? Or about any religion for that matter? What do you think is going on in the world out there?"

He glanced up and said, "I been to Korea, New York, Toronto. I boxed in Madison Square Garden in 1957. I seen how the White man takes everything, never has enough, always wants more. What do *you* want?"

"Something to drink," I said, digging around for my water jug in the back of the pickup. When I found it, I took a long drink and pondered. I decided I'd try to give him some kind of serious answer.

"Look, I'm learning this stuff to live it. Not to take it off to some university and get a degree with it. I don't know how all this came about, but this is where I am and what I'm doing. I sure didn't plan it. But it feels right.

"How else is a White man going to learn how to be a native in this world, if he doesn't learn from Indians? I don't mean the particulars of your religion. I mean the way of it. Heck, I'll never master your language or the meaning of all the things you have handed down for thousands of years. I'm a White man and I'll never be an Indian. But maybe I can find a way that works for us, or just me. I don't know . . ."

He scuffled the heels of his battered cowboy boots in the dust, his head down, saying nothing but the faintest of *aaa*'s so I knew he was listening.

"When I heard Margaret Sisencha tell the *chaptíkx* about how the Spirit Chief gave the Animal People their powers and then turned himself into Sweatlodge, I could see it. And how we don't really know anything unless they help us . . . it sounds right. My people don't have old sacred stories like this to tell how it was for all human beings to live in nature. This is far older than the Bible or anything else my people have handed down. We're cut off from our own native beginnings. We were thrown out of the Garden of Eden, but *you* weren't. See what I mean?

"So I'm trying to learn something that we left behind thousands of years ago. I don't know what it is, but I'm learning it. I can feel it, right here." I touched my chest, my heart. Johnny *aaa*'d again, nodding as he stared intently out at the heat waves obscuring the mountains.

"So things were decreed long ago, and they're still in force today, only my people ignore all that. They think they're the only ones that matter, and the whole world exists just for them to use any way they please. I know that's what's wrong with the world today. And it's insane. Well, I don't know why I feel this way, why me? But I do. And when I hear the *chaptíkx* I hear how to live by that. Maybe these are your private versions, for *Skélux* only, but they speak to me. Everybody knows the animals were here before people, and that by comparison with the animals, we are weak and ill-equipped to survive in nature. If the Animal People—all nature—had not helped us, we never would have survived. If they hadn't offered us their bodies as food and clothing and tools and shelter, in return for respect and careful treatment, we wouldn't be here on earth today. If they hadn't offered us special gifts, like talents, like knowing and seeing beyond appearances, we wouldn't have thrived.

"That's what I'm learning, Johnny. What do I want? I guess I want to live in the way we were made to live in the beginning.

"I get the stories, Johnny. Everything is alive. I always felt it. The stories make me think about it. They talk about all these Animal People living before humans came. A living earth and living sky. Winds and stars and trees and mountains talking to each other. All living by a code of creation that allows for all to live in their own way. Some old understanding, some old agreement.

"And they become aware a new people is coming. A pathetically weak and vulnerable people, but one that has just as much right to thrive on earth and under the sky as any other. And they know the coming of these new people will change everything. They put their heads together to decide how to order everything so that these ignorant humans will have a way to grasp the reality of things and thrive anyway. Am I getting it?"

"*Aaaa,*" Johnny affirmed.

"Some of those ancient ones resent the whole idea and declare themselves enemies of the new people. Because they break the old agreement and declare war on a whole species, they themselves have to be neutralized, rendered powerless as a threat to the order of creation. That was Coyote's job, and that's why he's like Jesus to you guys—the main man.

"And Coyote has a lot in common with us new people. He relies on his wits and false bravery in the face of more powerful creatures who he envies. The oldest of the old ones pities him as he pities the new people. So Coyote is the special champion. He's the one, all right.

"So the world changed. The Animal People are still here, but we have to seek them out, to find ways to see them without their animal masks on. The world cooled down and got solid. Or maybe the world just came to be seen through the eyes of the least able to see, I don't know . . . But there is one way for us to appeal to the old one who pities us, to slip for a while behind all this solid world in front of us. Something humble and simple—the sweatlodge. Because the ultimate source of life, the oldest power of creation, gave himself to us in this shape.

"That's the way I see it. It isn't about stealing Indian religion to me. It's about being a real human being. It's about making English into a Native language. If it's not right for a White man to go sweathousing, then I'm screwed."

I was quiet, wondering if Johnny thought I was crazy. Framing all my vague leanings into words to a rapt audience of one had somehow energized and cooled me. I felt the breeze moving stronger in the shade of rustling cottonwoods, stirring up clouds of insects sheltered in the limp leaves. Johnny got up and dusted off his pants. He broke apart one of his cigarettes until he had a small pile of tobacco in one palm, held out between us.

"*Aaaa, wai i hwi,*" he said. "I heard a lot of good talk. These things I never hear a White man say. I thought maybe them spirits burn you alive. Damn son of a bitchin' White man deserve it, got no respect. But now, even a Indian don't talk like that unless he have that family training, handed down. So here I feed 'em for you." He let the loose tobacco trickle through his fingers and tossed the last bit of it into the air.

"My words, that you are helped in what you're tryin' to do." He brushed his hands together. "Because you got only some idea in there. Talkin' about stuff you don't have no experience with like that, some of it sounds pretty weird. The Indian youth, now, just wantin' to go sweathousing is enough, just the desire. Don't see that much no more."

He peered at me as he put on his hat with both hands, front and back, wiggling it to just the right angle. There were no compulsory leave-takings among traditionals not steeped in White ways, so I knew he'd just walk away when he felt we were done.

"No, not many youth care about the old way," he said, and walked away. Then he surprised me by turning to call back, "*Wai nuhl wíkunchin!* (Well, be seeing you!)"

I watched him walk along the edge of mown hay toward the county road, the eagle feather flitting lightly off the back brim of his hat. Thinking: Nobody else wears a felt hat in this heat! Something arbitrary and inconvenient like that had to have something to do with his power. Doing something he was told to do by his spirit partner, his *shumíx*. Or something like that . . . I realized I could be reading things into the situation. And yet, even though my interpretation did "sound pretty weird," I felt convinced I was right.

There was no way for me to take time from the continuous round of summer work to go sweathousing with Clayton. He'd told me it would take at least ten days, and we'd have to go off somewhere free of distraction from daily life.

After the first two cuttings, the stubbled alfalfa fields were irrigated again in the long, dry days of the growing season, but after the last cutting in autumn, Stuart and I put away the sprinkler pipes on racks built along one wall of the horse barn. I was free. I had nothing to do until the snows of winter moved down Chopaka. Eventually they would cover the canary grass pastures at the head of the lake, and Stuart and I would start hauling stacks of hay to feed the cattle through the months of snow.

So I told Clayton it was now or never, but he was strangely unresponsive. It was like he was waiting for something. I didn't push it. I drove down to the Woods place every day to visit with him while he watched Jim gentling a young stud horse in the small log corral under long-dead cottonwoods hanging with garlands of gray, fibrous bark. Tractors crawled past on the paved road, moving wooden bins into the apple orchards in preparation for the harvest. Magpies argued dramatically behind the screen of poison ivy above the muddy bank of the Similkameen River, at its lowest level of the year but still flowing clear and cold from its mountain source. Aspens already glowed in patches of gold high up near timberline on Chopaka. It was the time we usually made plans to go hunting, but neither he nor Johnny would say anything definite about anything.

So I went hunting.

I had always hunted, ever since following my father and grandfather out across Midwestern fields as a boy, learning how to make meat from birds and animals. But it had never been the very passion of my life as it became in the Okanogan, where somehow going to ground had intensified my craving to experience and master the unimaginable natural richness of the world around me. Unless I was hunting with Indians, I hunted alone. I couldn't stand the cold killing and glorying in supposed proofs of manhood that made hunting with White men such a trial. Once Stuart barely paused in the middle of telling me a humorous story to stop his pickup, point a .30-.30 out the window, and blow away a porcupine waddling up a grassy hillside. When he drove on, his only response to my uncomprehending "why?" was to say, "If you had to yank out a hundred quills stuck in your dog's muzzle like I've had to, you'd blow 'em away every chance you got, too!"

Hunting was easy. Most of it was wandering in the hills with no great purpose, like my grandfather, who seldom shot anything. He was "drinking in nature," he said, and it always seemed enough to him just to be out there. That's how it was for me, yet I was a productive hunter, always bringing home meat, even though I hunted only whatever presented itself to me, whatever offered itself to me. It was always that easy, and always more than enough. Well—maybe when I was younger it hadn't been so easy. When you don't know how a thing works you have to chase after it until it turns and gives up its secret.

What was hard was the blood. Even when I was a boy, when the animal grew still and the blood ran out from the body lying on the ground, I felt an unbearable grief. It never got easier, that moment of death I brought about in another living creature. It may be that the best warriors are those who feel nothing when they kill the enemy. The ones I knew from Vietnam who killed that way were certainly the ones who fared best and who seemed to have an air of invulnerability about them. But I took solace in the words I'd heard somewhere to the effect that the best hunters really don't like to hunt. Meaning it hurts them to kill. Because I was one of the best, yet it never stopped hurting to send another soul out of this world. Hunting was what I seemed to have been made for, yet the killing gave no pleasure.

So I talked to them. I tried to be worthy of what I did to them. I left all my doubts and distractions at home and went off into the hills an upright, two-legged animal breathing in life fully, feeling only the need for food and the trueness of my momentary time here on this earth. We can't live without taking another life and using it as food. It's not an abstract fact, this law of survival. It's with us every time we sit at table and open our mouths to eat. Eating is not just taking in protein and carbohydrates—it's eating someone else's life. It's easier for a vegetarian to ignore this since plants don't have eyes that go dim.

And with me it was not just that something had to die so that I and others could live. I went and killed. Sometimes I was forced to finish the job with my bare hands, like the time I ran out of bullets and held a struggling, wounded doe down while I dug a knife into her beating heart. I held her as she took her last straining breaths and her life ran out red and foaming on the grass. And I cried, telling her how grateful I was for her gift of life, her body as food, holding her until the moment she ceased.

In those days I only hunted with a .22 rifle. It was so easy, I only took a few bullets with me. I never took a long shot, never pulled the trigger until I was sure. By then I never thought consciously about it, never questioned what to do. There were few imperatives: Give them a good death and treat what they gave me with respect.

How I came to be this way I had no idea. I was hunting this way before I ever knew Indians. My grandfather I hardly remembered, much less how he killed. And I certainly didn't get it from my father, who killed so indiscriminately it appalled me as a boy. He killed for the thrill of the bang-bang and the bullets ripping up dirt after a fleeing jackrabbit, the snap shot that knocked the pheasant out of the sky, the challenge of a long shot that dropped the coyote so far away he told the story for years to anybody who would listen. But he never went over to see the coyote's body. That's what made me stop going hunting with him: the way he'd kill anything that moved and then walk away as if that's all there was to it.

It was an overcast day. The endless sunny days of summer, touted in travel brochures for so long that "Sunny Okanogan" seemed to be the region's official name, were giving way to the great gray skies of Northwest winter. It was a reminder that only a few hundred miles to the west lay the rainforests of the coast. At this time of year the arid interior could be as cloudy as the coast, but the water gets squeezed out on the trip over the Cascades. Still, that left the cloudiness—day after day of it without a drop of rain, or maybe just a sprinkling here and there, a spit of snow to freshen up the peaks. Horizon to horizon watercolor gray vagueness. Perfect for hunting.

In the morning I walked away into the hills with my rifle and a few things in a pack. I was up there almost all day and thought only about what I was doing, what I saw and felt and smelled and heard. I instinctively knew as always that this was what we were made to do, this was the first and highest use of oneself all the way back to the first man: walking over the earth looking for food, calling on faculties honed by hundreds of thousands of years of hunting.

I climbed up Rattlesnake Draw, leaving the cactus and cheatgrass and mockorange of the lowlands behind, and entered the dark world of steep canyons thick with moss and the silence of fir. No trail, just a steep chute in granite scoured by snowmelt, damp in undercut shadows where poplar roots were exposed like dull bronze snakes lying in gravel. Up and up through cool grottoes of fern and maple brush, threading a maze of jagged rocks at the base of a rockslide, resting in groves of old-growth evergreens standing in pockets of deep soil left by glaciers. Squirrels announced my advance with long-winded warnings that sounded like old-fashioned alarm clocks going off. Ravens hung motionless in updrafts, croaking down at me.

Out onto the terraced heights, lighter but still a land without shadows, I wandered in a dreamy solitude of open grassland and bare, rounded granite, dotted with solitary, storm-twisted pines and boulders of milky vitreous quartz. Bumblebees droned past, red-shafted flickers preened their salmon-colored wing coverts from the tops of gunsight snags, and flocks of chukar partridges chuck-chucked a warning from screes of loose rock.

I was a silent observer in a world that had been going about its business with no help from my kind for time out of mind. Hours of intuitively blending with the rhythms of the world I moved in brought me to the timbered ridges that swung north, steepening toward the summit of Chopaka. I built a tiny fire out of the wind and made a cup of tea, resting and sipping the hot, sweet bitterness while coyotes sang faintly in the wind.

In the afternoon I found my second wind, following deer trails up and down south and east toward Rattlesnake Ridge. A startled "whoof!" and a glimpse of black bear disappearing into dense thickets of bitterbrush. A bit of woolly white hair on a clump of moss . . . what is it? When I pick it up, my hand remembers the feel of rabbit fur. Fresh tracks in mud show the recent passage of mountain lion. I pause to eat sour, hairy gooseberries from stiff canes armed with bristling thorns. I find more berries to taste: blue elderberries, coyoteberries, even late raspberries. More lion tracks, and fresh deer tracks. Then deer tracks everywhere, and fresh droppings.

A bluejay appeared, kwash-kwashing stridently as he hopped from limb to limb in a tall ponderosa pine, his glossy black crest wagging as he eyed me with one eye, then the other. *Kwásh'kai* is the Okanogan name, reminiscent of their call, like many bird names such as *xáw'xaw* for crow and *an'an* for magpie.

Bluejays usually lead me to game, something I never told anybody until I once told Clayton. He said his people had always followed bluejays to find game, adding, "and they laugh at you when you miss!"

When the jay took off to the east, I watched the line of his flight and followed. Every time I came close to whatever solitary tree he landed in, the bluejay flew on in the same general direction to another distant tree. He was leading me down the spine of Rattlesnake Ridge, and I realized my day's tramp had described a wide circle—I was returning toward the steep dropoff into the Sinlahekin Valley and Palmer Lake where I lived. Sagebrush flats cut by timbered ravines spread away toward the emptiness visible a mile away.

In a grove of pines the jay was suddenly gone. Or silent. I stood for a long time, listening to the huff of wind in pine boughs. Then I saw them, about twenty mule deer strung out on the open slopes beyond, blending so well with their surroundings I noticed them only because one took a step while feeding. Up and eating in the late afternoon, they weren't going anywhere particular. I waited until all heads were down at once, then oozed to the ground. With a mental map I crawled down into the nearest ravine, through tangles of coyoteberry and wild rose, up the other side where the rocky ground gave way to the deep loamy soil of tall grass and sagebrush. I left my pack and crawled silently, slowly, blindly toward where I knew the deer browsed, placing each hand, elbow, knee with care. It was a long time of relentless, slow-motion movement. Then I smelled them, the musky deer scent on the wind that blew over them to me. I sensed they had detected my approach, so instead of stalking, I began to move almost aimlessly in their general direction on all fours like another animal, stopping to sniff, chewing on the sagebrush leaves in front of my face, making no more movement than if I was a coyote casually poking around—except for the rifle I kept low in one hand.

Then I stopped. Something inside me said, "Now." I stood up. I was almost in their midst. Strung out to the left and right and directly in front of me, all of them had frozen at my upright appearance and were looking directly at me, their big ears erect. Does and yearlings and a few young bucks. I flipped off the safety and took a deep breath.

"Is there one among you who will come and live with me?" I said, loud enough in the windy blow of bushes so they all could hear me.

At this there was sudden motion. All but one began moving away, the ones to the right running uphill with that prancing, leaping gait so characteristic of mule deer, the ones to the left edging downhill in stiff-legged alarm. But one stood staring at me, a young buck with barely forked antlers. He turned his head to look at the others fleeing, then back at me. Our eyes locked. He was only about forty feet away.

"Are you the one?" I said to him. His head dipped down and up. "Thank you. I'll treat you good!"

I raised the rifle and placed the sights on his heart. He didn't move. The others were already out of sight. Bang—and I see it's a fatal blow to him, the quiver, knees bent. Then he turns and walks slowly, casually away from me, over a rise, and disappears.

The kill trance is upon me but I restrain myself from giving chase. I know what to do when they don't drop, when they go away like that. Sitting down right where I am, I break dry sagebrush branches for a fire, placing them just so while talking to him quietly. Thanking him with great emotion. Telling him I hope when my time comes to die I give myself so freely and to such good purpose. With a match I bring flame out of the twigs and smudge myself in the acrid yellow smoke. Then I sit there until the fire burns itself out. Words come into my mind. *Orésilip*, fire; *shmún'xu*, smoke; *skwa'skúlstin*, sagebrush. Out loud I say: *K'atlús la ch'máxt mi wíkuntum i stla'chínum.* Over the hill a mule deer might be seen. *En'kl'tán.* Dead. *Limlemt.* Thank you.

When the fire is out I'm calm and myself again. I get up and stroll in the direction the deer went. Over the rise, the land slopes gently down to the dropoff into the valley. Except for one leaning fir tree, it's all grass and sage and dried wildflowers, blowing in the wind. How beautiful and perfect the world is. Right at the edge of the dropoff I come across the buck on his side, lying on a flat rock with a stunning view of the valley opening up below and the mountains all around and the lake gleaming off to the north. He came here, to this spot on earth, to die. I am overcome by the unknowable way this speaks to me. I sit for a long time, my hand on his warm, furry body, immersed in the dreamlike beauty of this place he drew me to, this place he came to spend his last moments on earth.

The grief is strong, but so is gratitude for how he offered himself to me. Now he was food. So be it. No animal or plant wants to give its life to someone who doesn't appreciate the magnitude of the sacrifice, who doesn't show respect for what has been given. Hunters who don't know this don't have it easy like I do. So I thanked the deer again, telling him how sorrowful I felt to take his life like this, and promised to treat his body well. Then I went to work.

There's a way of doing things, and my way was something that had the familiarity of years of repetition. This was a big-bodied deer with a slight neck, well-developed legs from roaming his mountainous homeland, and showing the effects of a summer of rich feeding in the glow of russet hair and the full, rounded outline of muscles. Teeth and tongue stained with sage, youthful antlers hard and yellowing to the tines, smelling strong with the glandular musk of the rut, eyes glazed and staring blindly, unmoving in a thickening pool of his own blood, the deer was precious and beautiful in death. I stepped over to the lone fir and spoke to it, snapping off green boughs. I made a bed of boughs next to the deer and rolled him over onto it. There I slit him open with a knife and removed the steaming entrails, cut away the anus full of droppings, opened the chest cavity and cleaned out the dark, clotted handfuls of blood. The ravens and coyotes would eat well tonight. Then I went back for my pack, washed my hands, slung my rifle on my back, and began the long, tiresome, backbreaking labor of dragging the deer home.

By the time I got home with the deer, I was utterly exhausted. It was dusk, and the aftertaste of death and blood was a vague uneasiness now that I was back in the human world of houses, fences, cars, and electric lights. I dragged the deer into the unheated mud room, a wooden porchlike enclosure built onto the trailer at the front door, and then rested with my back against the body, watching night come to the Okanogan.

After supper I skinned the deer and began to butcher. I had the radio playing inside. Moths circled the bare lightbulb overhead and walked slowly up the cold, wet mounds of meat with wings fluttering like some kind of dance. I moved the big pieces of body to the kitchen sink and with a hatchet and knife made manageable chunks which I washed and wrapped in paper.

It was just work you did until it was done. The radio played songs of love and loss, the blood was everywhere, and I thought about how once I had a woman who always did this part after a hunt. It was moments like this that I remembered her: how she had shared my wandering life for awhile, how she loved to butcher and cook and sing. She had been so bold, her blue eyes staring fearlessly into mine. But I had been so grateful for her love I spoiled her—brought her coffee in bed in the morning, cherished the very sound of her voice. I too obviously feared losing her. When she turned selfish and demanding, as if my role in life was to please her and I wasn't doing a very good job, I was appalled. When she became a bully, and grew fat on her appetite to bend me and life to her will, I loaded my things and drove away. I had known the love they were singing about on the radio, and with the only woman I'd ever known who truly loved to butcher animals. But never again would I treat a woman like a goddess come to earth. And as the years passed in solitary regret, I wondered if I'd ever get another chance to do differently.

The next morning I loaded all the wrapped meat in boxes and drove off to find Clayton and give it all to him. It had been a sudden decision, made with no thought as I sat on the porch watching the geese fly over heading south in V-formation, honking softly under the same high gray roof as the day before. Somehow it felt gloomy to me, like a hangover. Driving the road along the lake I saw cars pulled off, parked in high grass, and people on ladders in the orchard trees, filling sacks with apples. Harvest was in full swing.

I met Stuart coming the other way driving a flatbed loaded with bales of hay for his horses. We stopped in the middle of the road, elbow to elbow with the motors running, and he quizzed me about where I went in the mountains, what I saw, where the deer were, and how I got one. His blue Australian cow dog rose from his perch on top of the bales and sniffed the air, trembling and whining at the smell wafting from the boxes behind my cab. We could hear snatches of song in Spanish from the rows of trees stretching up to the base of the mountain. When a car came up behind me and stopped patiently, we said so long and I drove on.

Clayton was at the corral by the river, leaning on the log rails and giving advice to Jim about the slow process of taming the stud horse. I saw the horse on the far side, stamping and rubbing his halter on a post. Empty burlap feed sacks were tied over the animal's withers and hanging from the halter under his mouth. Clayton and Jim had progressed to sacking him down—getting him used to things hanging and banging against him. He had one blue eye that stared crazily, but he stood with the pride and self-possession of all stallions, young as he was. Jim told me he had one flaw: He was skittish about any slight drop-off in the ground, balking at the edge of a one-foot creekbank as if it were a chasm, then leaping with an exaggerated, terrified burst of power as far as he could to get over it. Maybe it was his weird eye. Jim said he was going to train him for the Suicide Race at the Omak Stampede, held every summer, where horses are ridden full tilt over a cliff, down the soft bank, across the river a hundred feet below, and over the finish line inside the rodeo ring on the other side. I'd heard how Indians looked for horses that were afraid of going off edges and trained them into champion suicide racers. It baffled me how they did it. It was one of those things Indians could do that defied logic and common sense. Or so I thought.

"It's not so strange," Jim said, laughing at my bafflement. "Which would you rather ride over a cliff? A horse that doesn't have the sense to be afraid and goes blindly into something he don't know how to handle? Or one that's so afraid you have to talk him into doing it over and over again until he's got it down pat?"

"Sorta like choosin' a wife," Clayton said, obviously in good spirits this day. Jim had never settled down with any woman yet, and Clayton knew my story.

"Yeah, but there's no purse at the end of *that* race, eh?" Jim said, head down and the tip of his boot kicking the dried piles of horse droppings. "Besides, I'd break so many hearts out there if I settled down and stopped making the rounds! You're the one who should be choosin', uncle."

"Yah, but my *nak'wétstin* won't have me!"

They grinned at each other. Clayton was Jim's father's older and only brother. Ever since Jim's dad had died, Clayton had grown more like a father to him, although the old nephew-uncle ease and teasing still prevailed. When Clayton's wife died and Charlene, Jim's mother, had not remarried, Salish custom kicked in to give the two a special relationship, and a term to call each other, *nak'wétstin*. In *Skélux* eyes, the brother of a dead husband had first right to marry the widow. Or if a man's wife died, he had to look first for a wife among her sisters. In the old days, only if the *nak'wétstin* refused or was already married could the widow or widower look elsewhere. Or like Charlene, refuse to remarry. But nowadays it wasn't much observed. Clayton was already living with a woman, married "Indian way," and continued to treat Charlene like his sister-in-law.

Charlene came out with two young girls and started putting sliced apples and pears to dry. She wore a yellow apron and her hands moved so fast the slices piled up faster than the girls could spread them out on the screens. The screens looked like ordinary screen doors propped up between two rusted cars almost engulfed in wild rose brambles. Charlene turned and yelled at some dogs milling around my parked pickup. One leaped out of the bed. She looked over at me.

"They won't stay out of the back of your truck. What've you got in there?"

"Oh, yeah—I forgot," I said, and led Clayton and Jim to the truck. I picked up a stick and said, "Yesterday I killed a deer." I handed Clayton the stick. "All the meat is yours."

"*Aaaa.*" He beamed, accepting the stick from me and shaking my hand the way Indians do it, barely touching fingers. We leaned over the side of the truck and he touched the stick to individual wrapped cuts of meat oozing pink liquid in the boxes. Charlene and the girls came over and looked at all the meat with great interest. One of the girls climbed in and dug around, lifting packages of meat, going, "Oooh, it's so soft!"

Manna from heaven. Everything stops in the presence of a gift of value. I knew Clayton didn't have a freezer, but I also knew he'd distribute the meat so widely it would be gone in no time. He reached across the bed of the truck, proffering the stick to Charlene.

"*Wai, i nak'wétstin*, here, you give out this meat to our people!"

"*Loot awhá!*" she cried, recoiling in mock horror. "No! That woman of yours come lookin' for me with a gun!"

This exchange gave them both so much pleasure they had to wipe their eyes.

"Well, maybe somebody put it in your freezer for now," he said, and Jim and I started carrying the boxes to the mobile home. The sweatlodge retreat was still on my mind, so I asked Jim if he ever went on one.

"Yep, I sure did. When I was about fifteen," he said, lifting the freezer lid and stacking meat up one side.

"Was it hard?"

"Yeah, I got bored. But it cured me."

"Of what?"

"I had all these skin sores, and I used to have a big birthmark right here," he said, touching fingers to his cheek under one eye.

"Did your uncle do it with you?"

"No. Old Willie sponsored me. I was so afraid of him. We're related I can't remember how. But he still scared me to death."

I knew enough to stop there. We finished and he closed the lid, then we went to wash our hands. He grinned by the sink.

"It won't be bad. Just be willing to die and everything'll be all right!"

"Thanks a lot."

"You're welcome."

So I went to Clayton and asked him when we might be going.

"Come the new day, we go," he said, his eyes shining. "I come and get you." Evidently I just hadn't hit on the right way to ask him before today. It reminded me of something my father always said: "If you want something, make yourself useful to somebody."

But we didn't go the next day, or the next. There were feasts to attend—not surprisingly featuring venison in a variety of dishes. Clayton had me drive him in his car to a get-together way down in the wide openness of the main valley near Omak, at the house of his wife's daughter. His wife was already there, basking in the pleasure of feeding so many people, her graying hair newly styled in the fashion popular with teenagers, her front locks swept up in a gelled wave fixed at the point of cresting. It made me think of a peacock's sexual display, a thought I quickly squelched when she ushered me back to the place of honor at her table with a dignity and formality I hadn't seen in her before.

Then we all filled several cars and drove to a feast at the community center in Malott, farther down the valley. Clayton's old Ford barely got up to the speed limit with so many people packed in. I drove through Omak's busy apple shed district dodging forklifts crossing the street loaded with full bins balanced two or three high. Belching a cloud of blue smoke, drawing the amused attention of lounging truck drivers and shed workers, the old car finally broke free of town and chugged down the open highway. From the back seat, Jim's brother-in-law, as hostile as ever and drunk as usual, slurred, "Now this is livin' . . . Ev'ry Indian should have his *own* White chauffeur!"

In the Met'how band hall, a low, government-brown wooden building set off in the sagebrush near the rows of government housing, long tables lined up end to end were already filled with people. I found an empty seat next to a man I knew slightly, the only other White man present, and drank coffee with him. Lionel Burke, a janitor at the local

Indian school, was married to a Colville and had half a dozen children. I'd heard him speak fluent Okanogan with elders, so I struck up a conversation with him and mentioned I was about to go on a sweatlodge retreat with Clayton Tommy.

"*Aaaa.*" he said. "*K'ulsht.* Self-training. There's something you don't hear about much these days."

"What's it about?"

"It's not about anything."

"Have you ever sweated?"

"All my adult life."

"What do you mean, then, it's not about anything?"

He didn't answer. He sipped his coffee and looked straight ahead like nothing was happening. Like nothing had been said. It dawned on me that this guy sitting there in institutional khaki work clothes dusted with the chalk of schoolroom floors wasn't a White man at all, really, that he was as offended by my demanding questions as Clayton would have been. I was mortified to see my Anglo striving so openly displayed. How easily I fell back into the aggressive, abrasive ways of my own people when I thought I was talking to one.

On the table was a coffee cup filled with loose cigarettes for anyone to smoke. I reached for one and offered it to Lionel.

"Somebody spoke without thinking," I said.

He took the cigarette with a curious smile. Then after a long silence between us, he said, "If you go through with this, maybe you'll see what I'm talking about." He gave me a level look.

"If you don't say '*aaaa,*' they stop talking after awhile because they think you aren't listening, or you don't care."

"*Aaaa,*" I said, provoking his crooked, toothy smile.

"It's hard, that ten-day thing. Me, I came back with *asíl chásyakin*, two heads. The White man head and the Indian head. I didn't know *what* was true—disoriented, I guess. Clayton, that old bugger, he says: 'Aren't two heads better than one?'"

"It's no good split like that. Just like my wife. Only she went to school and got this head full of *Suyápi* ways. You don't know how to live with both of 'em. Have to sort it out, make some kind of peace. Maybe choose one way over the other. Or go crazy. Or stay drunk."

"*Aaaa.*"

He smelled the tobacco, tapped the cigarette on the table, said something to his daughters eating on the other side of him, looked back at me.

"But you'll be okay."

I smiled. He was a fine man, so measured in what he said and did. Like a rock for his family.

"Do you dance in the Winter Dances?" I asked him.

"I go, but I don't dance. My older kids do, and my wife. I just help."

That level, assessing look again.

"I'll tell you what Old Willie told me way back, when I married Feather. She's his *shnímat*, or grandchild, what we'd call, like, a grand-niece or something. You know how the elders just stand up and talk at public gatherings, like this one, make a speech? Well, I came here on the run, like you, twenty years ago. Old Willie gives this talk at the wedding reception, all in the Native language. Later he asks me, 'You know what I said?' I say no. He says: 'Stand still and let the good catch up to you!'"

So we were finally on our way, Clayton and I, heading north into British Columbia, me driving his ever-sputtering white Ford station wagon, and Clayton quietly looking at the mountainous world go by. If there was anything I'd learned about Native ways, it was that right time and place were everything. If the need is great, time and place will come looking for you. But if you're seeking something out, you have to sit tight and let it happen as it will. I was ready for anything after talking to Lionel Burke, filled with assent for whatever might happen in my life. I was going to stand still and let the good catch up to me.

We were heading up the same highway through the same mountain valley I'd driven down with Jim Woods when I first came to the Okanogan. It was autumn now, not high summer. There were no nighthawks. The orchards looked golden and bedraggled, harvest already over, the trees battered and listless, ravished of their fruit by an army of men and machines. It had been years since I'd come this way, up the narrow corridor of the Similkameen River, up into an even more mountainous world where the season was advanced farther along than back home.

For some reason I had envisioned us setting up a sweatlodge on Omak Lake where Clayton had sweathoused when he was a boy and where so many of his revelations to me had taken place, but here we were going in exactly the opposite direction, following the highway past Keremeos, going farther and farther to the northwest into the heart of British Columbia's mountainous bush. Past the lone boulder big as a house that stands dramatically in an open pasture where centuries of travelers along this ancient route had left red ochre pictures of spirit partners, mythological stories and advertisements of doctoring powers. And where Clayton had me pull off barely clear of the mad rush of cars and trucks along this main Canadian highway so he could throw out a cigarette and say a few words in Salish.

Around noon we pulled down onto an overgrown track, a long-unused road that skirted the swift-moving Similkameen. The golden leaves of poplar trees lit up the somber green of fir and pine, flew out in escaping clouds at each gust of wind, floated by clumped like rafts atop the shiny water. The track disappeared and Clayton guided me to a sandy clearing full of flowering goldenrod and clumps of crimson brush maple, where I parked.

Clayton, without a word or gesture, but carrying a fir bough he found lying on the ground, set off down a trail along the river. It was invigorating to stroll around in the crisp sunshine after hours of sitting at the steering wheel. Leisurely following in the old man's direction,

I walked upriver along grassy banks undercut by the current. Through the clear green roil I could see a bouldery bottom. Forested mountains rose up closer and closer on the opposite side of the river, their rocky summits flecked with white. I found Clayton standing and looking around intently on a flat sand shore overhung by towering trees that leaned out over the water. Some of the trees were coast cedars, limbs draped with a rich yellow-green lushness found only along the rivers in this more arid country.

Still silent, Clayton came up to me unraveling a length of twine. Holding one end on the ground at my foot, he measured up my leg to the hip bone, then tied a stick at that spot. As he walked back he tied another stick to the loose end of twine. With a river cobblestone, he pounded one stick into the hardpacked sand, then pulled the twine tight and scribed a circle around the fixed point with the other stick, ending up with a perfect circle marked on the ground, about six feet across. Tossing away the sticks, winding up the twine, Clayton regarded me with the beginnings of a smile.

"You got long legs there. This maybe the biggest sweathouse for two men I ever gonna see."

"Doesn't look that big to me." The ones I'd seen covered with tarps like rounded half-domes tucked away behind Indian homes looked as big as this was going to be.

"Yah, but we gonna do it the old way, no canvas or plastic, just like in the beginning. Mine, when I so young, to see my sponsor bend his head and barely fit, his long white hair almost touch the hot rocks, his chin on his knees!"

"I like this place. It's beautiful here." Bluejays screeched and scolded from the treetops, then flew across the river in a ragged flock. Clayton watched them, blinking in the wind.

"*Kwásh'kai* find things, more than just game to hunt. He find this place for you, show it to me."

"*Aaaa.*"

"This way, to train yourself in life. To walk through life the man, head up, who have that right to be here. This how we train to receive the healing, the power that come. That way of knowin'—it come from this old man we put together here." He looked at the circle on the ground before us. "So we do this how they always done it, way back to legend time."

"*Aaaa.*"

"Better to talk Indian much as you can. My want, that they hear you, come and see you here."

"Who?"

"Them *shumíx*. That why we can talk to animals, they understand the Indian language."

I felt totally inadequate to the task. What little I knew of Salish was going to be like baby talk.

"They miss to hear our beautiful Native language. Just a little bit, don't worry! They come runnin'!"

"They don't understand English?"

He looked at me in surprise, then pity.

"Sure, they know all languages. How could they not? But like, Indian language is *their* language. Not like English, cold, no feelin' in the words. Like that stud horse my nephew trainin', he understand what he say to him in Indian."

"Sometimes I think animals can understand me when I talk to them," I said. I was thinking about how I talked to the deer I killed. But I turned instead to pets. "Surely people who have dogs and cats, their pets understand them?"

"Oooh, Fifi! Oh, my sweet Fifi!" he said in a high-pitched voice, petting an imaginary lapdog held in his arms. "What you been up to? Naughty! Naughty doggie! Why you be so bad?" He looked at me. "That what you mean?"

"No, no, wait a minute," I said, laughing with him. "What about when I talk to the animals I hunt? I know they understand me. I can feel it." He had heard me talk to animals and plants in English, just like he and Johnny Stemilt did in *Skélux* when we were off hunting together. But he'd never made any mention of it.

"Maybe the time come for that. You put your heart into that, I hear you. Never hear a *Suyápi* talk to animals like that before. I dunno. I see the Whites so thrilled when a Indian give a speech, talk to our mother, to our mountain. They jealous, they have that envy. They hear our words, what is in our hearts, what we want, what we gonna do, how we just like the earth.

"To be embarrassed by such talk, like only children talk to animals, talk to mountains. Or maybe ashamed, maybe down deep he know what he doin' to the earth is wrong. If he try to speak from the heart, like we do in Indian, he have to say: 'Too bad, mountain, you in my way! I gonna bulldoze you outta my way!' Or, 'I dunno why I hunt you deer. Oooh, your body stinks! I guess I just kill you for your big horns, so I can show off to other guys!' Or like you see up here, 'Oh my gosh, you big trees is gonna make me a pile of money!'"

"*Aaaa.*"

"What good, to talk from your heart, when your heart is bad? So they don't. That cold English, hidin' behind those words that don't sing."

"You seem to do pretty good with it," I said.

"Yah," he sighed. "It all English now. That why them *shumíx* so lonesome to hear the real language. We inside the lodge, you do your best, eh? It be like love, like a blessing to them." He grinned at using my words like that.

"*Aaaa,*" I affirmed.

The insistent murmur of the river was soothing as we stood there quietly just being there. A loon shot by, close to the water, heading downriver. The chilling wind of autumn continued to shake the trees overhead, scattering more yellow leaves out onto the glossy surface.

With only brief words of instruction from Clayton and both of us working without pause, it took about four hours to construct the sweatlodge. While Clayton shoveled out a pit the size of the measured circle, I cut long willow poles from thickets growing along the river and dragged them back. We sharpened the butt ends of the poles and stuck them into holes around the perimeter, leaving slightly more space between two on the side closest to the river. Starting with one of these two, which would end up framing the entrance, we bent the flexible willow poles in a curve across the circle to meet one from the other side. When two poles were side by side, about waist-high, Clayton showed me how to wind the thin top parts of the poles around the thick lower part of the opposite one, tucking the twiggy brush at the ends into a slip knot. This left a stiff, free-standing, perfect curve of wood. We did this with ten poles, five on each side of the circle, leaving five parallel hoops, then started forming hoops at right angles to these. When we were done, there were five more perfectly curved hoops, running tightly over the first five. It was so simple, I was stunned. Here in no time we had a sturdy, graceful hemisphere, the basic framework of all sweatlodges. It was beautiful.

Then he sent me to find some young fir trees, as bushy as possible. After a long, wandering search in the surrounding bottomlands I found two about ten feet tall in a sunny clearing.

"*Ch'k'ílhp, áamp'sum, limlemt,* (Fir tree, such a pity, thank you)," I said, seeing how it felt to use what Salish I could come up with. My heart was in it. The fir tree knew. Sap ran freely as the hatchet sank into new wood. I returned, dragging a tree in each hand.

When I got back, Clayton had woven more willow poles into the original structure, in and out horizontally in three doubled ranks running around the circle, except the lowest rank which stopped at either side of the doorway. Right there he'd dug a sloping passage to the pit floor, which was about a foot deep on the river side and rose slightly to the rear. We went and gathered armfuls of wild rye grass that grew in immense clumps as tall as a man all over the clearing around us, all yellow and seeded out and dry as straw. He began to attach handfuls of this thatch to the willow framework and sent me for more. As I came and went, stocking up piles of rye grass all around the perimeter, he forced the ends of handfuls between the doubled horizontal poles, which held the thatch in place by tension. He started at the bottom and worked around, then higher with an overlapping layer. Seeing how he did it, I joined him in thatching the third rank and the topmost part, until all was covered, except the doorway, to a thickness of about eight inches. At the very crown, where it was thinnest, he used all the remaining grass to spread out a thick, loose layer and pinned it in place with small lengths of willow laid on, the ends poked into the framework underneath.

I could see Clayton was tiring, but there was such a glow, an intensity in his eyes, such a silence of concentration that I knew he was enjoying this work. Old-time work. Legend-time work.

I hauled buckets of water from the river which he threw over the thatched dome until it was all drenched and giving off the smell of wet straw. Then we shoveled the loose sandy soil of the excavation onto the thatch, smoothing it with our hands up the walls and over the top. It clung readily to the thatch. We had to dig more nearby to cover the sweatlodge to a thickness that satisfied Clayton, then turned to the two fir trees. While I lopped off boughs, he climbed inside with his *picha*, a three-foot-long, curved, sharpened stick of ironwood used for digging plant roots. He dug a small pit just inside the entrance to the right, and tossed the soil out. Then he took the fir boughs I handed in to him and showed me how to spread them smoothly on the floor. Starting at the pit with butt ends pointing to the rear, he worked back, overlapping so thickly he finished with a springy bed of fir tips.

Clayton crawled out and walked off to his car for something. I stood back and looked at what we'd accomplished. It looked like a symmetrical mound in the sandy ground, a natural bulge in the earth. It had been rough, dirty work, but simple and quick. No string or nail had been used. The whole structure was held in place by the tension of willow branches alone! Clayton Tommy sure had my respect. I had no idea how deep was his reservoir of practical bush knowledge and skill.

He came back with a big mountain goat skin folded around the padding of an old quilt and draped them over the small doorway from nearly over the top. Then he sent me to gather firewood.

"Bring only branches from the big fir trees," he said. "That old man *ch'k'ílhp*, he take pity on us, make it easy for us to take off his dry arms."

By trial and error I learned how even the longest dead fir branches, hanging from ten feet over my head, would break cleanly near the trunk when I pulled from the very tip-end. By experimenting with the other kinds of forest trees—the ponderosa pines, spruces, cedars and poplars—I found that this ease of breaking did not hold with them. The dead limbs of spruce wouldn't break no matter how far I bent them. The others took more force to break than fir, and never to the thickness or so close to the trunk. Only the fir was so easy and so productive, the Douglas fir, the most numerous of all trees in that country. By dusk, I had a chest-high pile of fir branchwood near the sweatlodge.

About fifty feet away in the trees, Clayton had set up a little bush camp while I had been gathering firewood. Under a lean-to constructed of poles tied to trees and covered with the old wagon tarp he used on our hunting trips, he'd piled our whole outfit—sleeping bags, blankets, cooking pot, buckets, food, and my backpack. The rush of the river was a steady, continuous presence at this spot. It was getting darker by the minute, and the wind had dropped to nothing. I stood off a ways, feeling a gathering moodiness, a gloom enveloping me like the dark forest closing in. Clayton lit a fire and unpacked gear, his motions stiff and weary, but I felt detached from him and unwilling to step across the invisible boundary from bush to camp. I was becoming some brooding thing of the night bush, wary of the flamelit familiarity under the tarp.

I heard Clayton humming a song, and looked over to see him slicing carrots and cutting up venison for stew. It was a captivating melody, simple and repetitive, vaguely similar to other Salish songs I'd heard. His voice made tone shifts never heard in White music. His voice spreading out into the forest dissolved my feeling of separation. My old feeling of joining easily into camp routine came back, I stepped into the light and knelt down to help him prepare dinner.

"This the time they come lookin'," he said, not raising his head from his work. "After sunset, before the full night, they come out. And again, at dawn. That dim time, before full dark, before sunrise. They know what we here for. Where that salt we throw in?" I dug in my backpack.

"I think it's . . . yeah, here." Clayton salted the stew and set it over the flames on a wire grille propped on rocks.

We settled back in comfort against our bedrolls.

"Now, won't be long, we eat good, *Skélux*. Come the new day, you not eat, not drink till after sunset again, like this. That how it go. Little bit less, little bit less, each day. Till maybe just a mouthful of water that night before the tenth day. This how we train ourself for life. With the sweatlodge, to train ourself, perhaps get an education. Lotta good things come from this. That old man heal whatever is wrong, whatever you ask him to.

"These things to hold in your mind as time go on. Not to hurry or struggle. Let this good come to you. Like the young say now'days, 'no big deal.' Ten days, a long time to look around this world and wonder. Think about how pitiful we are with no help from those powers, those forces of nature out there." He waved towards the darkness. "And how maybe they come and see you trainin' yourself, makin' yourself clean and fit to be a power man in this life."

I thought about his words, stirring the stew and adding sticks to the fire to keep it bubbling slowly.

"I appreciate this, what you're doing for me, Clayton. *Límtenun'tm* (Makes me feel glad)."

He nodded, staring at the flames, the buckles of his suspenders shining yellow in the firelight. He slipped off his soft leather shoes and wagged his stocking feet close to the fire's heat. He could have been home with his wife or hanging out in the social warmth of the Woods household, but here he was out in the British Columbia bush, out in the cold autumn night taking the time to teach me this old way of his people. I knew he felt a man's place was out in the hills or on the ranches, making his living. He had a hunter's aversion to any suggestion that he'd rather hang out at home with the women than be off with the men in the hills, even at his age. Yet now that we were here, I felt a little surprised that he was actually doing this with me. It was something elders did for family members, and despite the decline of interest in traditional lore among young Salish, Clayton didn't lack for requests for sponsorship from members of his extended family.

"I guess I wonder sometimes why you help me like this, when we're not related." He laughed unexpectedly.

"You such a card," he mused. "You got no other people, *Skélux*. Who else gonna do for you?"

"Nobody, I guess. *Skélux* . . . you keep calling me 'Indian.'"

"I like you, Indian. You like they say, down to earth. Love our mother. Why not you, instead of them 'apples' runnin' around the tribal center, think they're in charge?"

The contempt in Clayton's voice was not disguised. Jim Woods, I knew, had no use for the largely acculturated tribal office workers who approached Clayton with tobacco, calling on distant kinship ties to solicit his support, who flaunted or used their Native identity while behaving like White men. I'd heard their brassy, garrulous voices promoting the new plan to develop a huge molybdenum mine on Colville land with a powerful mining corporation. The promise of economic boom, destruction of a mountain, sudden social dislocations—

all these were heating up reservation politics, splitting the Colville Confederated Tribes into warring camps. I knew Clayton was involved in tribal affairs, but I was only beginning to understand how virulent reservation politics could get. And it was looking like a sure thing, this mechanized destruction of a mountain in exchange for comfort and security for tribal members, to the dismay of traditional *Skélux*, whose emotional reverence for the earth isolated them from their own supposed leaders.

"You just the opposite," he said, moving the stew pot off the grille. "On the outside is the White man, the smart mouth with a big mustache. But on the inside, you like the old-time Indian."

"Yeah, but you sponsor them. I know you never refuse them."

"They just come out here and pretend. Put up with it, tough it out. Then they go back, wear it like a big reputation. Look so solemn, but see, they just showin' off. They kill to be the boss. Don't change their mind, 'cause they buy the power they crave by sellin' off our mother. Don't know about any other.

"No . . . I help you, *Skélux*," he said warmly, handing me a bowl and spoon. "Bein' a Indian not about the color of your skin or how much Indian blood you got. It about what in your heart.

"That old-time way, we say, *en'hwl'hwl'tíls*, want to live. To have that want to be here. I see you walk over the earth. You want this thing you are. You want to live.

"Not like the apple, talkin' like he know what in our hearts. What best for us. Like the White man, he just pretending. Out for himself, he have to make a big show like he got something. *En'hwl'hwl'tsá*, just the opposite, how you say, his want to pretend. Make a show that other people think high of him."

Clayton looked at me waiting with empty bowl in hand, his brow furrowing as if he wondered what I thought of all he'd said.

"Want to eat!" I said, digging into the pot.

8

Just after dawn, I woke up smelling the rain and listening to it pattering on the tarp above me. Shivering as I climbed out of warm bedding into the cold and damp, I pulled on clothes. Clayton's old army sleeping bag was already rolled up and tied with twine. The sheltered ground under the wagon tarp was a dry island in a sea of rain, a ceaseless autumn downpour that snuffed out the memory of summer. Across the river, the dark, ragged forms of fir and cedar appeared cut in half by low, drifting clouds. Clayton walked up the trail from his car, soaking wet, carrying two battered metal buckets of rocks. Gray hair matted like a wet rat accentuated the roundness of his head. Rivulets of water running down his face, he seemed unconcerned with the rain. Instead of a coat he wore two wool shirts, one over the other, hanging wet-heavy as he stiff-armed the buckets to where I stood under the tarp.

"Hoh! There we go!" he puffed, buckets thudding to the ground. Gesturing to the rain, he said, "A perfect day. It a good sign, to start off on a day like this."

I was incredulous. "Raining like this?"

"Sure," he said, removing the outer shirt, wringing it out and wiping his face with it. "Sweatlodge bring here a day of his own. We have built his form as he instruct long, long ago. He know what we desire. This rain his doin'."

He ignored my puzzled look, dug among the piles of gear, saying, "Now. The good little student, to pay attention and remember." He produced a bundle of dry branchwood and kindling sticks, stored the night before, and looked up at me, eyes ready to laugh, knowing

I hadn't thought to be so prepared. "Plan for your fire, each day." He wrapped his poncho over the bundle of wood and strode off through wet bushes toward the sweatlodge. "Bring the rocks."

The buckets were so heavy I thought my arms would pop out of their sockets in the short distance to the lodge. The rain fell as a penetrating chill. Clayton went to work with no regard for the rain, except for how it might prevent the fire from getting started. About six feet from the goathide doorflap, he had me shovel out a pit in the soft earth. It was dry about a foot down, and using his body to shield his work from the rain, he quickly built a tipi of twigs, adding larger and larger sticks until he had a pile about a foot high. Igniting a wooden match with his thumbnail, he held the flame under the smallest twigs at the bottom.

"Fire, smoke, come forth," he said in a kind of singsong, repeating five times, then saying the same in Salish. A thin gray thread rose up into his eyes, flames appeared, snapping and popping. Clayton rocked back on his heels and dumped the last dry wood on the flames. Still sheltering the fire as much as possible with both our bodies, we began to lay on wet wood. The bright flames faltered, hissed, sent up a billow of white smoke. We stood side by side blocking the rain, and I was shivering dramatically from the water running down my neck under the collar of my military field coat. Shifting miserably from foot to foot, head lost in smoke, I waited as Clayton added bigger and bigger branches.

Ho, the mighty woodsman whimpering in the rain. It was laughable, really. I may have loved the wind and storm, but ceaseless cold-fingered downpour reaching in to chill my bones and squeeze my heart was not my cup of tea. Clayton, on the other hand, seemed to thrive on it.

When the flames finally roared, driving us back, Clayton spread the fire out with a long stick. He threw on more wood until he had a flat pile about three feet across and a foot high, barely burning again, but coming back slowly from below. One by one he placed the rounded volcanic rocks onto the bed of branches, piling them into a tightly clustered pyramid of fifteen or twenty, then covered them with heavy pieces of wood stacked up against the rocks in tipi form. The fire roared back, rising up in a pillar of flames that hissed and smoked heavily in the rain.

Clayton held a handful of tobacco, said a short Salish prayer in a high, almost keening voice that slid down to an emotional *"Wai i hwi!"* and then scattered the tobacco over the fire. Smoke hung threaded into overhanging branches. I had to step back in the face of blasting heat, and step back again, warm for the first time since getting out of bed. Our clothes steamed. He looked at me, as if it were my turn.

"I am warm, thank you," I said to the fire, and Clayton laughed.

Back at the bush camp he unrolled an old blanket and called me over. Wrapped up were some things we would use in the sweating ceremony. Two yard-long wooden tongs, fire-blackened on one end. I ran my fingers over the gray, scaly bark, and the smooth bumps where stout thorns had been removed, recognizing it as the local hawthorn. A big pile of fresh sagebrush. A gallon-size woven basket commonly called *yámhwa*, its insides covered with some dark, impervious substance. Pine pitch, Clayton said, and in the bottom of the basket, embedded in the pitch, was a small piece of translucent white quartz. The last thing was a fan of bluejay tail feathers, mounted beautifully on a beaded wooden handle that was short and flat. Blue, black, and light blue beads mimicked the pattern on each feather, the blue vanes ribbed with parallel black lines.

Clayton held the fan flat to his hand with his thumb curled under, holding it in place like extensions of his fingers. Then he gestured like a bluejay in flight, descending in wavy arcs, calling out in the bluejay's alarm cry, "Kwash-kwash-kwash-kwash!" It was so startlingly realistic, so loud, I was hardly surprised when I heard answering cries from out in the conifers. One especially noisy jay flew to a low branch nearby and kwash-kwashed at us, then shook himself in a spray of wet. Clayton threw some crackers out to the base of a tree. Silently, the bedraggled jay dropped to the ground and eyed us warily, hopping closer and closer to the crackers. Clayton jerked up the fan of feathers, then lowered them slowly and smoothly, then jerked them up again and repeated the slow, smooth descent. He was mimicking exactly what the jay was doing with its tail after each hop: jerk up, then slow lowering. It was some kind of signal or communication. Clayton synchronized his fan gestures with the jay's tail signal, both of them jerking up, then lowering in a smooth, slow motion.

"*Kwásh'kai, limlemt,*" he murmured. The jay nabbed the crackers all in a bunch, flew up, and was gone. It reminded me I wouldn't eat that day, until evening, and I was hungry.

Back at the sweatlodge, Clayton lifted the flap and placed some of the sage and the fan behind the pit. He walked around in the rain poking the fire and rearranging the burning wood to cover the rocks evenly. The fir wood popped loudly, sending glowing embers out to hiss and sputter on the wet ground. Even though my clothes were soaked through, I no longer shivered. He piled on more wood and sent me to the river to fill the basket, saying, "Now, all is ready and we wait for the rocks. Like the elders always say, go slow and easy. This your time of healin'. Take the time to look around, feel this place. Nothin' else goin' on. Nothin' to worry about, to figure out. This day, to feel how you want to live. What you got, that *shumíx,* comin' to see you purify yourself, train yourself for power."

Time and place had narrowed to here and now. As we got closer to the sweat, all other preoccupations and distractions fell away. I didn't know what to expect from moment to moment—it was all new—and I naturally adopted Clayton's outward appearance of quiet acceptance and simple enjoyment of doing tasks, or doing nothing at all. At the river's edge I stood for a long time mesmerized by the stippled pattern of rain on the glossy surface sliding by. I was slowing down almost to a halt inside, letting the rich, wet world around me sink in. Not one other thing to do in the world but get water and wait. Balance on the tip of a boulder just inches above the clear flow. Listen to the muscled murmur of river under the hiss of rain. See the crimson fringes of roots waving in the lap of water undercutting the bank. Dip the basket into ice water. Walk back slowly along, balancing the heavy, watertight basket . . . how the quartz pebble glows on the bottom. Set it down inside, behind the shallow pit to the right of the doorway, smelling the resinous, Christmas tree scent of the fir needles. Stand staring at the fire, so compelling to the eyes, so utterly mysterious how wood consumes in garish flame and rocks glow with an inner orange brightness. Stand staring at Indian television while raindrops patter on my clothes and bare head, and the front of me bakes and steams.

When Clayton judged the rocks to be ready, he shoveled the remaining burning branches to the back and exposed the rocks in a radiant bed of coals. He rolled them to one side of the pit, then picked up the tong sticks. Holding the two butt ends together with one hand, and manipulating the fire-blackened ends by spreading and squeezing together the middle part of the sticks with his other hand, he skillfully seized and carried rock after rock to the pit just inside the doorway. After he had transferred about half the rocks, he rubbed the smoking ends of the tongs in wet sand, then leaned them against the earth bank of the lodge. He covered the remaining rocks with fire and added more wood. Then we undressed, tucked folded clothes and shoes under his poncho, kneeled and crawled in.

It was already warm inside, the fir boughs a soft, scratchy cushion under me, and we sat facing the pit and the open doorway, Clayton on the pit side, tucking his bluejay fan into the willow wickerwork over his head. Then he pulled down the mountain goat hide doorflap and arranged it until it was totally dark inside. Instant stuffy blackness permeated with the fragrance of fir and wet sage. A cavelike silence, a clicking heat rising from translucent, glowing rocks.

A sharp sizzling and sputtering burst from the rocks, and an invisible choking cloud of steam rose up, enveloping us, smelling of burning sage. Again and again, Clayton dipped a branch of sagebrush in the water and splashed the glowing rocks. Then he poured cupped handfuls of water on, again and again. The burning vapor scalded my face and shoulders, threatening to collapse my lungs. The heat intensified until it was unbelievable.

Clayton said a few words in the *Skélux* language, naming me, calling on Sweatlodge to take pity on me, on us both. Then he began to sing in a quavering voice. His song began as rhythmic grunts that slowly became a distinct melody, as if it took time for him to recall it, or get to the place inside him where the song was. Then he sang with surprising emotion, and in a voice that gained strength. It was difficult for me even to breathe, much less sing, but I tried to hum along as best I could.

Again the old man sprinkled the rocks, crying out in a long rush of Salish spoken so rapidly I only registered the obvious pleading quality. At each splash of water the rocks dimmed, then glowed forth again. As time passed they became dimmer and dimmer until all was utter burning darkness. Clayton sang a new song, but in the scald of my throat and lungs I came face to face with my own threshold of pain. I toppled to the floor, pressing my face into the cool fir needles—I could breathe again! Here the air was cool and my head out of the cloud of burning steam, but the change made me light-headed, dizzy, nauseated.

More water splashing on the rocks, and another song, Clayton's voice sagging and becoming hoarse. Maybe five songs in all. I lost contact with the passage of time. There was only the rhythm of Clayton's singing voice, the splash and sizzle of water turning to steam, the unbelievable difficulty of breathing, and the slow, drumlike beating of my heart. I sat up as well as I could—it was less dizzying. Gripping my knees, rocking back and forth to withstand the agonizing, oven-like pressure, blinking my sightless eyes at the constant stream of sweat pouring down my face, my body oozed water from every pore.

A sudden blinding light and cool flow of air as the old man threw up the doorflap with a wet splat. He crawled out through the swirling fog of steam and I followed, standing up unsteadily, blinking in the bright rainy daylight. How green the world looked. Following him past the fire to the river, I was amazed to see our naked bodies swathed in clouds of effervescent steam. The rain felt like continuous pinpoints of touch. I waded into the pull of river with Clayton, slipped on the slick boulders, fell under the wonderful, awakening coolness. I held my breath and went under, into a blurry, vividly yellow world that kept trying to take me away with it. Then I eased into the lee of a boulder like Clayton did, only my head above water, remembering that this water was ice cold, yet marveling that it felt like tepid bath water. I was now more awake than ever before. Every sensation, every color, every sound clearly registered. A calm power surged from every part of my body. I oozed life and fitness.

I saw Clayton on the bank above, looking up at the thinning rain, the lifting of the clouds. I made my way to shore through the rush of water, slipped at the base of the bank, then, laughing for the sheer pleasure of it, I sprang like a deer to the top of the bank. I stood digging my toes into the sand, feeling each drop of rain touch me, for the first time in my life completely at one with the universe. Everything, including myself, existed in a state of beauty, perfection, rightness. I felt fused to eternity.

Clayton glanced at me and his eyes were pools of light. There was a palpable unwillingness for either of us to speak. There were no words. Without any sense of modesty I looked at how different his body was from mine. How hairless and dark and wrinkled from age he looked, his skin glistening in the rain with a bluish cast. How my hairy white body was red as a beet. He was short, compact, with a heavy torso on too-small legs, and no butt. I was tall and stooped, so "White man" with my beginnings of a spare tire around the waist, and my body covered with hair. I was especially hairy in a Northern European way, with dense tangles of wispy-curly hair on my forearms, chest and lower legs, and was even beginning to grow thick hair on the tops of my shoulders. I was truly the "hairy man from the east" that Indian legends spoke of. Standing side by side at the fire, Clayton looked at me several times. Then I saw the glimmer of humor in his eyes.

"I never realize before how the White man is the missing link between monkeys and Indians!"

The rain continued to fade out until it fell like a heavy mist. I marveled at the blood-red leaves of Oregon grape shiny in the woods. At the dark rough branchiness of the insides of the forest; the ridged, fissured, platy, gnarled, lichen-covered, dead-looking bark of northern conifers. Away through the trees to the south, the sun was trying to break through the gloom. The fire was a brilliant bed of fiery coals mounded over the remaining rocks, and its stovelike heat felt good. Lost again in television-locked gaze, I watched the garish metamorphosis of shape and color.

The old man shoveled the rocks free to one side, took up the tongs again, and carried the last of the glowing stones one by one to the lodge, mounding them up on top of the previous ones. Then he banked the coals with ash and we crawled back inside.

This time I welcomed the instant dark coziness, the smell and feel of fir boughs, the burning spread of steam. Clayton sang song after song with hardly a pause, his voice ranging high into beautiful whipsaw warbles and dropping to drone and rasp and fall away into a hiss. Most of the songs seemed to be composed of vocables, repetitions of "he-ya" following a melodic line that was repeated over and over, and I found it easier to join in and sing with him. The heat was clearly more intense, yet I didn't suffer as much from it. I noticed more things this time, like the smell of our bodies, the popping and sizzling sounds of water dripping into the pit of rocks, and a faint whitish glow visible yet illuminating nothing—and pulsing with the rhythm of our singing.

Pinpoints of light floated by, streaks, motes, garish clusters at the periphery of my vision, and Clayton called "*Aaaa, aaaa,*" in the midst of the song, as if acknowledging some other person's presence inside with us, manifesting as faint bluish sparks. I heard the flapping of wings, the motions of feathers moving the dense air, and realized he was shaking his bluejay fan in time with the beat of the song. The unearthly lights vanished, but I was filled with an emotional burst of energy, rocking on my seat cross-legged, feeling so humbled by the presence of mysterious things, yet galvanized into an itching, spasmodic, swaying strength of body. Our voices rose up louder, louder, the snapping of his feather fan brushed my face and chest, then his song faded away. With a roar, more burning steam raced over us, and I knew he'd poured water directly from the basket onto the rocks.

There's no way to describe the mingling of horror, pain, joy and willingness that brought me to another brink, a place where I simply could withstand no longer what I was enduring. Yet Clayton let out deep, satisfied *aaaa*'s, still flapping his fan. Something about this not harming him allowed me to let go. Okay, I thought: I'm willing to die if that's what this is. Instantly there was relief, but from what, I wasn't sure. It was just as hot—my skin felt like it was peeling away—but I knew it was not harming me. What I had let go of was my control.

"*Límtenun'tm! Límtenun'tm!*" I moaned, and Clayton responded, "*Aaaa!*"

This powerful presence pressing on me that we call pain or burning up (or being cooked alive) I knew now was not something bad or something to fear. It was something stronger than me. Something greater. The breath of the living Sweatlodge, and it was my task to humble myself, submit to it, breathe in this great one's breath.

From the waist up I was swaying to some deeply felt rhythm,

gradually aware that I was hearing a familiar melody. The sounds accurately vented an anguish that seethed inside me. It was like the rhapsodic sadness of dancing to rock music with a savage beat: some glimmer of awareness that we aren't much more than these sweaty bodies in motion, than these breathing, suffering, unknown living presences. Then I was singing in English:

Listen to my song, oh mother
As I dance alone here on you,
Listen to my song, oh father
As I dance alone before you . . .

Clayton started to follow the melody with his voice but gradually drew my irrigation prayer song away from the sharp, pentatonic sing-song into a more Salish-sounding rendition, blurring the tone shifts, registering the flats even flatter and giving the song an emotion that quavered audibly and vented even better exactly how I felt. As we sang, I began to have muscle spasms on the insides of my thighs, just above the knees. A sharp pain in my belly felt like something pulling on my navel from the inside.

The heat was incredible, enclosing me in a wet flame. I distinctly heard a third voice singing with us, almost a falsetto, faint at first, but growing, and singing half an octave off from us. It was the most stunning voice I'd ever heard. It had none of the suffering or human frailty that ours expressed, none of the horrible self-awareness of humans, alive now but certain someday to die. As if called by our human distress, attracted to it, this voice joined in and became a roaring in my ears. A roaring as under a waterfall, a ringing, a burning something in my ears that took away all sound but the beating of my heart.

Ahead of me a brightness beckoned. It seemed to be growing and vibrating. I could see a large oblong object like a balloon flying from a dark spot on the edge of brightness. Another balloon, exactly like the first, came floating by. Then another. The objects became audible, taking the form of sound as well as shape. It was a message of some kind, I thought. I strained to figure it out as another floated past. The sound pattern was familiar, a definite up and down that I was sure I recognized.

"We go outside now." Yes, yes! That's it. A misty scene coalesces before me: Clayton sitting to one side in the opened doorway of the sweatlodge, a halo of steaming light around his head, his hand gesturing with the bluejay fan timed to his words: "We go outside now."

"Yes," I said.

I could hear Clayton's knees creaking as he stood up and walked to the river. I followed him out and stood up, my body working perfectly, each movement a delight. My skin was almost as red as the Oregon grape leaves. Walking was weightless ease, gliding over the fragrant earth toward the green muscle of river.

Easing into the water, I floated away in the current, suspended in a buoyant coolness, bobbing past Clayton as he held onto a boulder, his eyes staring at nothing with an inward vagueness. It was easy to hold my breath and stay under for long minutes in the pull and push of current. It was easy to move my body. It was easy to be alive.

The river carried me along for a thoughtless time around bend after bend. Then it widened and slid shallowly over a rocky bed, bumped me over protruding stones, slowed into a circling pool where it floated me suspended over a glittering pebbly bottom moving with the shadowy shapes of fish. I crawled out onto a sand bar and stood up, a man, and the fish darted swiftly away. I had never felt so natural, so intimately belonging to nature, so clearly just another animal on a shore. I was slowly coming back to myself, thoughts intruding on the flow of raw perception. How far had the river taken me? Was the sun going down or was it just darkening for another rain? The river was mesmerizing. Golden leaves of poplar floated on the surface and turned lazily, suspended in the clear depths, a brilliant litter making a grand procession around the pool. Driftwood, rolled and rounded and smoothed into unlikely shapes, bobbed along in the parade or came to uneasy rest in a raft, trapped at the outlet by a dam of washed-down tree trunks.

I finally began to chill, and walked back upriver over the blankets of decayed leaves, a naked man on a popular trout stream. But I met nobody, passed Clayton's car back in the woods, and came out at the bush camp.

Clayton sat peacefully by the chirping campfire in a clean plaid wool shirt, black logger's denim trousers and red suspenders, his bare feet holding the wooden stock of his rifle at a certain angle as he forced a cotton patch down the barrel with a rod, so the patch would drop out the side breech.

I said, "*Wai, kch'kícht, kow'íwilux* (Hello, I'm here, elder)," and started to fumble around for my pants, with some reluctance.

"*Aaaa, ixí anewí istitl'wílilt* (Yes, that's you, my nephew)," he responded without looking up.

Pulling on blue jeans was all it took to satisfy the early childhood training in conventional modesty that now warred with my newfound nature-boy lack of inhibition. Something about clothes separated me from nature, made me something else, pulled me away from the pure flow of perception and into the reflective thought and distance of human beings. The denim seemed too tight, too abrasive on my skin, somehow alien. Yet the jeans did the trick. I squatted by the fire in easy familiarity with Clayton, smelling the rich gun-oil smell that called up vague memories of M-16 rifle training and military barracks.

"Somebody else was singing with us, there at the end," I said, unwilling to use any more words than I had to.

"*Aaaa*, we show them we want to live, so they come and help us."

The tiny fire didn't give off much heat, and I rocked slowly in my squatting position, feet planted apart, arms hung over my knees, body unfamiliarly like a well-oiled machine, shivering but so deeply at peace I wondered at it.

"You are cold," he said, not looking up from his hunting preparations.

"Yeah, I'm cold. But, I don't know . . . It feels good."

He looked up.

"I'm cold, but . . . so what?" I shrugged.

He understood, nodding.

The sun blazed through the dense evergreen in shafts and dapples. I moved away, strolling slowly to an open spot, standing in the faint warmth of autumn afternoon sunshine after rain, hugging myself, still shivering. Soon the warmth of the sun's rays penetrated the chill, stopped my shivering, and I slid to the base of a cedar tree, leaned back against the steaming bark. I must have sat there, thoughtless, doing nothing, for an hour.

Then something stirred inside me at the disappearance of the sun behind clouds wet and heavy on the western mountains. My mindless lack of concern for anything other than what I was experiencing faded. I saw myself as just lying around like an old dog. All my life had been spent in the familiar context of doing and thinking, circumstances and relationships, expectations and preparations. The busy hum of modern life. The unexpected pleasure of sitting without thought in the sunshine, feeling content, feeling fit, feeling the beauty of the world and my presence in it, now faded in the compulsion to get busy doing something.

Behind the cedar tree, the river at some previous flood time had scoured a channel down about six feet below the area where we had our camp, and the cedar stood precariously at the edge of this dry channel, its roots partially washed out and hanging clawlike over nothing but air. Under the cavelike overhang Clayton had placed a bucket under a drip of clear water for our drinking and cooking. I climbed down to check on the bucket, saw it was full and carried it over to where Clayton was heating up leftover stew. I found my damp clothes and hung them up to dry. Clayton mixed the spring water with a coarse flour mixture to make bannock.

"What can I do to help?"

"So, the White man come back."

"I just want to help. I don't feel right just hangin' out while you do all the work."

"You see somethin' to do, you do it, I guess."

The delicious odors of deer stew and pan bread were making me woozy with hunger. I sat down. He had everything under control with the ease of his years of bush life. There was nothing to do but wait, then eat.

"I guess I felt guilty. Like I wasn't doing anything."

"That how the crazy White man take back his sickness," he said, shaking his head. "*Suyápi kayús*. Start to be healed, then run back to his madness. I seen it lots of times. To be the natural man, same as all the world around, that not good enough. Gotta get busy. Gotta worry and lose touch with what's real so he feel okay inside."

Cut to the quick by the old man's uncharacteristically harsh assessment of me, I blurted out, "What? Just sitting around feeling physically good is all it takes to be healed?" He said nothing. "Anyway, I don't see what's wrong with wanting to help."

"Not that you want to help me, nephew," he said, cooling my anger with his appeal to me as a relative. "The White man head take over, say doin' nothin' but standin' around feeling pleasure to be alive is wrong."

I chewed on that for awhile.

"You know, once there was these two coyotes," he said, starting a story I knew wouldn't be one of the *chaptíkx*, which had more formalized beginnings. "Up on a hill together. One coyote says to the other: 'I'm a coyote, but you just another coyote.' That other coyote, he don't like that kind of talk, so he say, 'No, wait a minute. I'm a coyote too!'

"'Huh-uh, no way,' says the first coyote. 'I'm a coyote, but you're just *another* coyote.'

"'No, no. I'm a coyote! I'm a coyote, too!'

"Well, this go on for awhile, back and forth, till that first coyote, he say, 'I can prove it. You see that camp of people down there on the flat? You see that clump of aspen trees on the other side? Okay, I goin' to run down the hill, through that camp, and sit down in the shade of those trees. Soon as I get there, you follow me down, do the same thing.'

"That coyote dash down the hill and race through the camp of people. They look up to see this coyote run through their camp. Yell, 'Hey, look! There goes a coyote!'

"Soon as the second coyote see the first one reach the shade of aspens, he take off, race down through that village, too. The people look up again, yell, 'Look! There goes *another* coyote!'"

I had to laugh. Clayton's coyote jokes always put me into a good humor. I couldn't see any connection between the story and what we'd been talking about, but it didn't matter any more. The food was ready. Clayton cut a piece of bannock bread out of the pan and onto a half-bowl of stew, stuck a spoon into it, and handed it to me. I savored every mouthful, grateful for anything. It took my whole attention. Just chunks of venison and vegetables in a broth and a mouthful of unleavened bread still greasy from the pan, but it was like eating for the first time. The sweat and beginnings of fasting were transforming me—every littlest thing was a wonder.

I set my bowl down as Clayton ate on with the appetite of a logger and the manners of a teenage boy. It was a long time before he settled back content, slowly sipping a metal cup of spring water. Night was full on us, and the fire was down to coals. Individual stars appeared and disappeared in the drift of clouds. The river, as always, spoke of passing by.

"The White man, see, he a lot like those coyotes," Clayton said in the breezy darkness. I could only see his shape near me under the rustle of the tarp overhead.

"*Aaaa*," I said, not understanding, but willing to listen.

"They egg each other on with hurtful words, not feel good enough, not worthy to just be alive in this world. Have to prove something. Race against each other to be something more. But what?

"There you were, all that cleaned out of you, touched by the voice of the *shumíx*, standin' in the glow of the sun, full of life. Long time, you belong to the earth, earth belong to you. Burnin' steam, icy river, cold wind, just a man. If a man is alive, here in this world, he have that right to be here, that's all. You felt that, I seen it. That what we call knowin' somethin'."

I shook my head slowly, abashed, remembering it just like he said.

"This how we train ourself to live. What we know, we hold onto, keep with us. Like receiving a gift. A gift Sweatlodge give to us, fill us up with, that silent knowing that our body feel.

"*En'hlipokomínen*, to remember, that how we live. To wake up and remember what we know. Carry that with us. To want our heart to beat, to want our breath to come in and go out. To want this gift of life given to us, to want this, what we are, human people. To want to live.

"Nothin' to prove. Not anything we have to do to deserve this life, be worthy of it. Just accept it, live it, remember it."

In the silence that followed, I said, "*Aaaa, wai i hwi.*" The coals glimmered, the trees moved in increasing wind. I was there and I remembered.

"Besides," Clayton said, his voice dropping to a murmur as he spread out his sleeping bag. "Tomorrow *you* do all the work."

9

True to his word, Clayton lay around all the next morning under the tarp as I went about doing the work of preparing for the sweat. He said nothing, rousing himself once in a while to go through his hunting gear or repair a packstrap, and he even hollowed out a punky log with a hatchet for some use I couldn't divine. He came out from under the tarp into the drizzle of the day only when it was time to enter the lodge. In typical Indian fashion he didn't say anything about how I did things or make suggestions when I dropped superheated rocks on the ground. My unfamiliarity with the tongs was like trying to eat rice with chopsticks—finally so exasperating I carried the last rocks to the pit with a shovel. I poured the water now, and the silence in burning darkness was like the silence I felt inside. Utter dark scalding vacant silence.

"They know why we here," his voice said in the darkness beside me. "But they want that we tell them what in our heart. They want that we speak the words. Then we all together in this, what good they bring."

"Clayton, I hardly know how to pray in English. I don't know how to say . . . *Loot kn'* . . ."

"There no wrong way to pray," he said.

"*Aaaa* . . ." and my self-consciousness vanished. "*Xa'xá Iyilméhum, kwílsten, temxúlaux, chipchaptík'xwl! Awhá inchá . . .* (Here I am, pitiful, come here you help me, heal me, my want to live, so be it!)"

"*Aaaa*," Clayton said. Then, "That first one go like this," and I quickly picked up his opening song. Singing, paying attention to the pouring on of water and sage, remembering how the lilting songs went that filled the tiny, stuffy interior with something so emotionally human, I found it easier to endure the rush of horrible heat. Until the time came, as it always did, when I let go of something and ceased to suffer in self-pity, existing as a man somewhere else than where I did out there in the world of my familiar life.

As our voices trailed off after the fifth song, I leaned past the pit, throwing up the slippery mountain goat hide, light and coolness drawing us out into the visual world of forest and river. The slow but penetrating shock of cold river, two animals stumbling up the bank, standing to drip at the fiery thing on the ground drawing and holding their eyes. Aware only of breath, of heart beating, of the feel of earth underfoot.

More hot rocks, easier to tong somehow; the incandescent, translucent orange strangely pops but does not burn when I touch it. Sage leaves wither into acrid, sweet smoke, consumed by the clinking rocks. Then the flap is down and Clayton is settled again at my side. The rush of water driven up as steam, the throaty sputtering voice of earth forces brought together by a man asking for help to live, breathing the breath of such terrible power, a power greater than himself. Breathing Sweatlodge's breath, burning in the dragon breath of darkness. Oh, oh, it is so good to die this little death of the mind, to let my body go free into whatever the power is that we have invoked here.

The songs make me totter with emotion. I remember them like an instinct. Something about the focus, the singleness of purpose allows me to grasp them and sing them just as Clayton does. But even in the trance of becoming that works on me in the endless pour of sweat, I hear with increasing humor how I Anglicize the songs a little, impose the melodic feeling I'm used to on a song of profound pity.

"It not a campfire song," Clayton growls. "We not roastin' marshmallows!" I laugh so hard. Nothing so moving and releasing as this joking in the midst of suffering.

I emptied the basket onto the rocks and willingly breathed in the burn of boiling steam. My whole body was on fire, but it was good. It was what it was. We both called *aaaa* at how good it was to be alive, here, now, like this. The glow of white appeared again, like the house lights coming up, a misty, tunnel-like glow that illuminated nothing. Faint blue pinpoints of light appeared with a flourish, drifting by on the periphery of vision. I felt something or someone asking for my song, so I sang my walking-through-wet-alfalfa song, tapping fingers in time on the edge of the basket. Clayton joined me, then sang louder, making it into a Salish song again, and I let his changes sink into me.

Then, in the bubbling hiss of cooled rocks, in the waning heat and silence after countless songs, I was grateful. It was time to go out again. I had been through fire to a purified state of innocence and bare essentials. It was easier to say the Salish words of thanks, to lift out my chin and hold my mouth in the more facially controlled, loose-lipped way the Okanogans sing out their words, using more of the back of my mouth and throat to distinguish the kws and k'ws and hls and xws that make speaking a consonant-rich tongue such a trial. Clayton *aaa*'d and *aaa*'d, yessing my prayer, clearly grateful, too. We crawled out into the glare of sun, puffy white clouds drifting across the blue, sun at midday, noon, *en'tohox'káin*.

Again I swam in the river long after he climbed out. *En'hlapomítk il siúlhk*, diving in water, as much a prayer and purification and seeking the attention of the spirits as sweating, was not something I had to be urged to do. I dived into the rushing yellow clearness, swept along bumping slippery rocks, holding my breath longer than I'd believed possible. Seeking out configurations of beauty in the deep; rising to breathe the sweet air of the world above; lolling one-handed in the lee of mossy boulders; floating in particular simpleness beneath the lean of forest trees at a particular place along a particular river. So cold that only the obvious drop of my body temperature signaled by sluggish muscles and a refrigerator feel in my guts would draw me up into the wind, dragging up the bank, to walk in steps of perfect fitness to the fire. Wind, light, the movement of trees, the rush of river, the searing heat of a bed of coals in a pit. It was so simple, so pure, it ached.

Finally dressed, with that healthy smoothness of skin, that afterglow of peace and patient reserve, I saw the absent Clayton returning from the car, his eyes glancing at me from afar with a glow that was uncomfortable to look at. My eyes must be like that after a sweat, too . . . I saw that all his stuff was gone, loaded into his car, but he was leaving his tarp strung from the trees for me, and my few things in one corner of the dry space underneath.

We wandered away into the hills together without speaking. One last stroll before he left me alone to continue my self-training. Upriver along benches of ponderosa pine, and into the steep ravines that led up to the rocky heights. Clouds formed and darkened; it began to rain in brief showers. I was wearing my worn work boots, summer campaign coat, and a wool stocking cap. Clayton buttoned up his two wool shirts, laced up his hunting moccasins, and slipped on his deer-head hat. I'd seen him wear the hat before, on hunting trips, but he never wore it in camp or around women. It was stiff but flexible, the skinned and tanned hide of a deer's head, the ears on, eyes sewed shut, thick neck ruff hanging below his back collar and the shriveled black snout wedged out above his eyes like the bill of a baseball cap. A leather thong under his chin held the wild-looking headgear in place. Clayton claimed it never soaked through, that the long, coarse deer hair naturally shed rain and snow.

The ravines were dense with thickets of young conifers and burned deadfalls, and the going was awful in the sudden downpours. *Taku'út*, what Clayton called "strolling around," could be strenuous at the best of times, and his surprising ability to walk untiringly for miles always humbled me. It wasn't easy to be in my thirties, at the peak of my strength, and find it hard sometimes to keep up with a man in his sixties. We worked our way up, using game trails, to the summits wreathed in clouds, and he found a dry spot in the lee of rocks where we rested, looking down through openings in the veil of fog at the river below. New clouds appeared, swirling upward in wispy columns out of the dense timber, draped in smoke-like films obscuring the soggy sea of fir tops. A grouse perched motionless on the limb of a dead snag out away in the vast emptiness, right at our eye level. Beneath his deer-head hat, water dripping from the tip of his nose, Clayton quietly studied the world. Then he looked right at me, studying me.

For the first time, I noticed his right eye was distinctly larger than his left, as if he habitually held it open wide and squinted the other. As we looked at each other calmly, I examined his face with fascination. The two halves of his face seemed completely different, as if each were from a different face. His right side expressed almost an angry fierceness, while his left side was benignly soft and pool-like. We both smiled.

"We get back, you on your own," he said. "You do fine. I come sometime, check up on you. *Stim as pu'ús awhá sin'ka'íls?*"

"*Xast* (Good). I'm here to do this. I'll do it. My want to live!" Since I was learning to speak the Indian language by mimicking what Salish-speakers said, I found myself mimicking also their use of English. They commonly use a possessive with words we use as a verb. "My want" was correct in Okanogan but sounded odd in English.

"You know, Charlene do this when she just young, about twelve, thirteen, all by herself."

"Really?"

"Yeah, but her granny have a different family way. Point up to Chopaka one day, in summer, said 'Time to go.' She go by herself, stay up there long time, about a month."

"A month, huh. Sweating and fasting?"

"Yah, but different way. She take deer jerky, her *pícha* to dig roots, pick berries while she up there. Set up a tiny lodge by that first creek there on the south side. Sweat there, sleep inside each night, then maybe a week go by, she move to that next creek to the west. Set up her *kwílsten* just big enough for her, stay there awhile. Little by little she go all over our sacred mountain, stay on each of those creeks. Sweat. Eat less and less. Come home when the chokecherries ripe. Her uncle ride up a couple times to check on her, but never found her, she hide so good. Oh, she laugh about that, later. She tell me she not want to see anybody."

"Well, I'll stay put. I won't hide from you. But don't you forget I'm up here!"

"I be back in three, four days, *Skélux*."

The next four days alone in the bush were just like old times for me, a return to solitude, to living outdoors in the absence of my own kind, that gave heightened presence and personality to all the forces and forms of nature around me. But it was very different for me to live by the discipline imposed on me by the old man. Instead of the open-ended life of camping and hunting and traveling wherever I wanted, one spot and one purpose dictated all my actions.

Awake at first light. Quiet and alive, dreams to consider, the world in the light of day. A fire to build, rocks to heat, water to draw. Sweating and swimming with increased tolerance, improved skill, a ritual sense of timing. A waning of vigor, a hollowness in my stomach. Afternoons wandering in the hills, observing whatever nature presented, sitting in silence, gathering firewood, doing camp chores. Evening campfire and the wonder of something to eat. Shortening days and lengthening nights. It was simple, repetitive, and hard.

Silence and solitude, meaningful work, a ritual ordering of what to do, the mountain wilderness full of wind and smells and birds and rain, walking along the river under swaying trees, eating less each day, drinking only at specific times—even without sweathousing and diving in cold water it would have been a healing time for me. But with the daily sweat and swim my body sang with fitness, and my perception of myself and the world shifted into a dreamy, slow-motion, receptive place. There was only here and now and this.

So this was how we make ourselves attractive to spirits, to the sacred power of the world, to *xa'xá*. Self-training, I could see now, was me becoming something other than I was familiar with—a beauty of body, a silence of mind, an emptiness that cried out in my prayers to be filled by that alive, watching world out there. And how alive it became! After the sweat and swim every day, I emerged reborn into the wet, windy world. As the days passed and the change deepened I could more easily grasp how everything had life, how everything was aware—it leaped at me, it pushed itself on me.

Up on a rocky spine, the granite crystals peek out like eyes from matted coverings of lichen and moss, the wind so strong the reef of stone seems to sway like a ship at sea. The perfect shape of a fir top out over the edge catches my eye. I'm drawn that way to see such deep green color, such ranked ordering of limbs, leading out and down, then turned up at the ends. Closer, more of the tree in view, must be huge, an ancient one, vastly older than me, dried cones dangling. Closer to the vertical edge, the cliff opening below, my eyes following down the tree its full length, to its great bole six feet thick, held upright by yards of roots snaking through the rocks along a ledge. Such power and beauty, standing there for hundreds of years, never moving anywhere else, truly a mysterious power of this place. It feels good to share the world with this tree.

I say to it: "*Anewí k'shwinúmpt, ch'k'ílhp* (You are beautiful, fir tree)."

Then movement, and there on a tiny flat place above the trunk, a wide spot on the ledge, a deer lies at rest, legs tucked back, head up, looking around at the world, ears twitching, unaware of me watching from above. As long as there's cover and food, it doesn't matter how steep and rugged the land is, deer will live there. Deer and fir tree and granite cliff and me . . .

And another time, almost impossible to get to, scrabbling up and down narrow cliff chutes, across unstable rockslides, through tangles of ironwood bush, spiraea, brush maple. Then the very tops of an isolated grove appear as if floating in air over the abyss. The tender young candles of elderly firs hold forth like this every year, over this windswept chasm since before the coming of White people. Bluejays drew me here, screeching incessantly, their calls now echoing out over river and a sky remarkably clear. I feel drawn down into the shadowy grove, slide from rock to rock into a mass of green pressed against the cliff. A large owl bursts from cover and flies away, chased by scolding bluejays with tall black crests and crows so shiny black in the sunlight their flashing feathers dazzle the eye.

Down, down, down into the twisted barrier of long-dead branches pressed against the stone wall, until finally I find the great curving boles, enormous, sap-oozing, fissured. Roots the size of a man's body, the mountainside held in check here for centuries. Then it's easy to climb upward into the trees, limb by limb, into an arboreal world few enter, and sit in the living sway and creak. I can see almost nothing beyond the dense surroundings of fir boughs. A secret world; likely no other human has been here before or will find it in my lifetime. Or if one does, it would surely be someone I'd like to meet . . .

And another time, during a sleet storm with lightning and terrific winds, I was almost dancing along towards camp, laughing at how joyous such weather made me feel. Humming the melodies of sweatlodge songs, something I'd do without even knowing it. Finally pausing to stare at the sway of trees, the horizontal blow of sleet beginning to whiten the world, the flashes of lightning brightening the gloom of late afternoon. A word, *k'áshney*, came through my mind, and I wondered if that was the *Skélux* word for this kind of storm. When I said it aloud, there came a ferocious, cyclonic wind tearing through the treetops toward me. Sleet coated my face, trees shuddered and groaned, the wind arrived and nearly knocked me over, then fell to a quiver. "Only the wind is real."

Clark's nutcrackers, large black, gray, and white jays from the high-altitude, spruce-alpine fir country, would come and tell me when it was about to snow. The first time it happened, the birds fluttered down from the mountains in a flock, calling "kraa kraa" in their grating voices. One perched on a limb above me, looked right at me, kraaing with what could only be an attempt to tell me something, but what? Then she went silent, and after a few seconds the first flakes of a snow shower began to fall. As the snow increased, the nutcrackers flew away. After that, every snow or sleet shower was heralded by the appearance and guttural calling of nutcrackers, who would hush just before the fall of white.

As I sat marveling at the world one day, a rare pileated woodpecker, big as a raven, with a bright red crest and dark body, came and dug with slow power in the punk of a tree stump, stopped once to look at me, then resumed. Chickadees lived in the trees everywhere, tiny teenage pipsqueaks chick-chick-chickadee-ing in flocks, investigating everything. Water ouzels perched on rocks at the waterline on the river, doing knee-squats in calisthenic rhythm before throwing themselves into the icy water and emerging ten feet away. Robins came and went, standing sentinel at dawn and dusk on the ground of clearings, heads cocked to the sound of burrowing. In the wet hush after rains, Townsend's solitaires sang lonely, bittersweet, warbling songs that tugged at my emotions, held me rapt in my isolation from my own kind.

Two kinds of squirrels chattered every morning in the full light of day, one dark and one red. I surprised a weasel hunting the river edge as I went to the spring for water. Coyotes howled just after dark, sometimes splitting the night silence with such high-pitched yapping songs that the blue heron who roosted in a big cottonwood across the river woke up gabbling and flew to another tree. A beaver swam by, eyes and nose and flat tail on a level. Kingfishers perched on limbs over the water rasping "zzzzt!" and flying away like giant hummingbirds. And once when I was inside the sweatlodge, I heard something walking on the earth overhead. When I came out, nothing was there, but I saw the tracks of some large bird in the wet dirt.

Sweating alone made me aware that this was all about me and my personal relation to the powers of the world. There was nobody to make sure I did it right or did it at all. I could change my mind, strike camp, and hike out to the highway if I wanted. Clayton Tommy was just helping me do something his sponsor helped him to do. It was up to me to do it.

Alone in the darkness, the burning heat, the flood of sweat, the fear and suffering, I would give up and go to some other place within me. The singing of songs reminded me of what I was doing. Rubbing my body with fir boughs to receive their strength, with sage to make myself sweet-smelling to the spirits, I endured and stayed put. No light, no sound but the murmur of flowing river penetrating underground where I sat on a bed of fir, suspended in burning nothingness. No sense of the passage of time. An unimaginable grief, a terrifying sadness, a sighing and sobbing that faded only as I let myself dissolve into the nothingness around me. And then I could see a misty world opening up all around me, as if I sat on fir boughs on a vast plain, and saw figures coming to where I sat leaning over hot rocks.

Figures in the sky, figures walking, figures below ground, all moving slowly toward this place where I suffered. I saw bluish figures moving on the rocks. Figures vaguely human, vaguely animal. Presences outside the lodge scuffled at the doorflap, raising the hair at the nape of my neck. Flareups of light, like the flash of an arc welder seen by unshielded eyes, blinded me and stayed bright after I closed eyes burning from salty sweat. All the indefinable occurrences on the edge of consciousness penetrated my mind and heart so focused on receiving whatever might come.

In the river's sudden awakening, my body cooled and taken away in the current, I would marvel at the instinct that took over, making sure I breathed air, not water. And later, awakening under the tarp in the wee hours for a dreamy moment, I'd remember being in a river, the same river but different, a river speaking to me in a hollow, drifting voice about its ways and purposes. And wondering—wait a minute!—when was I swimming in that other Similkameen that I now remember so vividly? Memories piling up of things I don't remember happening. How can this be? Yet not really questioning it. Accepting it, holding it in my memory, knowing it must have some purpose, will have some use.

Awakening another night with my head out in the wet, looking through an opening between trees at the constellation Orion, the Hunter, the three stars in a row of his belt, and three fainter stars in a row, below at an angle, his quiver or his scabbard. Watching each star wink out as clouds slowly obscured it all.

In the morning there is a frost that disappears quickly with a wind that comes with daylight. There is a flat emptiness inside me. I begin to dress. I carry dry kindling to the sweatlodge, to the cold pit nearly full of damp charcoal and fragments of rocks. The rocks are breaking up badly—soon I'll be sweating with gravel. Then pebbles. Then sand. I smile, feel a laugh coming, but it passes. Too long away from people to laugh readily.

How long have I stood here, looking up at the low, racing clouds? They threaten rain or snow, but the sky grows calm and dark as the morning wears on. I stand at the lodge door, scratching idly, in no hurry to begin. Just the smell of fir boughs and willow and sage makes me feel good. It is all so familiar and homey now.

It's day seven. I get to work.

10

The fire stood up in the roar of six-foot flames when I heard the familiar valve lash of Clayton's car engine and the crunch of tires coming up the river track. My hearing had become so keen I heard many voices long before I saw a group of people, all Indians, walking slowly along the river toward where I stood. Clayton led the way, followed by Jim Woods carrying a bucket of fresh rocks. Behind them came Old Willie the Indian doctor, and a man and a boy who looked vaguely familiar.

All of them carried something. As they came closer I looked at their eyes. None of them would look me in the eye, nor even look in my direction, except the boy, who studied me briefly with curiosity. But they all took turns coming up to shake hands with me, just a touch of the hand but still an overwhelming presence of my own kind, eyes down or looking off somewhere, a mumbled "*Wai*" from Clayton, "Yo dude" from Jim. All I could say was "*Aaaa.*"

The father of the boy said, "Watermelon be good right now, eh?" and I remembered him and his son from that day I gave out watermelon from the tailgate of my truck. He was Roger Antoine, who had translated old Willie's joke about the three White women being my wives. Roger was Old Willie's grandson, and eight-year-old Bennett was his great-grandson. Bennett's gap-toothed smile lit up at the mention of watermelon, but he slunk away after a perfunctory, silent shake with me when he realized what it was really about.

Old Willie stared at a spot above and to the right of my head for a long time as he held my hand, his so soft and fragile. It was hard to say how old he was—he looked in his seventies or eighties—but he could have been a hundred for all I knew. Indian doctors live forever. He spoke Salish—or maybe it was English—with such a slurring, faint voice that I had no idea what he said to me. He wore a heavy wool Pendleton coat open in front so I could see rainbow-striped suspenders holding up his baggy trousers. I took him in as I took in nature, as I studied the deer at rest, but there was something in his bearing that made me back off. He usually looked sleepy or droopy-eyed, but with his eyes up like that, I could see he had one lazy eye that wandered off and came back while the other held steady. He was very wrinkled around the eyes. I didn't like the way he held onto my hand, not letting go for about a minute, but it made me pay attention and really register him: a truly formidable old man used to commanding respect. I couldn't see what made Jim Woods so scared of him, but then this was only the second or third time I'd been around him.

When he finally turned away, he spit in the fire and said some words in Salish. Roger, off to one side, repeated everything he said in a loud, even voice. The old man mumbled and Roger repeated without appearing to listen, even digging in a burlap bag and pulling out a decorated stick with his back turned. I had never heard a *tl'kwánchin* before, a sort of ceremonial repeater, but everything he repeated was met with *aaa*'s from Clayton, Jim and the boy, so I joined in. Roger handed old Willie a bag of Bull Durham tobacco and the stick, which looked like the dance sticks they carry in the Winter Dances, about four feet long and hung with fur, feathers, a metal bell and a stuffed bird that looked like a tiny nuthatch.

The old man had Roger open my fire and count the rocks I had heating. Roger added a few more fresh ones from the bucket, then recovered the heap and added more wood to the fire. Old Willie walked over to the sweatlodge doorway, even more bowlegged than Clayton, looking like the old-time cowboy he had been so long ago. He took a branch of fir from the floor inside and used it to sweep a spot on the ground to the right outside the doorway, then stuck his power stick in the ground firmly upright. He kneeled looking inside for a long time, then got up stiffly and said something to Clayton, something funny about the old-time construction. Clayton laughed and held his hand flat at arm's length over his head as he answered. Old Willie looked at me and said, obviously trying to be heard and understood, "Two-story house!"

It felt good to laugh again, but it made me aware of how starved I was, how flat and empty my guts were. How much more I breathed. I was eating mainly air now.

There was a lull where everyone stood still and seemed to sense something. Old Willie zipped up his coat, pulled a wool hat out of his pocket and put it on his head, covering his thin, silvery hair. Clayton ignored this, but both Roger and Jim did some quick covering up. Jim was already wearing his beaded baseball cap with ponytail through the rear opening, so he zipped up a jersey hockey blazer around his heavy body and stepped closer to the fire in his running shoes. Roger, slim like me and dressed in jeans and a western shirt with snap buttons, pulled on a denim jacket. It immediately started to rain. I would never have believed it if I hadn't seen it. How did they know?

The boy, Bennett, ignored the rain, too, even though all he wore was a dirty T-shirt. He graduated from feeding sticks to the fire to climbing up onto the muddy sweatlodge roof until his dad said somebody didn't know how dangerous it was for young boys to play around sweatlodges. He ignored his father's words for a while, but finally followed Old Willie and Clayton as they walked away to the bush camp to sit under the tarp and smoke Willie's pipe.

We three men in our thirties stood close to the bonfire, letting the blasting heat keep us comfortable in the steady downpour. Once Old Willie was gone, Jim relaxed into his usual swagger, but was still careful not to laugh out loud. Roger spoke with a strong Canadian accent, his sparse mustache no more than individual hairs hanging over his upper lip. As close relative and assistant to Willie, he had none of Jim's inhibition. He cracked joke after joke while Jim stifled his guffaws and I had no strength to do more than wheeze. But god it felt good to be in the company of humans. I wondered if I was going to pour water for them all.

"No, you'd just burn us up," Jim said. "You been sweating for how long?"

"Seven days . . . today."

"Ah, you don't even feel it any more."

"Yeah, right."

"Old Willie will do it," Roger said. "He's here to look into something. When he 'sticks' like that, he's gonna call his powers."

The speed and fluidity of their talk was more than I could participate in. I was awash in a newness that held my attention but left me incapable of holding up my end of a conversation. The smell of our wet clothes steaming by the fire, the sounds of their voices, the unlikely information, the complexity of human interaction. They both sensed where I was at and didn't require my active involvement, even deferring to my state of mind with asides to elaborate on what I couldn't be expected to know. They were including me just as I was.

There had been a car wreck. Jim's brother-in-law, sober for a change and hunting deer with Jim and Clayton on the Native timber lands on the Canadian side north of Chopaka, got a call when they stopped in at Old Willie's place. His wife, Jim's sister, told him on the phone that his own sister had been in a car wreck that morning near Penticton, and had been taken away by ambulance in bad shape. There was no more information than that—all from a sobbing, incoherent woman who'd been asleep in the back seat, telling the little she knew from a phone booth.

The sister had been like a mother, raising him after their mother had died. He was shaken; he wanted to borrow Clayton's car and drive immediately to Penticton. But Clayton told him the best thing he could do was go into a sweatlodge and pray for his sister. With Old

Willie sitting in his big easy chair staring at him, Jim's brother-in-law caved in. Clayton had been about to drive out to check on me, so Willie said they'd all go and sweat where somebody already had a fire going and rocks heating. He sent the poor man down the road for Roger, and here they were.

"So . . . where . . . is he?" I asked.

"Stayed in the car," Jim said.

"He'll be along," Roger added. "I about lost it when he showed up, sayin' he wanted to sweathouse, eh? The only spirits he believes in are the kind that come in a bottle!"

"I don't know," Jim mused. "I remember that time he told Bennett to stop cryin'. When he was about three, that time you'n me were out in the pasture tryin' to load those horses into the horse trailer? So dark, no moon, and Bennett wailing. Remember? He told Bennett cryin' like that brings the spirits."

"Yeah, but he was just trying to hush him up. He knew Bennett could see the spirits."

"Sure, but he knew Bennett never got scared when he saw 'em. Just talked to 'em or pointed 'em out to you."

"Yah, I never thought of that."

"I thought *he* was the one who was scared," Jim said. Then to me: "Bennett is like some kids, sees the spirits when grownups can't. Specially the house kind, little troublemakers who play with the kids."

Roger added, "I'd be sittin' there watching television and he'd shake my arm, point to the corner and say, 'Da', stick mans!' Scare the piss right out of me, eh? Oh, he see 'em all right," Roger said, lapsing into the Native English of the older generations. "He tell me what they say. *Ax'éy!* Stuff I don't wanna know 'bout."

"He still see 'em?"

"Don't think so. Once he started school with the White kids, that was that. He doesn't talk about it any more."

"I tell you about the dream I had about the shooting at the

laundromat?" Jim said, turning to heat his backside. We followed suit, facing into the rain.

"*Loot.*"

"I woke up in the middle of the night. Dreamed I was at that laundromat in Loomis. There was these hippies washin' their clothes and drinkin' beer in their cars outside. This biker-lookin' chick comes up and starts shootin' with a pistol, and I'm runnin' when I wake up in a real sweat. Didn't feel like no ordinary dream. Something telling me something."

"Like happening without you, going on like watching TV? Real-like, but you just watchin'?"

"Yeah, that kind. But the bullets went whizzing by me and that woke me up. I thought about it for a while, then I remembered the washing machine was broke and Mom was going into Loomis the next day to do the laundry. I went and woke her up and told her about it. Told her I didn't want her to go to Loomis. She got up and burned some cedar, told me she wouldn't go wash in Loomis. She'd put off the laundry.

"Well, the next day we heard about the shooting at the Loomis laundromat. Drunk hippies doing their laundry, just like in the dream. Some woman mad at her man for sneaking around with another woman. Shot him sitting in the car with her. Said she didn't know it was loaded, just wanted to scare 'em. After that, Mom said it was probably safe to go do the laundry, but she went the other way, down to Oroville."

Roger was rearranging the fire, adding pieces of fir wood to keep the rocks covered. "*Aaaa*, that's how it goes," he said. "You keep it up and you'll be a *Smohalla* like your mum, eh?" He laughed.

"She's no *Smohalla*. She just dreams ahead sometimes, and I got a little of it from her." For me, he said, "Down south there, Yakima, Warm Springs, they got a different way. Like a dreamer religion, real strong dreamers, mainly women. They call 'em *Smohallas*. They live by their dreams, go through life dreaming everything, they say.

Like if they dream something, they gotta go do it, or they lose their power. Like they dream they're driving a red car, they go out and buy a red car!"

"I never heard they did that," Roger said. "That sounds like when our power men have to do something their power tell 'em to. What they got show 'em something in a dream they gotta do or they leave 'em. Like that time Old Willie's son-in-law swam across Lake Okanagan at night in a snowstorm. He said he knew he was dead if he didn't do it, but if he did, that power of his would help him. But he has one of those strong partners, real strong, like Grizzly or Cougar, or maybe Wolf by the way he swam so easy."

"Doesn't happen very often," Jim said.

"Good thing, eh? Bad enough how hard it is to suffer for the power like some people, even the non-Native." To me: "How you holdin' up? Want some coffee and doughnuts?"

I wheezed along with his laughter.

"You know, that breakfast this morning was a real treat," he said with an innocent look to Jim. "Hotcakes with maple syrup, bacon and eggs, big hot bran muffin with butter drippin' out of it, strong coffee with cream and sugar . . . I'm so stuffed I don't know how I'm gonna take it sweathousin', eh?"

Wheeze. Wheeze.

"No, no, eh," he went on. "What you're doing is a good thing, eh? Long time ago, all peoples did this, that's what Old Willie says. This is how you gotta do if you want to bring the power to you. The power is out there in the bush, waiting. You gotta make yourself attractive to it. This sweathousing give you the good looks, the strong body they like. No smell of food or the city or of havin' sex. Cryin' for it, so pitiful, like Bennett. Like puttin' on new clothes, you put it on you, and the power gotta come, eh?

"Of course, that old bugger, Clayton Tommy, he sort of specializes in takin' snoopy White guys out into the bush and accidentally losing 'em. The last White guy he sweathoused had a heart attack and they had to rush him to Vancouver in an ambulance!"

Wheeze. Wheeze. But Jim didn't crack a smile. Old Willie and Clayton were approaching the fire. Willie studied the rocks glowing incandescent orange like cantaloupes in their bed of coals, every raindrop striking with a cut-short hiss. He sent Jim to get his brother-in-law and we got ready to go in. Roger took up the shovel and began rolling rocks to one side free of the burning wood. Old Willie picked up the tongs and held them out to him with a coy smile.

"What the devil are these? Don't you guys have a pitchfork?"

Jim's brother-in-law came up listlessly, looking hollow-cheeked, and at Old Willie's insistence, gave me a tight-lipped handshake. At the naked lineup, Old Willie had him follow him in. Then Clayton, then Jim, then me, then little Bennett who stood waiting, shivering in the rain, still wearing his tennis shoes right up to the doorway. We crowded in like sardines in a circle, starting with Willie by the pit and ending with Bennett to my right at the door. We were out of the rain, but it was still cold. Roger kneeled outside the door, still dressed, and handed in a beaded leather bag to Willie. As the old man opened the bag in silence, Roger began to fill the pit with glowing rocks, using the shovel. He was so fast and efficient I was blown away. Then it got hot, real hot. He was bringing in all the rocks at once.

Sprinkling dried cedar on the rocks, Old Willie prayed in his gruff, snuffling voice, so faint and slurred that Roger repeating everything outside in such clear, unhesitating Salish while he carried rocks made me think the words were some often-repeated formula. Jim's brother-in-law looked bad. He stared at the rocks, drew cedar smoke to himself with a hand like others did, and said nothing until old Willie asked him his sister's Indian name.

"She don't have one."

Clayton cleared his throat. There was expectant silence. He said in Okanogan, "That one they call _____," pronouncing her name in a high voice.

"Oh yeah, _____. I forget she have one." It was the first time I ever heard a Salish word pass his lips.

Roger appeared at the door undressed and handed in the basket of water and a bunch of fresh sagebrush. Jim vigorously rubbed his arms and chest with fir needles, and Bennett crowded his little body next to me to make room for his dad, who sat back, knees up like the rest of us. The heap of clinking rocks stood up a foot above the level of the floor, searing our legs, already making us sweat with the door open.

It was clearly not going to be a mild sweat.

Roger had brought in a two-sided hide drum stretched with thongs over a six-sided cedar framework, painted with figures and designs, and a leather-tipped drumstick. He heated the drum over the rocks.

Bennett piped up beside me, "What's your name?" I looked down at him gazing up at me wide-eyed. "I have to know who I'm sitting next to. What's your name?"

"Tom."

"Hello, Tom. My name's Bennett Antoine." He held his hand up and we shook formally to the easy male laughter that rippled through the tightly packed group.

Then Roger pulled down the doorflap and the darkness roared with the splash of water on glowing rocks. Burning steam raced up to the ceiling and descended over all of us. Hotter and hotter, Old Willie praying and coughing, Jim pressing back from the blast, spreading out so I had to brace myself with one hand gripping the willow overhead to keep from crushing Bennett against his father. Coughing, fir boughs rubbed on skin, moaned *aaa*'s, and at a word from Willie, Roger began to drum and sing.

It seemed like everybody knew the songs Roger sang but me and Jim's brother-in-law. Even Bennett hummed along with obvious familiarity. They had a different feel from the sweatlodge songs Clayton taught me, more rhythmic and syncopated, more like songs you could dance to, and the beat of the drum by my right ear took hold of me as I withstood the relentlessly growing heat. My familiar little dark space, so roomy before, crowded now with so many sweating bodies there was no way to shift position or lie down, filled up with a deafening pulse of voices singing in unison and the throb of Roger's drum.

It was the hottest sweat I'd ever experienced. There was nothing to do but hold on and try to pay attention. Men whooped or cried *"aaaa"* in the boiling darkness, meeting each new roar of steam with pitiful cries that strangely translated to yes! more! this is good! Poor Bennett squirmed back half behind me in a fetal position, no longer singing, but not giving up. I followed the sound of Jim's voice singing close to my left ear, trying to learn the songs by lagging behind his melodic changes. But there was nothing I could do about how it all blended, roared, burned, and time stood still. I was carried away without knowing it into the white glow, the bitter sage smell, the faint blue lights shimmering and floating about.

Under the flood of singing, I hear old Willie's voice muttering, then praying with agonizing emotion. Little human-looking figures move back and forth from the rocks to where I hear his voice. The song ends and Willie speaks as if in conversation with someone, answering himself in an oddly distorted voice, using slurred Salish that seems to be spoken from overhead. Long pauses punctuated by *aaa*'s of surprise, grief, gratitude from the men around me to what they're hearing said. And the drum laid by my bare feet swirls with faint blue lights, as if Roger had run in an electric cord and had flashing lights going off in a circle inside the drum. Everything heard and seen without thinking. Voices and the creaking of the lodge willows. Sand filtering down through the grassy thatch onto my head. Old Willie still pouring on water, Roger repeating what he's saying, voice muffled as if he's speaking with his head between his knees. Then Roger throws up the doorflap, and the steam is so dense, light barely penetrates. A long silence, a stir of bodies finally getting relief as cool air flows in along the floor, a blinking in the light of day, a long time for the steam to clear out enough for me to see other faces.

Bennett came back to life, sat up, whispered to his dad.

"Yah, you can go," he said. Then as the boy slipped behind him and out the opening, Old Willie handed out the empty basket. Roger had him go fill it at the river.

There's a long silence. Nobody goes out to bathe in the river. Clayton's head is back, eyes closed, and he looks done in. A flicker of thought comes feebly after such a beating: starts up, fades, starts up again. The wet forest smell—still raining out there. Jim's brother-in-law, tightly pressed against Clayton, a big space between him and Old Willie. He is fearful, keeping his distance, which causes the flutter of a laugh in my empty belly.

Willie spoke in a low, exhausted voice, and Roger responded by interpreting in a hoarse voice, speaking in an old man's English, the kind so close to Salish thought patterns he didn't distinguish pronouns. He turned slightly toward me.

"What he got, her helpers, go look at those women. That one drivin', *áaamp'sum* (such a pity), she dead, hit hard on head. That one, he his wife, that one, he have leg broke, two places, ain't it? She okay, sleepin'. That little girl asleep in front of car, he not wake up, hit head on back, big bump. But she wake up later, not remember nothin'. He wife, hurt but okay. They pregnant, but not know it. Just broke leg, bumped around, ain't it? *Ax'éy. Wai i hwi.*"

Little hands handed in a full basket of water, then pulled down the goathide flap from the outside. Bennett had had enough. In the darkness Clayton said, "I guess he guard the door for us," and there was some wry laughter. With Bennett gone, I relaxed back against the twisted ranks of willow with more room to spread out. The songs Roger led us in were familiar, so I sang easily with everyone else, joining in the grateful, joyous mood. Hotter and hotter, but more steam this time than radiant heat from the rocks. Cries of thanks, "*limlemt! limt! límtenun'tm!*" During a song the house lights went up for me again. A glow on the ceiling brought on odd thoughts. It looked like the framework was on fire, glowing as though ready to burst into flame right where the apex should be. It didn't seem strange to me that the willow framework was burning, but as the song ended and Old Willie kept pouring on water handful by handful, each bursting upward of steam seemed to make the burning place grow brighter instead of extinguishing it. I could only stare in incomprehension.

"They goin' now," Roger said. When I lowered my eyes, the door was already open, light streaming in below the outflow of hot fog. It felt like coming back from somewhere far away. Men crawled out one by one. I sat outside for a long time, feeling the tap-tap-tap of rain on my steaming skin as men bathed in the river, some staying in for a long time, others ducking once or twice and climbing out to look for clothing. I was weak but I made it into the river and revived a little.

At the fire, Roger was back in his fluent Canadian voice, speaking earnestly to Jim's brother-in-law about arrangements to get him to his wife at the hospital in Penticton. I dressed and sat under the tarp alone, too tired to think. They all drifted downriver toward Clayton's car without a word to me, except for Clayton who came to say, "*Wai, Skélux.* I be back in a day or two."

"*Aaaa.*" He looked at me for a moment, then walked off. I had just enough energy to pull a blanket over me before I fell asleep.

11

I woke up to the wet smell of evening, a dreamy twilight with trees dripping after rain. I was alone again, my mind held by the images from the crowded sweatlodge. But I was oddly indifferent to the memory of how tiny humanlike figures had run back and forth from the rocks to Old Willie's feet, or to the surprising suggestion that his helpers had gone to find out what happened after the car wreck and reported back to us in the sweatlodge. It was all vivid and real, but it meant nothing to me.

What I felt was a palpable loneliness, a sense of separation from my own kind that was deeper than just being left alone in the bush again. The faces of those who had been so important to me as a child, as a young man, floated by with an ache. Hours passed as I examined a lifetime of released memories. It was as Clayton had predicted: a lot of what *k'ulsht* was about was getting to know myself, seeing myself with some honesty for the first time in my life. In this peculiar reverie things floated by without my intention, relatives spoke in their own voices, I suddenly grasped situations or events that had always baffled me, and I saw that I'd been on the run for so long I hadn't realized how alone I really was. Various flaws of character stood out clearly and made me smile, since I was probably the last to notice them. Ruefully, I saw the limits to what I'd done in life and what I could hope to do if I continued living according to my own devices. It was obvious something had been given to me when I was young, something that came into play at dark hours to spirit me out of dangerous situations, keep me going strong, bring me back to life when everything seemed hopeless. Something that drew me off into the heart of nature to hunt and wander and feel at home. I could see it was time to acknowledge this help and make it a conscious part of my life. But that was as far as I got.

It was midnight, or what I called midnight—Orion at the highpoint in the sky—when it came to me I'd forgotten to eat or drink. I was down to a morsel and three sips. But all I did was sit and wrap the blanket tightly around me, thinking about how we aren't aware that putting food and water in our mouths every day is what keeps us alive. Then I forgot about it. The wind rose and fell, the trees dripped. I let go of everything and sat passively, alert to what was out there around me. Silent, receiving, alone in the darkness.

The first hint of light in the sky after a long night's vigil is like God coming. A great power coming to change everything. "Pray to the day," as one song repeated over and over. It grows and spreads. Then it seems to fall back into a vagueness as the things of night grope for ways to escape into hiding. Then with a blush of silent power, the world takes visible form. Full day arrives before the sun actually rises in this mountainous world. I see there is no other way to experience the heart of mystery in this waking world without being out here like this. No talk could take me here. I pray to the day, to this dawn, this power coming on in the world. You are real, I see you. *Aaaa* . . . Thank you.

When I finally stand up, I know I have fasted myself to the place of no longer wanting to eat or drink. Such a flat, empty slowness. I fold the blanket into a carefully squared bundle and place it just so under the tarp, everything being done with a sense of gratitude now. I marvel at how my body can walk on its own without me intending every little movement, and at the same time I concentrate on the very act of walking, as if it was something I'd never experienced before.

Doing everything in slow motion, I built the sweatlodge fire stack, moved rocks one by one from the lodge to the firepit, heaped more wood, lit the tinder and sat back against the doorframe as the fire took off. The sun moved upward from the east, showing through the trees. Warm sun, blue sky, a balmy day as if now Sweatlodge was bringing a day of pity for me.

In the sweat my voice was so unfamiliar, the voice of someone else. There was so little force behind my breath that I sang the songs in a whisper. I spent long minutes just breathing, breathing in life. The heat was somehow unfelt, just there, burning, outside me somewhere. And the river was a chill, but remotely, as if I floated in a bubble. Then as the Similkameen swept by as usual and the last wisps of firepit smoke drifted into a sunny sky, I crawled back into the warm sweatlodge, dropped the hide flap, and slept.

I realize they're talking above me. I look up and there's a hole in the ceiling of the lodge. Bluejays are perched around the opening, looking down at me, kwash-kwashing. Only I can also hear them talking in English to each other, then to me. I can see the white stripes by their eyes, the wag of black crests, the stridence of their bluejay calls, but translating as I do when I hear Salish spoken to me, I hear them saying, "They're coming now." "Yes, they're coming." I suddenly awaken from sleep looking upward. No hole. Bluejays are making a racket outside, above, in the trees. I have the feeling they were telling me something, that I could understand the talk of bluejays.

I was awake all night again. Under the tarp, I found that animals had finally got into the last of the food. It seemed appropriate that they had waited until I had given up eating. I put the last little bit in the cookpot and set it out at the base of a tree with the half-full bucket of water. It was a precious offering by someone who truly knew its value.

Then I walked away into the night, wearing only the blanket, feeling my way along with bare feet. I made it up to the first bench, a flat, open place where I sat leaning against the bark of a big ponderosa pine, shielded a little from the cold wind by a thicket of brush. A new moon was setting in the west. The silver line of the river threaded through the shadowy forest below. Above the freshly snow-covered mountains beyond, the north star glimmered in clear sky. The wind rose and fell.

I listened to the sound of the wind, especially the huffing sound it made in the tops of pine trees. *Sniwt*, as the Okanogans say, "wind blows." Both noun and verb in one word. The doing is the thing. I simply paid attention to it. It came to me that wind was some great thing breathing, like the earth's breath. In time, a thought drifted by: Nothing is breathing the wind, it is just breath, moving. Then I became aware of my own breathing, how it went on, keeping me alive, without my even being aware of it until a moment like this one. How it, too, was just breath, moving.

I was suddenly, intimately connected to the wind blowing, for there was an uninterrupted flow of it coming into my lungs, going out, coming in, going out. With nothing else entering my body to keep me alive, no food or water, it was only the wind, the great breath, that was sustaining me. By breathing, I was a part of that vast invisible movement that stretched away forever. A laugh bubbled out of me, and the feeling in my chest was like playing with the flow of air, delighting in it, grabbing and releasing it. Laughing, like speaking, was a playing with the flow of breath that gave me life. *Aaaa* . . . Then the words came out of nowhere: "Only the wind is real."

Unaccountably hot, I slipped the blanket off. As long as I sensed the wind as alive and breathing me, I burned from some inner fire and sat exposed to the icy wind unchilled. I felt as though I almost knew something important, but then it faded and I shivered. I pulled the blanket up, wrapped it tightly around my body and head, with only my face exposed.

The last hours of night are the hardest. The wee hours when the wee people come out to look at this strange thing, a man sitting alone in the hills, eyes open, breathing. Or so my aimless wandering mind told me like a story. I saw my mind as loosened, floating, fragile. As something that could be easily taken away if I did not look right and remain silent. In silence I perceived the great windy emptiness and solid earth and trees and stars and me as simply existing, here, now. I wanted to live, so I waited and watched and endured.

Another dawn. Voices in the wind. Somebody walking this way, calling. But so indistinct, so unclear. Then nothing more in the growing light of day. Something moves in the sky. My eye identifies a jet. Then I hear it, the roar of jet engines, and see the thin white trail behind. The sun rises and it's another balmy day, sunny, breezy, only a hint of clouds to the west, a few curled threads high above. From up here I hear the faint sound of a semi on the highway miles away, and then the whine of a chainsaw off in the other direction.

It's day nine. I rise and walk slowly downhill to the river.

As I went about building yet another fire of fir branchwood, I saw how slow I moved. When I finished a task I would forget to move on to the next thing until I stirred from a long lapse, wondering where I'd gone. Sometimes I'd realize I hadn't taken a breath in so long I'd force myself to take a long, deep one.

In the lodge I forgot who I was and what I was doing. I found myself playing with the water in the basket, marveling at the feel of water swirling on my fingers. I lost count of the songs and simply felt my way through my time sweating. Trying to make it feel hot, I stayed inside one long, long time, pouring more and more water on the rocks until the white glow came and formed a huge doughnut in front of my eyes staring in darkness. Little people moved along the edges. I knew it was hot, but didn't really suffer from it until I suddenly felt like I was dying. I knew I wasn't dying, but it was so painful and consuming I crawled weakly out into the light without the strength to throw up the flap. I kept crawling all the way to the river, where I sat in water up to my neck. Then, barely able to stand, I wobbled to the tarp, lay down, and drew my blanket over me.

I stared at one corner of the blanket where I read the words on a label: Hudson's Bay Company. This was the blanket given to me when I first arrived in Canada, ten years before. A gift from the committee that supported American draft dodgers and deserters seeking escape from the Vietnam war machine. So long ago and far away, it seemed. It smelled like wet, rainy nights on the coast . . .

Sleep was short, like a momentary blackout, a brief blotting out of the sounds of river and wind. I was refreshed. With the blanket around my skinny body, I walked slowly upriver as the sun sank behind a silent oncoming of clouds. When I walked slowly back, mesmerized at the gradual diminishing of light and the stillness of twilight, I smelled smoke. It could have been the remains of the sweatlodge fire, but it wasn't. Clayton sat feeding sticks to the campfire when I got back. Neither of us spoke as I sat down weakly under the tarp. He lit a bough of cedar in the flames, let it burn brightly and resinously for a few seconds, then blew it out and smudged me and himself in the smoke. It was good to see him.

"*Wai. Xeláp*, tomorrow, after sweat, you come back to us. That last one, to bring you back. Your time with them over, after that last one."

"*Aaaa.*" My voice cracked. I saw Clayton looking at the cooking pot and water bucket, both empty and tipped over, illuminated by flames.

"*Loot kúnta'aks'cháoot*," I said slowly, pronouncing the humorous Salish equivalent to "I didn't do it." Clayton laughed softly. I had little power to talk. It was so hard to form thoughts, then make my mouth voice the words. Clayton sat quietly feeding the fire.

"Don't try to talk too much. I talk. Tell you somethin'. My nephew, Jim, his brother-in-law go to Penticton, see about his wife. Roger take 'em, come back today.

"She just like they tell Old Willie. He send 'em to see that, report back. See just how they are doin'. That what they tell 'em. She have that leg broke twice. Doctor in hospital, he tell her she pregnant. She guess she know that already, but she tell her husband what the doctor say, and he laugh.

"'I already know it,' he say.

"That dead one, her people already took her away. Little girl wake up, all like they say. Wake up with no mother, poor thing. All that his power tell him. What they seen.

"So that's it."

He unrolled his sleeping bag and climbed in. The fire burned down to coals, and I stayed sitting up, listening to him sleep. There were no stars and the wind was unnaturally warm and damp. Finally at some point I dozed off.

Explosive, ripping sounds woke me in the pre-dawn of the tenth day. I'd been sleeping in a sitting position, head hanging, and I blinked awake in a wildly thrashing windstorm, unable to see anything more than faint shadows in motion all around our bush camp.

"*Nt'a!* They comin' now," Clayton's voice exclaimed muffled from the sleeping bag. I remembered the bluejays speaking those words, and my ears popped. The tarp flapped and slapped madly overhead, then broke loose and fell across swaying bushes. I heard an unearthly splintering moan, then a shudder of release as a huge tree fell somewhere near us, hitting the ground with a thunderous boom. The ground beneath us rippled with the shock wave, branches and twigs fell in a spray, and a heady smell of evergreen sap came on the wind.

In a few minutes the worst of the wind was past. A steady breeze blew downriver from the high mountains to the west. As the light grew I could distinguish the forest around us, and noticed Clayton sitting upright in his bedding with a beautiful, enlivened look on his sleepy face, looking around in wonder at the wind moving trees. Then the feeling of the wind changed, bringing a familiar, musty smell.

"Snow," Clayton said, climbing quickly out of his sleeping bag. He pulled on his baggy trousers, slipped suspenders over his shoulders, and stood, nose to the wind. "Winter has come."

Telling me to sit tight, he broke camp and carried everything to where he parked his car. I had forgotten to stash kindling so we walked to the branch pile near the sweatlodge where I had chopped a pile of highly flammable chips from a pitchy limb. We saw the wreckage caused by the fallen tree. The very top of a tall spruce pointed stiffly, horizontally out of a jungle of splintered branches just inside the clearing. A long avenue lined with skinned and mangled trees showed the path of the spruce's descent. Beyond, the mountains were blotted out by an ominous slate-black nothingness. The first flakes of snow appeared, somersaulting downwind.

I was grateful to sit wrapped in my blanket and let Clayton take over. He built a fire with great speed. By the time he had it spread out to receive the rocks, the wind had fallen further but was driving snow so thickly it was impossible to look into the wind without our faces becoming instantly blanketed with stinging snow. With careful positioning of wood and a windbreak of propped limbs, he coaxed the fire into a roaring, hissing blaze.

For the last time, and with a feeling of regret, I waited as the fire transformed dull volcanic rocks into glowing orange orbs. Clayton gathered all the unused rocks and fragments into a pile and patted them affectionately.

"They give themself to us, sacrifice themself for us," he said.

I watched the flames, the falling whiteness, the growing wintry gloom of the forest. I became more and more stupefied by the transformation taking place around us. The wind dropped to nothing and the snow floated down vertically through a muffled silence. Except for the bare ground around the fire and the river washing by, the world was turning white. Snow began to mound up on our shoulders and heads.

Clayton had me climb inside the lodge and wait while he carried rocks with the tongs. The fir boughs and peeled willows never smelled sweeter. Another pang of regret, the same feeling as moving out of a house: the familiar smells and shapes and sounds are being left behind forever. The little lodge had become my home, my place of healing and strength and change. Ten days with Sweatlodge and Similkameen had given me a habitual awareness of my body in harmony with nature, and of the undefinable presence of those others who showed themselves to me. But I was also ready for my ordeal to be over.

"*Wai*, let's do this, uncle!" I said in Salish as he crawled in and pulled down the flap.

"*Aaaa, aaaa*," he said with feeling. "*Wai, Kwílsten,* here in you we come like this, pitiful, one last time. Look here at me, at us, our want to live, so now we breathe your breath." And he splashed water sputtering onto the rocks with a branch of sagebrush, the bitter burning sagey steam scorching my nose and throat. A large, brightly glowing rock on the top of the heap slid off and fell towards me, landing with a sizzle where I barely yanked my feet away.

"Goodness!" Clayton said, laughing. "That one want you to pick him up, hold him in your lap!"

"*Loot inchá!*" I said, coughing at the sudden cloud of smoke from burning evergreen needles.

Still laughing, but praying with strong feeling, he poured repeated handfuls of water on the rocks, then I heard another sizzle and saw the escaped rock flip up onto the pile with the others. He'd done it with his bare hands.

"Sometimes they do things like that, jump out and roll around, show you they alive, they move," he said in a reverent voice.

As he splashed the rocks more and more and the burning spread of steam became intense, I gave thanks and offered myself for one more time. Then we sang together again, the songs he taught me and some new ones. It amazed me how I was able to pick them up quickly, to match his voice and anticipate the shifts and changes in melody. His last song was intricate and driving, like a war dance song, and repeated the phrase *kwich'kwácht* (real strong) over and over. Then he led the way out into the swirling whiteness. Snowflakes hissed as they touched our bodies. The river, a vivid green in the whiteout, cooled us quickly. We climbed dripping from the river at the same time and stood in ankle-deep snow, gazing at the fire, waiting as it warmed us in the endless fall of snow. I was completely without thoughts. I breathed, pumped blood, listened to silence.

So tired, so very tired. I crawled into the cozy darkness for the last time and sat as Clayton called on the powers of nature and made the lodge so hot I reeled weakly in pain. My eyes burned from yet another flood of salty sweat, my ears ached. I sang feebly along with his voice, but everything gradually became remote as a ringing in my ears grew louder and louder. The house lights came up and I sagged sideways in the white glow, unable to stay upright. Clayton sang as if from a great distance. My own wheezing voice was close and unfamiliar. I was going somewhere else, somewhere more powerful, beautiful, compelling. I saw humans with animalistic features, glowing stars that opened into talking mouths, feathers floating on a wind, and heard a quiet voice talking to me about all kinds of things. I saw a great serpent beneath the earth and a rainbow arching overhead from its head to the tip of its tail. I saw all kinds of things, heard hours of talk, and yet knew these things were not mine, were not for me to have. I was here just to see, to know, nothing more. I knew I was seeing the world powers with power eyes, and hearing a power voice. Then the voice became silent. There was nothing but a roaring in my ears, and such cold! Oh, such freezing cold!

I became aware that I was lying naked out in the snow. When I sat up and looked around, shivering uncontrollably, I recognized nothing. The heavy snowfall had transformed the landscape beyond recognition. I could be next to the sweatlodge and not know it, I thought. But no rounded mound could be seen in the snowy flat of forest floor. The falling snow was beginning to thin out and the temperature was dropping. I struggled to my feet and began walking vaguely downhill.

I had no strength to call out, but as I walked I drew great breaths and my shivering subsided.

When I found the river flowing at a murmur in the snowhush, I got my bearings and turned to follow it downstream. Everywhere the snow-covered conifers towered, every bough, every branch neatly mounded in fluffy white. My feet grew numb and I stumbled on branches and rocks hidden in the snow. After miles, I heard Clayton's voice singing ahead. I came into the clearing and saw him crouched by the sweatlodge fire, his deerhead hat covered in snow, his poncho tented around him.

He stood up when he heard me, turned, our eyes met and he threw my blanket around my shoulders.

"*W-w-wai*, I f-f-found you," I said, and my feet ached as I heated them over the fire. He offered me water and I sipped. It was so unfamiliar it tasted like gasoline, but I continued to sip.

"So, the wild man of the timber come back!" It felt good to laugh again. "I thought maybe you went bigfoot!"

As I thawed out at the fire, he went and warmed up his car. When he came back, he said, "Maybe we go pretty quick. I don't know, got those bald tires, maybe can't get out in this snow."

It was a wild, spinning ride, fishtailing and bucking along the almost invisible track in Clayton's car, but he kept his speed up and we made it to the highway where snowplows screamed by in sprays of slush and sand. I must have fallen asleep immediately after we got going on the highway because the next thing I remembered I woke up as Clayton pulled off the road and roared up the hill to where my trailer sat.

Home at last, my beat-up old trailer a faded turquoise green under fresh snow. The trailer had been through so many winters, so many blizzard winds and heavy dumps of snow, the tin siding was collapsed in on itself, molded to the wooden framework underneath, like my body, showing the structure of bones. A thread of smoke drifted from the woodstove pipe.

Clayton helped me carry my gear inside. I was surprised to find it warm and cleaned up, a fire in the stove, and pots of food waiting for me, already cooked. I lifted lids and sniffed.

"Yah, Charlene, Grandma, them others, they cook for you, *Skélux*. Look like they fix your place up. Look like a woman live here."

He'd already told me that after the sweatlodge retreat "somebody" ought to stay home, stay quiet for a few days. Take it easy, let it all sink in, eat, drink, sleep. Maybe a few visitors. Come back gradually. Slow and easy.

"Think about what happen," he said now. "Your time to come back, bring all that back with you. Ponder on it. Two, three days I come and see how you doin'."

In the mirror there was a vaguely familiar man looking back at me, hair in dreadlocks, dark whiskers, mustache covering his mouth. Fir needles stuck to his skin. And eyes like pools of endless depth, eyes so alive I could feel the reflected feel of them. Eyes like power beams searching and touching the world. No wonder they don't look in your eyes . . .

Clayton stood impassively at the door, as if waiting to be dismissed. Then I remembered: I hadn't said a word since the sweatlodge fire. He had been doing all the talking, and I had not voiced my thoughts. I could see the concern on his face, the wondering if I was back or not. I cleared my throat.

"*Wai*. There is something . . . I wonder about. I was in the lodge, with you, singing. Then I was out there, in the snow, alone. Lost, and I had to find my way back . . ." I looked at him questioningly from my chair by the stove.

"*Aaaa, tlakwílux* (power man). I dunno. When I went to the river, you walk away. I not follow. *Xwu'xóoy uhl k'wap. Wai, xwu'púhlem il skwilekwált.* (You left and it was quiet. So then, you came out of the woods)."

"*Aaaa*," I said, and I wanted to tell him somebody had been talking to me, showing me things, narrating the structure and powers of the world I'd been seeing. But there were no words to say it. It felt fragile, barely on the surface of my memory, scarcely on a par with the richness of talk, of the smell of food, of the feel of being home. I instinctively knew that to speak of it would dispel it. To put it into words would strip it of something vital.

What had he said? Ponder on it. Yes, I would ponder on it, let it sink in.

12

Getting back to everyday life was slow going. Before my ten-day *k'ulsht,* I'd been looking at the suggestions of something powerful from the perspective of ordinary life—at the lore in the *chaptíkx* stories, at Clayton's unusual abilities, at the vague sense of something irrationally "meant to be" in my life. Now I was coming the other way. I was looking at ordinary life from the point of view of one who had been out of this world. But it was obviously all one world, like two different versions, two opposite poles. And one seemed to animate the other.

The paint peeling from the kitchen ceiling, the scuffling of a pack rat in her brush nest under the trailer skirting, the smells of food cooking, the faint skunk of propane from the stove flame—things I had before simply taken for granted had a sense of inherent magic about them. I was like a child discovering the things of the world for the first time.

But as time passed, my customary routines began to assert themselves again, and in the ordinary light of day, my experiences began to seem amazing. Sitting quietly in the kitchen after a meal or out on the porch idly gathering strength, I'd find myself reliving the crushing heat, the "house lights" coming up in a white glow, the drifting pinpoints of light. I wondered at the memory of how dimly visible human-like figures moved obscurely on the rocks and ran back and forth to Old Willie, or how the blue lights flashed in a circle inside Roger's drum, or how the ceiling of the sweatlodge glowed like it was slowly burning up.

In the steady flow of everyday doings in my trailer on the hill above the lake, cars driving by on the pavement, tractors humming up and down rows of orchard trees, plaintive country and western songs twanging away on the radio, dishes to wash and laundry to hang out on the line, I found the sweatlodge images to be so ephemeral, so ineffable, I couldn't describe them or comprehend them like I did the things of ordinary life. Little human figures? How little? About a foot high? How did they look? Were they like Indians or Whites? It was all irrelevant. They just were. I saw them, yet I couldn't make out anything like the detail I was used to in remembering things or people in ordinary life. But they were as real as anything I was seeing now: snow melting in bright sun, my truck parked out front, the familiar shape of Grandma's blue ceramic pot on my stove.

And just as real were the experiences that because of their context seemed like dreams or visions. Hearing the bluejays speaking in English through the hole in the sweatlodge roof. Seeing figures coming toward me as I sat on a vast plain. Or the long time I spent seeing the powers of another world and listening to a voice telling me all about it. I knew they were all things I was shown, I was allowed to see, because they didn't exist in my mind or memory before I went on the sweatlodge retreat. They weren't the result of wishful thinking or suggestion by Clayton or others, they were the result of trying to live up to my commitment to suffer, and receiving whatever came from praying for the world out there to take pity on me. I had stood still and let the good catch up to me.

Food was a marvel. I didn't stray far from the kitchen. The first day home I ate seven full meals, seven sit-downs with all food groups represented, except the coffee group, the junk food group, and the sweets group. These three were disgusting to me. I would learn to eat and drink them again someday, but for now it was real food that held all my interest. Soup and meat and vegetables and bread and fruit and water. Cold water in a glass, nothing sweeter.

Seven meals the first day. So much for Jim's prediction that my stomach would be so shrunk and shut down after my fast that I'd only be able to nibble at first, that it would take days before I could eat as much as I used to. Actually it took days for me to taper off to my previous three squares a day. Maybe it was the old campaigner in me, used to privation followed by gluttonous catch-up. Whatever, I was easily packing it in and fat began to form in the hollows of my body again. I began to feel like my old self and took walks through the nearby orchards that looked so desolate after harvest and a heavy snow.

The snow melted quickly in the lowlands around the lake. In the orchard I looked at from my front porch, grass emerged still green, flattened by the passage of tractors and littered with wooden poles used as props to hold up limbs when they were heavy with fruit. Bending down from the weight of growing, ripening apples, limbs would break if not supported. I walked along the rows up and down the hilly slopes, stepping over the props that had fallen after the fruit was picked, strewn like matchsticks, being covered by the fall of leaves that stripped the trees with each breeze. At the far end of the orchard I came to the unpainted plank shacks in a row the owner had built for his seasonal workers. Two Mexican men called me over to their doorway, the last ones remaining since all others had left after harvest. We talked about how well they did picking and what kind of work I did, in a combination of their sparse English and my high-school and street-slang Spanish. They invited me in to share the supper they were about to cook, so I sat on a cot in their plain ten-by-ten shack as they cooked food on a hotplate illuminated by one naked light bulb in the ceiling overhead.

Carlos was older, about forty, with a wife and kids back in Guerrero where he'd been an electrician and courier for ranchers. He had one arm that didn't work right and he told me how he was once robbed by banditos as he carried a payroll from town to ranch. They shot him and left him for dead, and he showed me the bullet scars and how his upper arm bone had healed in a crooked S-shape. Marvín was in his twenties and had been in the Mexican army in Chihuahua during Operation Bootstrap when, at Yanqui instigation, they had attacked and burned marijuana plantations. He talked vaguely about shooting growers when they tried to run, and how important it was for a man to kill like that. Carlos told me how sometimes he heard "diableros" or witches singing in the orchard at night. Marvín laughed and said the older man was too "chicken" to go outside the cabin at night. They both thought I was a rich rancher and were surprised to learn that I didn't own the land I lived on.

Meanwhile, I watched them prepare food, that being the main focus of life for me. They halved a pound of lard that came in a cardboard square, each half plunked into a cast-iron skillet to melt on the hotplate. In one, a full bag of red chili was dumped into the melted grease, then followed by all they had on hand, which was sliced zucchini and a can of mackerel. Carlos stirred the red, greasy mess while Marvín fried a stack of corn tortillas in the other skillet of hot grease. We stood around the smoking skillets spooning the burning chili mixture onto tortillas dripping with grease and ate until it was all gone.

The next day I spent a lot of time contemplating the world from the doorless opening of my outhouse. A pickup truck intruded on my outhouse retreat, pounding too fast up the steep road to my trailer, the horse rack on the back rattling like hammers pounding on steel. It was Stuart Bolster, his ten-year-old son "Boot" perched on the pipes above the cab, hands free, in the leg-hold of a bull rider he hoped someday to become. Away in the orchard, Carlos and Marvín were driving a tractor along the rows of trees, picking up props and piling them on a trailer pulled behind. Being undocumented workers, "lambristos" who had hopped the fence at the U.S.-Mexican border, they froze and studied the approaching pickup as it veered toward my trailer and skidded to a muddy stop next to my truck. Stuart got out and strolled casually towards my porch. Not wanting to draw attention to myself or my plight, I stayed seated and saw the two Mexican men go back to work.

At that moment a falcon flew directly across my line of sight, darting this way and that toward the tall, bushy ponderosa pine at the edge of the orchard beyond Stuart's truck. I realized I'd been hearing bluejays screeching from the pine tree ever since Stuart turned off his truck, and as the falcon zoomed toward the tree, their calls suddenly silenced. I watched the falcon wiggle expertly through the pine limbs and then barrel down and away through the apple trees. I was craning my neck out the outhouse doorway to watch the bird's graceful, primordial, sharp-winged flight disappearing into the sea of apple trees when I saw two men about where it disappeared. Two men walking slowly, cautiously uphill through the orchard towards the two Mexicans. I instantly recognized their uniforms—U.S. Border Patrol.

"Aguas! Aguas!" I shouted. "Hay viene la migra!"

Carlos and Marvín abandoned the tractor and ran like soccer players. The two uniformed men split up and gave pursuit, but they stumbled unfamiliarly over the props. I could see they'd never catch my friends. Stuart and Boot came toward the voice from the outhouse, so I pulled up my pants and emerged, heart pounding in the rush of adrenaline.

"We almost had them dumb wetbacks!" Boot crowed. I recalled that one of Stuart's cousins was a Border Patrol officer at the nearby Oroville barracks. Stuart grinned at me.

"Howdy, Tom. They said you been up in the Queen's country. I guess you're back."

"Yeah. That your cousin jogging in the orchard there?"

"Yeah. He can use the exercise. Work off all them doughnuts."

He sat on the woodpile, crossed his legs, tilted his cowboy hat back to reveal a pale brow above his sun-darkened face, and rolled a cigarette.

Boot said, "What'd you do? Warn 'em?"

I didn't answer. Stuart looked at me out of the corner of his eyes as he licked his rollie and twisted it tight.

"I didn't know you se habla'd their lingo." He lit up and the rich, sweet reek of Prince Albert tobacco smoke wafted by. "Well, my cousin has his quota to fill. It's a toss up between the Mexicans and the hippies. I'll take the Mexicans any day!"

"I don't get it," I said. "During harvest there's hundreds of illegals all around the lake, and the Border Patrol never even drives by."

"Who knows? Maybe old man Smith doesn't feel like paying these birds what he owes 'em. If a rancher calls, they can't very well ignore it." He shrugged. "So what you been up to?"

"I was sweathousing up near Princeton. Clayton took me."

Stuart burst out laughing. "Mexicans and hippies and Indians!"

"And rednecks," I added. "Who ride to school on cows."

"It was a calf," he corrected. Then, looking sharply at me, "You know what they say about White men goin' in a sweatlodge, huh?"

"No, what?"

"It's like a dog goin' inside a house." The local Whites didn't let their dogs come inside their houses. Stuart's face looked poised to laugh again.

"I don't get it."

"Neither does the dog!" he said, then stood up laughing at his own joke and tossed his pinched-out butt.

"See ya later," he called as he headed for his pickup, Boot already scrambling up the pipe rack to his perch.

When he was gone I sat on the porch and stared at the pine tree and the orchard. Something powerful and beyond the ordinary had happened. Like Clayton had said, I could explain it away if I wanted to. I could say that a peregrine falcon had just been cruising by and attacked the tree full of bluejays for one that wasn't alert enough and then went on in his opportunistic way of hunting across the orchard. Where "just by chance" the Border Patrol was sneaking up on my newfound, unsuspecting friends, my fellow border-runners just trying to make a better living for themselves and their families. I could say all that, and then I would have nothing, no power, "all gone." But

I knew in my gut, queasy and flushed out as it was, that things like this in life could not be that ordinary. The jays had been screeching a warning. The falcon flew directly across my line of sight, then took my eyes to where the uniformed men were sneaking up through the apple trees. It was a gift for me. Something offered, and it had been up to me to act on it, or not. I felt a warm suffusion of something like love, or a blessing, spreading through my chest as I accepted the fact of having received this gesture from the powers of nature.

"Yah, that how they do for us," Clayton said the next day as we sat across from each other in a restaurant. "Them *shumíx*, they don't like how plain people, earth people, get stomped on. They watchin' out. Maybe another time no power man around, can't give no warning. That one guy, like you say, hear spirits at night, singin'. See, maybe they watch out for him. And you, they know your heart. They see if you awake, if you still payin' attention. They know what in your heart, that you would help those men. Everything like that, you eat their food, you get sick and have to sit out there in a outhouse, right at the time those border cops come lookin'—all that no accident. Everything that happen like set up. That how they give us their power."

He smiled at me. The restaurant was filled with people, and I had been taken aback by the crowded presence of so many human bodies and voices when we came in. The drive down to the Okanogan Valley with Clayton had been a sudden reentry into the mess the *Suyápi* make in the world. Flashing neon signs and houses crammed together and busy streets and smoking lumber mills. Then the absurdity of the international border crossing, the suspicious eyes of the uniformed customs officer taking us in, scanning the inside of Clayton's car, and the standard questions in a dry voice faintly reminiscent of Scottish origins. Miles of orchards on rolling glacial hills with stucco houses and wrought-iron trim, a legacy of the Spanish and Portuguese immigrant farmers who settled here in the only part of Canada that even faintly reminded them of their arid homelands. A bitter wind carried low cumulus clouds across a wintry blue sky as we made our way across the truck stop parking lot. And in the privacy of our own booth, the slick plastic seat covers and smells of food, I sensed Clayton's playful desire to see me fully back in the world we all have to live in.

"This old way, this Indian way, how power men keep that alive, always from way back to right now. Keep it alive so the people can live well. Go up in the mountains, in the timber, way out there away from people where the power is. Bring it back to where it's needed. Right to here." He tapped the table top with his fingers.

"See now, the *Suyápi* don't see it like we do. I watch 'em, listen to 'em. I'm the detective, like that guy on TV, just watchin' and thinkin' about things till he figure out who done it." He grinned, pleased with himself. "The White people, they got this crazy way. Somethin' is real, or it's not. Like if it's hard and you can touch it, see it, why then it's real. Like that bird that chase after them bluejays, how you say that in English?"

"Falcon."

"Yah, kind of like a hawk, but hunt other birds, sneak around low and fast. *Suyápi* say what you saw is *real*. But now, somethin' else, that bird a person, maybe some see him as a man, as a woman. That bird person, maybe he thinkin' he do somethin' for somebody. Just like a man, his want to help, show you somethin' like those border cops sneakin' around. *Suyápi* don't see that. Act dumb, throw up their hands. Because they didn't see that. Their want to believe that bird is just a dumb bird! They don't see that bird person who just like us. That other is like . . . like . . ."

"Invisible?"

"Yah, like that. Invisible. So it's not real. That some kind of insanity, if you ask me. But that how it is now. That what we got here in this coffee shop. All these *Suyápi* stopped in their cars and trucks, eatin' lunch. Real or not real.

"I think about this a lot. What they call real, we call just ordinary, common, pitiful, like that, see? But that other, that *xa'xá*, that like 'powerful.' Anybody can see that, unless they crazy, they got no heart. Have to see that other way, see with what you feel in your heart. But so, crazy world all over now, gotta hold on to what we got, keep that way alive, even here.

"Maybe you see now how we draw that *xa'xá* to us. That what we want, to be close to that power in the world. Go sweathousin', train ourself, fill up with it, to where we don't see no more like we did. Ordinary, pitiful. We get that other way of seein', of knowin'. We see that other Chopaka. We see that old man in the timber, go down on all fours and walk away the bear. We see that woman sittin' in the shade, all comfortable on her grass bed, then stand up the doe deer, run off sorta teasin' us."

His eyes had an inward look, like he was remembering things he'd seen in his life, out there in the hills. I looked around, then felt his eyes on me and became aware that I was watching the movements of an attractive waitress weaving between the crowded tables. Ordinary urges were definitely returning with a vengeance.

"Gotta get you a Indian woman, you bugger," Clayton muttered. "Somebody not crazy. You be some strong woman's squaw man. Live off her per capita money, like Leonard!"

"*Loot inchá!*"

"You be hunkered down with all them other squaw men, down in Nespelem, bribin' the tribal council for reservation land in her name. Raise a big pack of kids, mixed blood. Go round to all the powwows, head held high, show off all your kids fancy dancin'."

Another waitress brought our food, apologizing for the delay. "It always gets like this after the first snowfall, eh?" she said. "Like a bloody social club!" I thought her voice was beautiful, her eyes compelling, her plump body in a somewhat milkmaid-looking uniform quite fetching. In fact, every woman in the room had something appealing about her. After two weeks of nary a thought about the opposite sex, I was coming into rut.

The hot food on plates before us smelled slightly off. Oh yeah, one step removed from the homemade simplicity of Charlene and Grandma's cooking. The uniform, institutional way of preparing food. We fell to. It wasn't so bad. I told Clayton about the blue lights, the white glow, the little figures I'd seen moving about inside the dark sweatlodge. He listened while he ate, *aaa*-ing occasionally.

"I wonder what those lights were? Who those little people were?" I said.

"Different man see different things," he said. "One man go deep, take it inside his heart, breathe in that powerful breath, become *xa'xá*. Another man sit there, think about some girl he want to be with. Or maybe he don't think it's real, think it's a lot of talk, this spirit stuff. Those *shumíx* don't even see 'em, go right by 'em. Like they're not even there. But that other man, they take pity on him. Let him look inside, like through a doorway. See inside their sweatlodge where they dancin' on the rocks. Same sweatlodge, only different. Different eyes, different ears. Some, they just look, see nothin' but darkness. Others, they see, that world have its own light.

"This so you know Sweatlodge is always there, you can go to 'em, to clean off and get close to the power. So you can wake up and show what you got, that you tryin' to live like he want. Call up what is *xa'xá* in your life, ponder things, get ready for things, know things."

I told him about the experience of seeing the ceiling of the sweatlodge glowing like it was smoldering, ready to burst out in flames, glowing brighter with each splash of water.

"*Aaaa*. When they leave, when it all done, some they go down, straight down, under the earth, like you can hear 'em, a sound like no other. Wet, burstin' right into the earth. Some they go up, they leave by goin' straight up into the sky. They ride that steam, right through the roof." He tilted his chin up, asked, "When you see that?

We sayin' thanks? We gettin' ready to go out?"

"Yes. We were getting about done. I was looking up at it, then I saw you had thrown up the doorflap."

"*Aaaa, wai i hwi.*"

About the lights revolving in the drum, he said: "That little drum Roger have, lotta power there. That drum like a person, a spirit person, talk to 'em, tell 'em things. Roger, he can hear that, understand what he say. Someday, he gonna heal a lotta people with that drum. He never let it touch the ground, always keep it in that bag of his. Except in the lodge, or maybe at the pole during the Winter Dance. Then, lay it on the earth and it charge up, like chargin' a battery. They come and dance on it for him. Charge it up. Whew! That some kinda power, then! Thunder in the drum. I seen little lightning shoot out, touch people, make 'em well. Roger not ready yet, still learnin' about that power in the drum. But it do what it want, have its own life."

When I told of seeing the bluejays gathered around the hole in the sweatlodge roof, and of hearing them talk, of understanding what they said, he laughed. "I don't think you got Bluejay. He watch what everybody doin'. Make a big noise, mess around with other people's power. He the only one who get away with, like, criticizin', tellin' what they doing wrong. Embarrass people, make 'em feel ashamed. Like they cheatin' on their wife, he come and sit up there in the tree above, call down to his wife, say 'Go look over there, he cheatin' on you!'"

I told him I heard them say, "They're coming now." "Yes, they're coming." "Then, the next day, you came back, and in the morning, when the windstorm woke us up, you said, 'They're coming now.'"

"*Aaaa*," he said, thinking about how things appeared to me. "I don't know, *Skélux*, maybe they playin' a trick on you. They do that. Mess with people. See if they can trick 'em. Their want that the people be *talht*. How you say? True, right, something like that. That their hearts be true. Maybe they testin' you. See what you do about it."

The meal over, we sipped coffee. Halfway through a cup of coffee, my heart started pounding from the caffeine. I switched back to water. The restaurant began to clear out, and I stared out the window, trying to find the words to describe my last vision, or dream, or whatever it was—like wandering in a world behind this one, where the powers that animate this one were revealed. He listened to me tell about the more clearly remembered images like a big snake under the earth with a rainbow arching over aboveground from nose to tail, like stars with mouths that spoke, like people with animalistic features, shifting from animal to human form and back. Clayton grew increasingly uneasy, ceased to say *aaaa*, and as I stumbled on talking about what I'd seen anyway, finally held up his hand to stop me.

"*Loot xast*, not good, not here." He stood up and when I got up, too, I felt dizzy and distracted. We paused at the cash register digging in our wallets and pockets for Canadian money, then paid and walked out to his car. He drove in silence, north up the main Okanogan highway, for nearly half an hour. He turned off into a small wooded park on the shore of a shallow lake, a public picnic ground. The reedy lake sat against a scenic bowl of bare rock cliffs, the whole area designated by the government as a wildlife preserve. Bighorn sheep came down by ones and twos to drink at the shore opposite. The water was covered by hundreds of ducks and geese of every kind, taking a breather on the seasonal migration south. There were even a few white swans, long necks gracefully arched, drawing shyly away from us into the cover of cattails and bulrushes. At a spot hidden from view from the highway, Clayton broke dry branches and kindled a fire by a thick grove of birch, then laid some of the dried cedar boughs from his dashboard onto the tiny flames. He smudged us both in the resinous smoke, naming the tree it came from: "*Púh'nilhp.*"

We sat by the fire and looked around. It was so peaceful there, the sky becoming overcast over the western cliffs, the lush growth at the base of the cliffs lining the lake looking faded in the autumn gloom, leaves falling steadily around us. And the sounds of water-fowl calling across the lake, echoing back from the cliffs. It felt good to be back out somewhere like this.

"Now we can talk," Clayton said. "That kinda talk, gotta be careful. Maybe they come, see nothin' wrong with us, don't like a place like that. Somethin' bad happen. Come out here, wipe all that off. Bad enough to talk about 'em in English. Gotta be careful what I say about 'em. Maybe they punish me."

Feeling differently about what I told him now, I said, "Well, I knew it was something I was getting to look at. It wasn't like I was gaining some power. It's hard to talk about. Like I was just shown around."

"That kind of talk, real deep, calling it up, better to save it for the sweatlodge, or like out here like this. You see stuff very few people see. We know about 'em because Indian doctors talk about 'em. I know about that one, that big snake with that rainbow. But I never seen 'em. That one like a superpower, real big medicine. Most powers, they up in the sky, or down in the earth, or on the ground here, like us, or in the waters. That one, he all places at once. Or maybe she, I dunno. Big power, deep in the earth, but after a rain, shimmer in the sky for all to see. Hold everything together, the whole world under us, alive and full of power.

"Them stars, of course they talk to us. Have mouths to speak because they the people who came before. Generation after generation, see, once they die, they go away, but they can talk to us. Some have that, they picked by those dead, to receive their power, to hear what go on with those that pass on. That other place where they go to. Maybe the dead want somethin' from the relatives they leave behind. Talk through that one that has that gift from them, tell 'em maybe they want deer meat, lotta fat. They give that, cook it up, put that food in the fire. Then those dead, that one that ask, he happy now, he bless his relatives.

"Them feathers blowin' in the wind, I dunno, maybe just

somethin' for you, I guess.

"And them people that are like animals, too. That would be the *chip'chaptík'xwul*, the Animal People we say, out there waitin' for us, just like we always know. *Aaaa*, you get to see it like it is."

"The whole time," I said, "there was this voice talking to me, telling me about what I was seeing, like showing me around, just a voice. Like a guy talking in my ear. Like somebody I know but don't quite recognize, somebody who's been there all along . . . very familiar, like a relative's voice. But I don't really remember anything specific that he said."

"*Aaaa, aaaa . . .*" Clayton said, visibly moved. "Who you think? This yours, this yours to hold your whole life. Nobody else's. Maybe little by little this come to you in life. Like come out when you need it, be there, just the knowing when something come up. Already know because it there, inside you, but another kind of talk. The kind that is like the talk of bluejays, but different. Just come out of you when the time come, somethin' in front of you, and you just *know*.

"Good we come out here. Too easy to throw away. Not there with truck drivers, there we just ordinary, no power, food, smells, pretty girls checkin' us out. *Shumíx* don't like a place like that. You try to say what he tell you, he hear his words, he come there and see you not really callin' him. You not need him. He go away, maybe never come back. No respect. Leave you to fall sick, easy to have bad things happen.

"No, much better out here." He lit more cedar on the flames and waved a smoking twig over us.

It hits me he's saying the narrator was my *shumíx*. The voice so familiar, the feeling of knowing him, of being comfortable having him tell me all about that world . . . I'm right on the edge of knowing who he is, of remembering something vital, but not quite. Clayton says nothing for a long time as I put the pieces together that I have available in my conscious mind. In some kind of blackout I climbed out of the sweatlodge and walked a mile in the snow naked, to wake up lying somewhere lost. During that time I was shown bits and pieces of a powerful world of nature behind (?) this world I was now looking at. All the while I listened to the voice of someone so familiar it felt like listening to my own father or brother, yet I couldn't quite call up the memory of who it was.

It was good that I was so mentally healthy. I smiled, remembering the government psychiatrist who interviewed a bunch of us in a military stockade when we faced charges for going AWOL and escaping confinement. After listening to me go on and on about all the insane things I'd seen or thought or done or experienced, he slammed the folder shut and said, "Yes, but you don't suffer from any of that. You're not crazy. Next!" It was good enough for me. Official validation for what I already knew. Besides, I already knew *he* was the crazy one.

Clayton Tommy, on the other hand, a man I knew to be practical, intelligent and down to earth about most things, took seriously everything I said. His calm, confident, almost reverent revelation that what I'd seen and experienced was recognizable and fit into age-old lore touched me deeply. These things were already familiar to him. The sense that I had seen what Native people have seen and shared with each other for ages washed over me. I had been granted a glimpse into the spiritual government of the natural world, the forces of nature, of which I was a weak, pitiful member. And I had a guide, no more than a voice at this point, someone from "over there" who was showing me what was what.

"I guess this is all they think I can handle for now," I said to Clayton. "I'm grateful. *Wai i hwi.*"

"*Aaaa,*" Clayton murmured. "Next, come the hot time, when the serviceberries ripen, that bird come back. We call him *shumíx* bird. You know that bird?"

"No, what's he look like?"

"Real small, like maybe a robin. Not see him now, gone away

south. Be back when the *shia* ripe, ready to pick. About June. Not see him in the daytime, he walk around in the brush at night. Maybe see him at dawn, at dusk. Dark bird, with little white on the wings. Have a mustache, just like you. Just walk around at night, callin' out real spooky voice. Shoo-MEEuh! Shoo-MEEuh!"

His rendition of the bird's call was immediately recognizable. He meant the bird named in English "poor-will." On hot nights in the sagebrush country, I'd heard the eerie, plaintive, compelling call as this relative of the eastern whip-poor-will wandered on foot through the brush, eating insects.

"Oh yeah, I know that bird."

"When he come back, we hear him out there in the dark. He speak our language, say our word for spirit power, *shumíx*. He tell us they out there waitin' to give us power, talk to us. Tell us it time to send the young people on a mission. Seek to gain spirit. That how it used to be, anyway. Hardly anybody send their kids out nowadays. A few. And still happen when they all alone, not bein' sent, but just out there for somethin' in the dark, like to find lost horse, or broke down and have to walk home in the dark. Somethin' speak to 'em, give 'em a song. Give 'em a power to live by.

"*Kúlstim*, that what we call it. Send 'em on a mission. Go for something. That what next for you. Come the hot time again, that *shumíx* bird callin' in the dark, out in the brush.

"So you think about that. Practice, maybe. Once ever so often, fast for a day, a night. Don't eat, don't drink. Go out in the brush, out in the hills all alone. Stay awake all night. Try to get good at stayin' awake all night.

"Come the hot time, the serviceberries ready to eat, I send you on a mission. Maybe what you got take pity on you. Show hisself. Then it all come back to you."

13

I wake up, alive for another day, aware of my body lying in bed. Yes, here in this body I've come for another day of waking life. Thank you, *oaaa* . . . I think of the deer I killed, the young buck, how his aware self left his body on the hill up there where he lay down to die. The last panoramic look at the world, so achingly beautiful in the last moments.

I am here now, back somewhere in this body, behind these eyes. But someday I'll not come back like this. Someday I won't open my eyes from vivid dreams, back in the form of my body, ready to get up in the sunlight of another day. I'll leave this body and have no way to be here with these people around me, this life of talking and touching and being together. I'll be like the buck, give my body to unmoving decay, food for someone else. And then . . . and then what? What's next for this *me* who comes and goes from this body?

But meanwhile get up, get out of bed. The pale outside light on the windows, the body moving without knowing how, the thoughts of food, drink, a fire. Again reminded of my breathing, the breath that has been there all night, all along, as always. And a body still itching from unaccustomed warmth and still air, from bed and closed-up trailer house far from the wind and wet ground and sound of rushing river.

But it's winter now, ice sheen on window panes, so bitter when I open the door to load an armful of firewood in the mud room my lungs constrict in the pain of it. A naked body fresh from a warm bed can take a lot of cold in the first, say, five or ten minutes, but I know I have to get the fire roaring quickly, or I'll soon shiver uncontrollably as I pull on stiff clothes with numb fingers.

Another winter in the Okanogan. Making it through the dreamtime of deep winter in the north, the valleys socked in with low, leaden clouds, the highlands freezing and still in pale sunshine. Or the storms with great silent dumps of snow that hush the world for days, followed by blindingly bright clear days riding on the breath of a fierce north wind. *Iyoh'músh* himself happy only when it's twenty below zero, pipes freeze and pickups stall. Or like this morning: a glimpse of snow squalls blotting out whole areas of the mountains while other parts bask in a pallid subarctic sunrise.

It doesn't matter what it's doing out there. We'll feed the cattle on the flats as we do every day. It's light enough to start at eight, but we always linger inside Stuart's frame house near the horse barn, drinking sweet hot tea and telling stories and looking out the window and putting off the moment we finally dress like polar bears and waddle out to the diesel tractor idling in the yard. His numerous children have already left for school—they have to stand bundled in the dark waiting for the bus to pick them up. It arrives half-loaded with the young from the other side of the lake, the Waters girls in the last seat in back so they don't have to put up with boisterous ranch kids crowding by them at every stop. And the bus trailing a steamy cloud of exhaust, rounding the curves on brittle snow so loud you can hear the tires rolling a mile off, taking them twenty miles to school in the main valley.

Then it's the backbreaking work of forking off hay for the cows, stack after stack, and if we're lucky the sun will show when it clears the shoulder of Palmer Mountain at eleven, glowing pink on breath clouds hiding cow faces. And if we're real lucky, we'll bask in the feeble sunlight low in the sky until the sun disappears behind Rattlesnake Ridge at two in the afternoon. That's when we finish, but it's still light for another couple of hours. Then the long dark night of winter settles over our frozen world.

That day it snowed off and on, and the sun never shined on us down in the valley bottom. One good thing about snowy, unsettled weather, it's often warmer than usual. So after work I went wandering. The snow was about a foot and a half deep, but the top inches were fresh and kicked loosely ahead with each step of my boots, making things easier. Not powdery, but loose and formless and what Clayton called "baby snow," it didn't clump up until it was disturbed. Pretty good snow for making time, and for tracking.

Since I'd spent years now wandering this particular landscape, just observing, listening, smelling, studying, thinking about what came to my attention, things had a familiar form that I took for granted. I knew the common things so well, it was the odd things that stood out. Like footsteps appearing as oval hollows in dewy grass up a hillside, or like the disturbance of a campfire from decades before still showing through the pine needles as bits of charcoal ringed by half-hidden stones. Against the background of what I came to expect, my attention was drawn to what stood out, and my thoughts turned to the stories they told.

I circled around the back of Gold Hill, following the old mining road, then turned back east, downward along the timbered ridge to the brow of the drop-off into the unnamed valley that separated Gold Hill from Lucky Hill. Looking down the slope of snow dotted with firs and pines, what stood out were the drift trails of deer angling from high on my left to low on my right. Rounded, half-melted depressions in the snow near tree trunks showed where they bedded down during the day. All the trails converged toward the south where the land tipped away invisibly into the deep draw of Cecile Creek. The deer were probably down in the brushlands out of sight on the south-facing banks of the creek, browsing and drinking before night fell.

To the north, the flat-bottomed valley narrowed as it rose up to a densely forested divide, then fell away toward the next drainage over, which ran below the steep face of Rattlesnake Ridge. Through the notch in the hills I could see the summit of Chopaka lost in vague cloudiness, and at its feet the vast expanse of frozen and snow-covered Palmer Lake where home was. A black and white world with very little contrast. Subdued by the old man of the north, held in a white grip, everything seemed to be turned inward, even the sun, hidden behind clouds and mountains behind me. There were no shadows because it was all in shadow. And it was all familiar.

Then I saw the odd thing: a single animal track crossing the deer trails, veering only slightly from what looked like a beeline for some point on distant Lucky Hill. Here was something. The line of tracks were a little to my left, so I waded over that way and stood by them, studied them, followed them as they led down the hill across the meandering trails of many deer. I stayed to one side, careful not to disturb the individual tracks, never knowing when I'd have to go back for another look. I studied the length of stride, the depth, the position of placing the paws. It wasn't long before I was convinced I was following the fresh trail of a coyote: hind foot usually placed into the track of the front foot on that side, a narrow gait for the length of stride. And then the clincher, a track with no snow knocked in on it so I could carefully break away the long hollow of snow and study a clear print down deep. Definitely the dog family—claws clearly showing, and the wide spread of toes so unlike domestic dogs. And wolves hadn't been seen this far south for a generation of aggressive trapping.

So on I followed, becoming more and more mystified by this coyote who trotted steadily along in a straight line down the hill, across a half mile of ponderosa woods and up the rough ravines and deep fir timber of Lucky Hill. The trail appeared as fresh as the one I was making, so the coyote couldn't have been more than an hour ahead of me. Up and up, through the deep snow of hollows, through dark stands of hushed forest, the trail led unerringly in a straight line. Huffing and puffing, forcing my way through tangles of branches to stay with the tracks, floundering through drifts of waist-deep snow which the coyote leaped, I was tiring and not very attentive when I neared the summit ridgeline and saw the coyote trail turn abruptly left and lead away over rocky ridges blown almost bare of snow.

I followed for about a hundred yards, but realized that the coyote had begun to wander aimlessly. It was a more ordinary coyote trail now, poking into this and that, turning any which way. Just trotting along looking into whatever. I was winded, my boots and jeans caked with snow that was stiffening in the drop of temperature heralding the coming of night. Weary from heavy work and miles of trudging through snow, I stopped and thought. What was the trail telling me? I must have missed something, so I went back to where the coyote had veered aside from a singleminded straight line. There I stood, carefully studying every print.

Every mark in the snow was accounted for in the fading light, every step clearly visible, except for two unusual holes in the snow. Beyond the very last step the coyote took in a straight line, there was a different-looking hole showing the marks of ears and neck ruff, and I could see bare ground at the bottom of the snow, like the burrow of a small animal hollowed out at ground level. The story was beginning to emerge: The coyote walked unerringly in a straight line for a mile over rough terrain, single-mindedly ignoring fresh deer tracks, droppings, urine-soaked snow, to scale this steep snowy hill and stick its snout in the snow, in this little critter's burrow, then turned left and trotted away. Okay, what's this other fresh hole in the snow, smaller, obviously not from a snout or a paw, about four steps from the turn? Looks like something dropped. I feel with bared fingers into the hole and find something, pull it up. A tiny clump of fresh guts. And for the first time I see the pinholes in the snow, discolored faintly pink, which when I dig them up turn out to be congealed drops of blood.

Wai i hwi. So that's it—all the evidence comes together in a story I can "see." A coyote on faraway Gold Hill smelled or heard (or both) a mouse or a vole under the snow here, made its way here without pause or distraction or undo hurry, stuck its snout in the snow to snag the mouse, stood for awhile chomping (I see now, half-hidden by snow kicked in, the deeper, half-melted imprints of standing still) and as the coyote turned and trotted away after supper, spit out the guts, something I'd seen sign of them doing before.

It was all here in front of me. All I had to do was give the sign all my attention and think about what story it told.

It was late, time to head home, so I started downhill but purposely sidetracked—went down into the darkening draw of Cecile Creek to see if the deer were where their sign had told me they would be. Sure enough, there they were, scattered in a loose herd along the edge of the lowest bench, some already lying down for the night, some staring unmoving as I passed tramp-tramp-tramp only forty feet away. And some ignoring me as they continued to strip off mouthfuls of bitterbrush. They knew I wasn't hunting for meat.

I was hunting for the trail in the snow that would tell me about my own life. As I slogged slowly back toward home in deepening twilight, I thought about how I'd been following the sign of some other presence in my life, a trail that was slowly yielding parts of its story, thanks to Clayton Tommy and his knowledgeable belief that he knew the outline, the age-old pattern of spirit help in a man's life, if not the identity of the one who made the tracks.

Or did he? It would be just like him to refrain from saying anything more than what he felt I had already suspected or discovered on my own. Or maybe even Jim or Charlene or Old Willie . . . already discussing among themselves who the power might be that had touched my life, as I had heard them speculate about other people's spirit partners. I had to laugh. It would be just like them, given the Indian stubbornness about not interfering in the lives of others.

I could see the sign. The tracks had been leading me step by step toward the fullness of the story. Was I just not reading the sign of my own life well enough? Maybe I unknowingly had all the evidence in my memory and simply couldn't put it together and "see" it the way I saw the coyote snap up the mouse and spit out the guts.

Out of left field came the memory of the falcon on Chopaka, the one who landed on the very summit, looked at me and flew away. And the falcon who showed me the Border Patrol officers sneaking up on my Mexican friends. I came to a stop in the snow, startled by the implication. A flock of bluejays went crazy in the orchard trees ahead, kwash-kwashing at my sudden stop. A flicker of recognition became a fire of distinct possibility. Could my *shumíx* be Falcon?

Kwash-kwashing in manic alarm, the bluejays noisily gave up their roost and scattered. I hit the county road and clipped along easily on the plowed, compact surface toward the lake and home, my frozen pantlegs slapping stiffly with each step, my mind flooded with memories of encounters with falcons.

The time just last summer when I was driving my pickup out from the corrals on Skull and Crossbones Ridge, crawling slowly through a fog blanketing the summits after days of rain. I saw the covey of quail crossing the road ahead of me, thinking they'd disappear into the tall, wet grass before I got to them, but as I drove through their crossing place I saw them all bunched up, a few feet uphill from the road, milling around as if there was no danger from me. So I stopped the truck, grabbed my .22 rifle and stepped around the back to shoot some for dinner. If a man suddenly appears, quail will flee into hiding or burst into flight and disappear. Yet these quail milled around tup-tupping quietly to each other, only ten feet away, as if I wasn't even there drawing a bead on one. Bang, one down. And the others acted as if nothing had happened, as if they were all in a trance. So disoriented by the fog, I figured. Boy, this was going to be easy, I thought, swinging to draw a bead on another.

At that moment a falcon appeared, diving out of nowhere between me and the quail, doing a crazy, threatening, zigzagging dance on beating wings above them. Swooping back and forth in front of my pointed rifle only a few feet above the quail, tail spread, tilting back and forth, so crisply and achingly beautiful in the vague whiteout of fog, the falcon put the quail into a panic. Most scattered in an instant, but a few that lagged the falcon made feints at, mock-stooping on the easy prey, but pulling up when they fled. Making no attempt to capture one, satisfied at scaring the quail into fleeing from my rifle, the falcon flew up to a lone spruce tree standing like a phantom in the fog, landed, and perched staring down at me twenty feet away. Dumbfounded, I stared back. Breaking the silence with a slurring tlaaa! tlaaa! tlaaakw! the falcon lifted off and disappeared into the fog. Awed, I stepped uphill into the wet grass and retrieved the one dead quail.

I knew something important had just happened. A falcon had come and shooed away the vulnerable quail, had purposely thwarted me from taking further advantage of their disoriented, senseless behavior. At the time I had felt chastened, like a master hunter of the wild had interfered with my lazy opportunism to make some kind of point, to give me some kind of lesson. Now I thought of the quail's mysterious behavior as *xa'xá*, and the falcon's intervention as a slap upside the head about being such a White man, coldly motivated only by what I wanted—meat.

Sure, the quail slaughter would have been easy . . . too easy. How could I so heartlessly take the lives of those quail people when they were transformed by the mystery of the fog? They had been so senseless, so utterly oblivious to danger from me. The falcon had intervened like a chiding elder brother, stopping me at a moment of failing to live up to my own convictions about hunting. The quail hadn't been giving themselves to me. I felt a horror at what I had done, and gratitude to the falcon for stopping me.

Years before, at the most difficult and dangerous point in my escape from a military stockade, I had tricked the single guard in our detail and managed to run through an open gate before he could sound the alarm. It was south Texas, the day before Christmas, at sunset. I was running like my Mexican friends, full tilt I knew only vaguely where, the sudden scream of the alarm siren making the guard dogs locked in kennels bark and howl behind me. Running on blind instinct I turned a corner onto a residential street of officers' homes with well-groomed yards, where I saw a car coming toward me down the hill. I slowed, panting, trying to recover my pounding heart and look normal, like someone who just happened to be wearing fatigues. Repeating the chant in my mind: "Gotta get free. Gotta get free." Powered by thoughts of making my way to Canada and living like a man was supposed to. Slower. Full alert as the car approached. Walls about chin high between the houses, forming walled-in back yards. No side streets. Trapped if . . . and then I saw the familiar military police markings on the car, the twin bubble lights on a bar across the roof. Crushed at the inevitability of capture, I sent out a silent, despairing plea, straight from the heart.

And at that moment a falcon soared by between me and the approaching MPs, about eye level, about twenty feet out, his head turned to me and looking me in the eye. I followed his barreling flight between the two houses to my right, above the wall that divided the back yards, and out of sight into the Texas brushlands beyond. In complete abandon, I turned and ran the way he'd flown. Red flashing lights began to sweep the house fronts as I reached the wall, leaped up, and ran like a tightrope walker along the wall dividing the two back yards. A crackle of radio voices and shouts of running men burst out behind me. And wouldn't you know it—a big, vicious dog in each yard raced up to leap wildly snapping and snarling at my shoes tippy-toeing along the cinder blocks like a fullback running in a minefield. One on each side trying desperately to get me and all I see is snapping teeth with my eyes locked on the narrow wall top so far from the ground. Their ear-splitting indignation could have wakened the dead, and their disappointment howled behind me as I leaped off the back wall to bare ground. I raced across the soft dirt of a firebreak and into the meanest bush I would ever see in my life: nothing but mesquite, prickly pear cactus, and the chest-high yucca they call Spanish bayonet.

But it was like home to me. Brer Rabbit would understand. Temporary refuge, though, so I moved as fast as I could, knowing only that somewhere ahead, about a half mile away, was a paved highway that was the outer limit of where they secured the area in the event of an escape. I knew this because they made the prisoners clean the correctional confinement offices in the evenings, and when they weren't watching me I studied the maps and escape procedures posted prominently on the guardhouse wall.

But the going was brutal: impenetrable tangles of thorny mesquite and spiny cactus made me back up and go around many times, yucca spikes bayoneted my legs and clothing, and in the gathering dusk I slowed to a crawl, bleeding, lungs aching, still going only because I could see the crisscrossing headlights of cars ahead and I was almost there.

Then the thing I feared happened. Flashing red lights appeared on the highway ahead, vehicles stopped a couple hundred yards apart. I stopped, trembling with fatigue and the mushy aftereffects of burning so long on adrenaline. I heard voices, dogs barking. Then came spotlights searching through the brushy gloom for me. I backtracked to an enormous expanse of prickly pear cactus I had just gone around. A huge, ancient clump of cactus about thirty feet across and rising taller than my head in the middle, with pads a foot long and half as wide. Dropping to the ground, I burrowed under the cactus, worming my way along through the older, decayed underparts, snagging and freeing myself over and over, forcing my way to the very center of the dark mass by feel. Then I dug in the soft earth and leaves and fallen pads, covering my whole body until only my eyes and nose were exposed.

There I waited most of the night. Hours of men calling, searchlights stabbing right into my hidden cavelike world, dogs sniffing and whimpering along on leashes held by military police with heavy booted footsteps cursing the cactus and yucca and mesquite that hid me. To relieve the tension I sang in my mind: "I was born in the briar patch, the briar patch, the briar patch . . ." Hours until I shivered so badly in the December cold that I knew anybody nearby could hear the rustling. But by then, no voices, no red lights, no dogs. I climbed out into total dark—only an occasional car passing on the highway. Nobody wanted to be out bushwhacking for me on Christmas Eve. It wasn't like I was a dangerous felon. I was just this lowlife who refused to serve anymore, just a "political prisoner" as we used to call ourselves to distinguish ourselves from thieves, drunks, and murderers.

Then I crept silently to the edge of the highway, waited until I felt the way was clear, and slipped across unmolested. I eventually made it to Canada, but in the rush and intensity of events after my race along the top of backyard walls, I forgot the falcon that flew by, looking me in the eye.

I've been out in the hills all my life. So many birds and animals have looked at me, looked me in the eye, that I never thought to single out one among so many. But now I remembered falcons looking me in the eye many times. The time one flew past me while I was walking in the forest, a shadowy form in the trees, and landed on a branch ahead of me to look at me. The time I heard a small bird crying in alarm in shadowy aspens, followed by a blur of movement, and a falcon emerged in a clearing to perch on a limb, limp feathery meal in his claws, paused in the only spot of direct sunlight penetrating dense woods, staring at me for a few seconds before darting away.

And then I remembered a different kind of falcon encounter, something that happened when I lived on the Washington coast. A time when I was free, but stuck in a city, and chafing at the pointlessness of a dead-end job in a gas station. It was my birthday so I ran off into the woods, into the refuge of nature, to wander and be who I really was. I came out on the ocean in the endless rain and salt-muck smell of tide flats, then walked the cliffs and beaches of Chuckanut Bay for hours. Near the end of the day the sun broke through clouds hanging low over offshore islands and sunlight glowed with red richness on the smooth bark of madrona trees hanging over jewel-like pools hidden in rocky coves. Always stopped and held thoughtlessly spellbound by such sudden changes in the world around me, I sat in the sand near the wash of waves, my back against a drift log thrown up by winter storms, gazing out to sea from a little bay where enormous fir trees dripped in the last, amber rays of the sun.

Still and utterly at peace for the moment, I lost myself in the beauty of sunset as the clouds turned from blazing gold to rose pink to fading buff. At the last moment when the light seemed swallowed by a horizon of darkening clouds, the top of the disappearing sun appeared through an opening and the miles of saltwater glittered blindingly one last time. That's when I glimpsed something being washed ashore in the brilliant sheen of crashing, transparent waves before me. What could it be? I stood and looked closer just as the flat-looking thing washed up on the sand in a glitter of foamy backwash. When I picked it up, it turned out to be the tail fan of a falcon.

So fresh, so beautiful, the dark and light striped vanes spreading easily and folding back, feathers held in place by a chunk of muscle hanging raw. Who ever heard of such a thing? The sun set and I studied this gift from the sea in the fading light. What killed or ate falcons? How did it happen in the sea? My mind could not fathom it. It seemed more significant that it had washed up in the last rays of the sun at my feet, a birthday present from the world I loved. I took the feathers home, and still had them. After salt-curing the flesh so the feathers held rigid in a spread fan, I used to let it hang from the rear-view mirror in my truck, but then put it away. That had been years ago. It was still in my belongings somewhere . . .

By the time I got home to my trailer in the snow above the lake, I had to admit there was something extraordinary about my encounters with falcons. The things I had experienced simply did not happen to people. If any creature or natural force had repeatedly and force-fully made me aware of its presence, it had to be falcons. And nothing else had so obviously helped me in time of need, or used me to help somebody else.

Exhausted but elated, I built up the fire and sat close to the woodstove so my pants and boots could thaw enough to get them off, then dug out the fan of falcon feathers and pulled out my copy of a popular bird identification book. The eyes of the falcon I'd seen all my life stared out at me from the page. *Falco peregrinus.* Peregrine falcon. Peregrine as in roving, wandering. Yes, that was the story of my life up to now. "Consummate hunter . . . catches birds on the wing . . . widespread but rare . . . secretive and swift . . . the only bird of prey that lives almost entirely on birds."

I laughed at the utter foolishness of what I was doing. Sure, there were unmistakable parallels between the characteristics of falcons recorded in books and my lifetime urge and ability in the hunt. But what was I doing? Looking for proof? I put away the book and considered the falcon tail with new eyes, fingering the slightly faded pattern of dark and light bands, the fluffy down at the dried base. I had discovered so many treasures in my life outdoors—crystals, obsidian arrowheads, antlers, bones, feathers of every kind, even a dead eagle and a bear tooth embedded in the bark of a tree. But of all of them, only this fan was still with me after all the passing of years. Something had moved me to hang onto it.

My Native friends had a long tradition of not openly identifying what they had. Maybe when they got old and their spirit partner left them, they might. Or just as commonly their relatives guessed by their behavior and inclinations who had given them a gift. Most of the talk about what *shumíx* a person had was from a seemingly endless supply of stories about such things, and most of the time it wasn't clear if the person told about in the story was somebody the teller knew or was lore from the distant past.

But I decided I could talk to Clayton privately about this and see how he responded. My falcon encounters were just too uncanny and suggestive for me to keep it to myself. And there seemed to be something missing from all of it, something I couldn't put my finger on but somehow figured Clayton could. Anyway, if nothing more, this bird of prey had made several gestures toward me in life, had pointed my way to freedom, had given me an opportunity to help friends in need, and had taught me a lesson with the quail. To honor that, I hung the falcon tail, tied with a leather thong, from a nail on the wall, in a prominent spot above the stove and my favorite chair.

14

There's never a hurry when it comes to doing things like a Native. Things happen so indirectly anyway, like oncoming headlights that may or may not be high beams. And it's done that way on purpose, slowly and indirectly, so the heart will have its way, so the heart will be the one to know and decide. I'd long since kept my eyes open to what was actually happening rather than trying to make things happen or to figure out more than I could know for real in my heart. So the falcon thing just sat there in the back of my mind, another opened door, as winter weighed in like a champion who couldn't be beaten and made to go away. Snow covering the world for so long now that bare ground is unimaginable. Everything done on cold soft white or brittle glittering white or blowing drifting white or the white that flutters silently from the vague above for days without end.

Winter was impossible to ignore. I had to pay attention and work just to survive. Fasting and staying out all night were out of the question. I needed so much animal fat I was even craving bacon. I never could understand how vegetarians managed in the dead of winter. They probably did fine, but I imagined they didn't fork hay off a bouncing, swaying trailer in a blizzard wind chill of minus 65 as comfortably as I did, sweating under my parka from the deer fat blaze in my belly.

And I was going to sweats. I came home one dusk to find Jim Woods in my trailer, sitting by the cranked-up woodstove, drinking instant coffee he'd found in my cupboard that I didn't even know was there. He looked long at the falcon tail but said nothing about it.

"I'm on my way to sweat at Johnny Stemilt's," he said, as if he were in motion instead of stationary, boots off, feet up to the heat of the stove, leaning back so far he was making my favorite chair creak with his great weight. Nothing more needed to be said. I would go, or not, whenever he shoved off. At least I didn't have to cook supper if I went. There was always good food after a sweat at Johnny's.

"Your pack rat was pretty pissed off when I came in. She was trying to make off with a spoon." I saw the spoon halfway across the floor toward the hole I futilely boarded up to keep her out. She always chewed through in a matter of days. But when she took something, she usually left something in exchange. Not things I really needed, like the cactus pad I found in the utensil drawer, but then what was she going to do with a spoon anyway? Just an exchange of pretty things to look at, I guess. Why couldn't she bring me something useful?

"That's where the coffee came from," Jim said, deadpan. "She made a pretty good trade for that spoon!" We both broke up.

"Yeah, I better let her have it," I said, dropping the spoon down the hole in the floor.

None of my White friends would let themselves in and make themselves at home like Jim and Clayton and, in fact, every Indian who came to my home did. Oh, maybe if there was something serious, a winter emergency, a car broke down on the highway at night— bush etiquette was still alive here. But the Native way was to behave like a relative, like it was their own home, and they assumed, rightly, that I was like them, that I would be offended if they didn't make my home theirs.

It took a while, of course, to get used to walking into other people's houses without knocking, or like Jim Woods with his extensive traveling and exposure to White expectations, maybe a knock or a scratch on the door as he opened it and went in. Once in the early days of knowing him I knocked and stood thoughtlessly outside the door to his mom's mobile home, waiting to hear "Come in!" or have the door opened. He burst open the door and stood there glaring at me.

"Enemies knock," he finally said. "People you know just walk in, dude!"

Once I went to visit Johnny Stemilt because I'd heard he was in bed sick from the flu or something. I'd never been there before, and when I simply walked in and stood in the tiny living room full of children and teenagers watching a video of *Billy Jack*, they ignored the scene where the Indian hero stands off a gang of White thugs with single-handed karate expertise, all of them with heads turned towards me, solemnly staring at this White man in their midst. Johnny's wife, who'd never met me before, stood and blocked me moving anywhere farther than just inside the door. It was not enough for me to say who I was and that I was there to "visit the sick"—a traditional and highly valued thing to do that was such a part of how they saw health and well-being flowing from the concern of others that there was a separate verb for it in Salish. She grilled me in a much more aggressive way than Jim's grandma did the first time I met her.

I could tell Johnny's wife was feeling me out to satisfy herself that I was no threat to her ill husband. I didn't know at the time that his family suspected his persistent illness was the result of someone "witching" him. In fact, I knew very little about the dark side of Native power and had no idea her persistent questioning was designed to hurt my feelings so I'd tip my hand if I was an enemy—lose my good-natured composure and show the anger and impatience I would be hiding if I really had it in for Johnny.

I finally sat down on the kitchen chair by the door where people coming in sat to take off muddy boots, and she sat in a chair facing the door. Resigned to my fate at the hands of a forceful and unrelenting elder, I told her much of my life story and gave the names, ages and current whereabouts of all my blood relatives. The young people grew bored and returned to the violent doom of Billy Jack, all but one who appeared to have Down's syndrome, a milk-eyed boy who came and told me it wasn't hard—I could unlace my own boots—here, he'd show me.

She softened at her grandson's gesture, stood up and put her apron on, waving me down the hallway to a tiny bedroom where I found Johnny awake, dressed, lying on his bed staring out the window. He actually sat up and swung his feet to the floor, sitting that way with obvious discomfort the whole time I was there. I did most of the talking, bringing him up to date on what was going on down my way and what people were saying about things. Except for telling me about his symptoms and his pains, he sat with his head down, watching the unmolested deer mice running along the baseboards, saying *aaaa* at appropriate moments. But I could tell he appreciated me coming to see him. When I left he gave me a baseball cap he had picked up in Seattle. It was bright red and had been fixed up with eagle down above white lettering that said: "NO MORE SECOND-HAND VERSIONS OF GOD."

He chuckled when I put it on. "That just right for you," he said, coughing. "You one goddamn White man gonna find out for yourself even if it kill you!"

Then I had given the hat to Jim, the true lover of baseball caps in all weather, and he wore it even stocking-footed in front of my stove, ponytail of a longhair through the hole in back as expected. After an hour of instant coffee and talk, he still hadn't moved, and all I'd done was dig up a towel, and then a pair of shorts in case there were women at the sweat. When he saw my sign of going along, all he said was, "*Awháha* (In a little while)."

We were in the middle of talking about his experiences years before when he went to South Dakota to support the AIM takeover of Wounded Knee, something he hadn't openly discussed for all the years I'd known him. I was curious about it because after charges were dropped against him as they were for most of the participants, he ceased traveling to AIM confrontations and stayed close to home, getting deeply involved in the local issues of his own people. He told me he actually left early in the siege, but worked on the outside to smuggle in food and ammunition. Then he was on the run, hanging out in remote areas of the Lakota reservations, going home only rarely until his legal problem was resolved. But something had happened to disenchant him with AIM.

"It was the sweatlodge that really showed me where they were at. City guys mostly ran things. They had that education and that rap and that big ego to be the boss. When I was little, hunting deer and gentlin' horses and talkin' Indian, they was in some big city playin' basketball and smokin' dope."

He began to lace up his boots. I got ready to go with him.

"Like there at the Knee, after a sweat, if a dude felt really wasted, wiped out, unable to think, he'd say there was bad medicine in the lodge. Or that somebody was witching 'em. It was like from a book!

"I been sweathousing since I was a little boy, since before I remember. The elders told me all kinds of things. When you're like that after a sweat, or maybe the next day, it means you came in with a lot to be pulled out of you. And they did that for you, but it feels like you been run over by a truck. Sweatlodge hangovers are about so much stickin' to you, so much to be purified. And like tryin' to stay like you are instead of letting go to be like they tryin' to do for you—like reborn.

"And those warrior sweats! Big competitions to see who could take the most heat, like showin' off how strong you are. That's not what a sweat is about. You know how it goes, everybody inside is just fine but maybe one guy layin' on the floor cryin'. Well, he's the one needs the most taken out of him, or he's the one that's fightin' it. Or he's tryin' to be strong when you're there to humble yourself, let go into the hands of *real* power."

We got into Jim's new car that he got in trade for his trained Suicide Race horse, a '67 Plymouth Barracuda jokingly known as the "honey wagon" because there was always a different woman pressed against him, perched on the console between bucket seats when he drove by. With cheater slicks on the back and summer tires on the front, we barely made it down my snowy road to the highway, but from then on it was bare pavement all the way to Johnny's. The moon was full, and it rose crisp and pale white and perfectly round over the glittering white countryside as we cruised along.

"And then you got a medicine man in his twenties—where's that at? Who ever heard of a guy in the middle of boozin' and leching and not knowin' nothing about life havin' great powers to doctor people? It was just too much. Things like that don't come to a person until later in life.

"It got to be too much for me. Like how they treated all the White people that were there, that helped and believed in things and made a big difference. A lot of 'em want to be Indians, sweat and learn and be on our side. AIMsters don't get it that White people wantin' to go native, that's a good thing. They're all hung up on the Indian way as an identity. Even if they grew up in Chicago and never saw the inside of a sweatlodge till they were twenty, they think it's in their blood, and no White man can get it.

"They don't want the Whites to change. They gotta stay put as the bad guys. That way they're better than everything the White man is.

"The way I see it, all these White people showin' up like you, gotta find their own way. Receive their own White way from the great power just like the Lakota and Okanogan did. Sure, you guys gotta learn how it really is in the world. How it works. But then, you're not gonna be a Sioux, you're not gonna be an Okanogan. Once you get it, you're on your own. That's how I see it anyway."

What Jim said about Whites going native was pretty much what I thought, too, when I thought that far ahead. We were quiet the rest of the way up into the forested mountains where Johnny lived. Jim found a place to park just off the pavement and not blocking the other cars and pickups lining the road in. It looked like a pretty big crowd for the dead of winter, but then Johnny was back in good health and this was the first chance for a lot of people to give thanks for that. It turned out a lot of people were there for the good food and company—only about nine of us men hanging around the fire out back were going to go in the sweatlodge.

Behind a sloping-roofed shed open on one side where people could shelter to undress, an area had been cleared of snow on the bank of a creek where it came out of dense spruce and tamarack forest. The creek flowed under foot-thick ice by the flat clearing where Johnny's sweatlodge and fire pit were, then disappeared over a frozen waterfall into a canyon below his house. I remembered hearing the dull roar of the falls when I'd visited when he was sick, but now all I heard was a muffled undertone, a glumping of turgid waters held in the grip of ice.

The sweatlodge was one of the few earth-covered ones I'd seen, built into the steep bank with a willow framework covered with slabs of cottonwood bark, then thick dirt, and now looking like a doorway into a huge snowbank, with several layers of carpet scraps as a doorflap thrown up onto the snow above. On the creek ice a hole had been chopped down to open water and a bucket and hatchet sat to one side. It was a cold, clear night, below zero, stars faint in the overshadowing brilliance of the full moon peeking between towering trees heavy with snow, and anybody walking from the house to the fire could be heard crunching along the path like an elephant.

Johnny's nephew had built the fire with four-foot-long sawed logs of tamarack, a wood so high in volatile oils that the chest-high flames continuously popped and exploded with burning embers we had to brush quickly off our clothes before they burned through to bare skin. Everybody but Jim was dressed for winter with layers of sweaters and coats, or a parka, or like me in a heavy military campaign coat. Jim was one of those big men who act like it never gets too cold for them, standing in the circle of illuminated male faces wearing only a thin down vest, unzipped, over a sweatshirt that didn't quite cover the last inch of bare belly above his rodeo belt buckle. He laughed at the jokes of his old high school buddy, Johnny's nephew, who everybody called "Kootch," from the Salish word for "fat." It suited him, and he seemed unashamedly happy with his nickname and great girth, laughing and sweaty under his parka, standing spreadlegged with a pitchfork poking at the fire, ready to do whatever his uncle hinted he wanted done.

As host, Johnny Stemilt stood quietly between his two brothers, felt cowboy hat tipped up, eagle feather hanging off the back, listening and observing and assessing the needs and condition of the men who had come to his home for purification and prayer. His profanity conspicuously absent, saying very little in English, he leaned around the flickering flames that highlighted the scars under his chin, holding out a pack of Salems, offering everybody a cigarette before lighting one up himself with his beaded lighter. Even nonsmokers don't refuse tobacco offered at a sweat. Some of the older men pinched off the tip of their cigarette and tossed it into the fire with mumbled prayer before lighting up. Then we all smoked together.

I smiled, remembering the summer before when Johnny confronted me about learning Indian ways, remembering him saying, "Nobody doin' that sweatlodge crap any more!" And here he had greeted my arrival at his own sweatlodge fire with a warm smile and a toothy "*Cha'kwínkshinchin!* (Let's shake hands!)" But then he ignored my presence, too preoccupied with the arrival of two other White guys who came with a short, self-consciously solemn Indian man in his forties. The two Whites were a little younger than me, long hair tied back in ponytails, clean-shaven, dressed like fur trappers in leathers and wool, their eyes more than anything showing how proud and scared they were in this unfamiliar setting. Johnny thought he knew the Native man with a broad, bright red bandanna tied around his head to hold his long, loose hair back behind his ears that made him look like the photos of nineteenth-century Apache warriors.

"*Wai*," he said, offering him a Salem. "Clyde, ain't it?"

"*Loot!*" he replied with a vigorous shake of his head. "They call me Coyote now. These are my two nephews."

More cigarettes and they shook hands all around that side of the fire. One White guy, shaking Johnny's hand, said, "Uncle Coyote told us maybe we could sweat with you tonight."

"*Aaaa*," Johnny said.

Openly calling somebody Coyote was so outrageous and unheard-of, I thought it was a joke. But nobody was laughing. I never saw Johnny's or Jim's faces go blank so quickly. As much as the Okanogans revered and laughingly delighted in the character of Coyote in their stories and lore, nobody would dare to call someone by that name. It signified the negative example of Coyote's blind pride, insatiable appetites, and imitating of others to his repeated demise. Calling somebody a coyote to their face was an insult, something used to provoke a fight in a bar, yet here was a charming Salish Indian pleased to have people call him by that name.

His talkative White nephew went on: "We been sweathousin' down at Uncle Coyote's place. We been to lotta sweats, respect the sacred kweelstun, just wanna come here and pray with our Indian brothers." His affectation of how he thought traditionals spoke English, glottal stops in odd places, intonation flat and folksy, was painfully obvious. I could see the older men pitied him as they would any adult who pretended like a child.

Uncle Coyote, on the other hand, had a way of signaling he was going to say something significant by closing his eyes, tilting his head and jerking like some outside power was taking over his mind. His pudgy cheeks would wobble, then he'd mumble something like, "Good to . . . we here like this . . . huh! . . . they always sayin' . . . yeah! . . . it's time . . . the White man learn from the Indian!"

I thought it was just about the coolest parody of an old Indian wise man I'd ever seen. The guy was a consummate actor, imitating the speech of Indian medicine men I'd seen in movies. But his *Suyápi* nephews hung on his every word, no doubt trying to decipher the deeper significance behind his cryptic words, flanking him with heads nodding, saying, "*Aaaa, aaaa.*"

Unlike what I was used to from Indians, Uncle Coyote stared at me significantly across the fire, giving me a look full of mysterious import, our eyes locking for a moment and grappling like power beams before I looked away. I had the distinct impression he was trying to make me think he saw something powerfully compelling in me. It was the irresistible appeal to White people's exaggerated sense of self-importance used by con men everywhere. He was trying to set the hook in a new fish, another White guy looking for his very own Native guru. I was supposed to become haunted by what his penetrating look might mean and seek him out to teach me his secret lore. But I could read him like a book.

I felt like the suspicious youngest brother in Salish Coyote stories, the one who saw through Coyote's disguise. Only White people failed to see the point of how Coyote manipulated appearances and appealed to their own unexamined wishful thinking and vanity to trick them and place himself in a position of power and authority. They thought they could emulate Coyote, picturing him as some infinitely wise and marvelous creature outside the loop of ordinary restraint. Dangerous, attractive stuff. I began to understand the hold Uncle Coyote had on the two White guys.

Then Coyote turned to Jim and read the words on his hat about no more second-hand versions of God and made a sly, disconnected comment about God being White and maybe the spirits didn't like it when a Christian went in the sweatlodge.

"I go to church," one of Johnny's brothers said. "The priest knows I go to sweats. I told 'em they both good ways to pray."

Uncle Coyote nodded, eyes closed, head tilted, smiling slightly like he was orchestrating a seminar on religion.

"They say . . . lotta good things . . . huh! . . . those old ones . . . But

Christian missionaries take away our . . . now all one . . . yeah, but we keep our old ways . . . that kinda priest . . . don't listen to men wearin' dresses . . ."

We laughed at the old joke, some of us too loudly for being at a sweat. Johnny glanced up.

"Okay, maybe we get ready now."

The shed had a hard dirt floor and one faint lightbulb glowing amid cobwebs. We undressed and hung our clothes on nails, joking to each other in loud voices, then abruptly clamming up at the sense of having gone too far. Feet numb and shivering by the time we made it barefoot to the sweatlodge, we knelt and crawled inside the equally cold interior in no particular order. Naked strangers crowding together in the dark. There was an edge to the shivering banter, uncharacteristically harsh and hostile.

Kootch, still dressed, pitchforked the rocks in, handed in a white plastic bucket of water with a long-handled tin dipper and handfuls of fir and sage, then, at a word from Johnny, pulled down the mildewy-smelling carpet flap from the outside and secured it tightly around the opening. Steam burst from the glowing rocks and in no time I was hot and happily sweating in the cozy darkness I'd come to welcome and look forward to.

It was a good, hot sweat, the scalding vapor smelling faintly herbal, the songs mostly ones I knew, the prayers in both Salish and English. Johnny tapped the dipper handle on the bucket rim in time with the songs, and had Kootch open the door several times for those who wanted to tiptoe out onto the ice to dip the bucket into the creek and douse themselves with icy water. They'd return shuddering and laughing and we'd go on with the mood shifting in utter darkness, each round hotter and longer than the one before. I finally recognized the herbal smell—it came from a handful of dried plants soaking in the bucket water, a wildflower called avens that I'd seen Johnny gathering under aspen trees when we were up in the mountains hunting.

Some men switched themselves with fir boughs, or rubbed needles on their skin, but I chewed the bitter sage leaves and swallowed the tonic juice to help me hold up in the searing heat. The Indian prayers, simple and to the point, were about how grateful they were for Johnny's recovery and pleas for intervention in disasters, stresses, illnesses, hopes, and losses of loved ones. One man prayed to Our Lord Jesus Christ instead of the more usual addresses to Sweatlodge, *Iyilméhum Xa'xá*, Chopaka, or even North Wind. I recognized his voice as the brother who told his priest he went to sweats.

My own prayer was not much different, adding my voice to the chorus grateful for Johnny's good health in the broken Salish-English combination I fell so easily into while sweating. I remembered Carlos and Marvín wintering in their poorly heated picker's shack and Stuart's son Boot down with the flu. I asked for what I hoped for: Clayton's safe return from Winter Dances in Canada and Grandma's full recovery from a fall that broke her hip. And I gave thanks for my life, my health, my having a job and a warm place to live. It was easy to be grateful—sweating always made working out in the cold that much easier.

Then I listened, astonished, as the talkative White guy spoke in his stilted version of Red English for a good ten minutes. He started out, "Oh Great Spirit, hear me, this is White Eagle speakin' to you, still carryin' the sacred bundle you entrusted to me, come here tonight to sit down in this sacred circle with my uncle and my elders, callin' out to you with a humble voice that you grant me the power and the wisdom to carry out the sacred vision that you blessed me with as I sat alone beseechin' you, sufferin' in the good ancient way up on top of our sacred Bonaparte Mountain . . ." His long-winded blah-blah-blah soon featured words that revealed his university education and lifted him up into the abstract center of the universe with his trembling fingers on the pulse of the Great Spirit's intentions for people of all colors to become as one in the balance of nature's dichotomy. Not one *aaaa* punctuated his performance. Boring us into numb indifference, he spoke in a high, grandiose voice that aped the reverence of a preacher speaking from the pulpit, but his voice held no emotion, no acknowledgment that who he was speaking to might have more power than he did. And he mentioned other people—his dad, his brother, and his ex-wife—reflecting on how they had so blindly wronged him in life, and instructed the Great Spirit in how they should be "brought into balance" and made to see the error of their ways. He finished with gratitude for his Uncle Coyote, heaping on his humble shoulders a litany of blessings that, had they showered down on the guy, would have set him up for life like a prince in old fairy tales.

No doubt fearing the worst—that this outbreak of White man's madness might be contagious—Johnny had been pouring on so much water during this speech that it was almost impossible to breathe and stay upright. Fortunately the next White guy prayed briefly and simply for his mother to live through her upcoming surgery, sobbing, "She gave me life . . . so please . . . I beg you . . . don't take her away."

"*Aaaa, aaaa,*" voices called out, adding their emotional pleas to his.

Then Johnny drowned out Uncle Coyote's brief incoherent mutterings from somewhere near the floor with endless splashes of water and roaring bursts of steam that, if nothing else, brought Sweatlodge's sputtering voice to our attention as the real power making us aware of our fragile hold on life at that moment. When Coyote's voice was no longer heard, Johnny pushed on the doorflap and Kootch threw it up from outside. Relief was instantaneous in the rush of welcome, frigid air.

After a long silence and the gradual return to using our eyes to see ordinary things by moonlight, Johnny cleared his throat and spoke up.

"There another person here with us tonight. He like a superpower, somebody so full of power right now, we can't ignore him. Somebody not sittin' inside, but still real strong."

"Real big, don'cha mean?" Jim said, referring to Kootch kneeling outside the door. Kootch led the easy laughter that followed. Then Johnny went on.

"That one, we gotta pay respect, show him we feel his presence. So I tell his story.

"*Ksaaaaaaaa'pi*, way back, before there was people, there was only the animals, which were huge, like monsters. The world was cold, like this, but without light. The animals held a conference to plan for the comin' of the human race, so that the people would have daytime and nighttime.

"The frogs were many and their constant yelling of '*Xeláp! Xeláp! Xeláp!* (Tomorrow! Tomorrow! Tomorrow!)' got the leaders to hold up their hands and say, 'Fine, we shall have the daytime and the nighttime.'

"A lotta animals tried out for the job of bein' the sun and the moon and they all got rejected. Coyote hear about this and he said he would apply for the role of sun, he will come up in the sky just lukewarm so the human race can enjoy themselves while he watches over them.

"Coyote went to the conference and told the main heads of his want to enjoy himself as the sun. The leaders decide to give him a chance. As the new day come with the lukewarm heat from the Coyote sun in the sky, there was a couple down on the earth, makin' love on the grass. A man and a woman goin' at it like nobody's business! All of a sudden the sun yelled real loud, 'Shame! Shame on you! What are you doin' down there?'

"The leaders called Coyote down and scolded him that it was not nice to yell at the people on earth, and that he could not be the sun. Coyote felt hurt that he could no longer shine all lukewarm for others to enjoy.

"Then Coyote's two handsome twin sons stepped forward and volunteered to serve as the sun and the moon. They didn't care which one was chosen as the sun or the moon. While the twins were talkin' to the leaders, one tiny ugly lady frog fell in love with the handsome twins. She spoke up boldly and said, 'If one of you twins take me as your wife, I will do all in my power to make you happy.'

"One of the handsome twins, just to clown around, pulled his eyelid down and said, 'Here, wife, is where you stay and be mine forever!'"

Kootch, laughing louder and louder outside as the familiar tale unfolded, burst out with childish glee at the twin's words, and stabbed the pitchfork into frozen ground by his knees. There were answering laughs inside, as much at Kootch's unrestrained enjoyment as at the dramatically ridiculous high point of the story.

Johnny repeated, "'Here, wife, is where you stay and be mine forever!'

"Snap! The tiny ugly lady frog leaped and latched onto the twin's eyelid. When they tried to pull her off, the twin cried out in pain and said, 'Leave her be. After all, I told her here is where you stay. But to have my wife hanging from my eyelid, this makes me kinda dim, so I want to be the moon, and my handsome twin brother, you can have him be the sun.'

"Now, as you can see, the twin's wishes came true. We have the sun so very handsome we cannot hardly look long at him, we have to turn our eyes away. His twin brother is the moon and his frog wife. They are kinda dim at night so that men and women can have romance in the moonlight. If you look up at the full moon, like tonight, you can see the tiny frog wife with her legs outstretched, holding tightly to her handsome husband's eyelid.

"So that's it," Johnny said to a chorus of appreciative *aaaa*'s. He closed the door for one more song and poured all the rest of the water and avens onto the rocks, then opened the door and we all climbed out.

I stood comfortably steaming in the snow, looking up like others at the full moon so radiantly and palpably powerful at the high point of his passage overhead. I made out the moon's eyes and the shape hanging off to the right side like a frog's body with legs outstretched.

"There's the proof that the story is true," Johnny said as he passed us to get in line for the bucket on the creek ice. I was the last one in line and shuffled along listening to the guys joking and laughing as each bucket of ice water splashed over a man's head made him suck in air and stiffen in bellowing delight. Smoking bodies passed quickly by me and up the path to the shed. When it was my turn, the current under the ice nearly sucked the bucket handle out of my hand, but then I pulled it up full, and like my dad said, teaching me to dive in the Missouri River when I was a kid, "Don't think about it. Just do it." Unbelievable cold enveloped my body and for an instant I had no skin and the cold air went right through me. Then the aftershock—heart and lungs in full speed, a body leaping and dancing and shouting out how alive it was, slowing to a walk up the trail with the air feeling like a summer night.

Inside the house, the arrival of inward-looking, flush-faced sweatbathers got people busy loading paper plates of food and filling paper cups with water. Johnny and Kootch carried some of these outside to throw in the fire for relatives who had died but came to such gatherings to share in the blessings of those they left behind. Then he and Kootch helped their wives serve everyone sitting down wherever they were, at tables, on the couches, in every chair available. Kootch's son, the milk-eyed boy who had showed me how to unlace my boots, brought me my loaded plate and cup.

Nobody is shy about eating their fill and then some at an Indian gathering, so it was a long time of easy sociability and lots of laughing before I was full and feeling sleepy. The emotional White guy ended up sitting next to me, and seemed to be an okay sort of guy, telling me about his tour in the army as an electronics specialist in Germany, and how his desire to live on the land had brought him to the Okanogan country where he worked as an electrician in the apple sheds. But as I warmed to him, he showed signs of trying to impress me with his insight.

"Yeah, those Indian legends are so cryptic," he said softly behind his hand, rolling his eyes. "What the hell is that frog all about? The 'tiny ugly lady frog'—god! it's so hokey! I thought I'd learn something. Turns out it's just something for kids after all."

"It's about what the power of the full moon does to people. How it affects us," I said.

Johnny, four plates to my right and facing us, lifted his head at my words and looked long and thoughtfully in our direction. I said no more. Maybe I was way off, but that's what I'd gotten out of the story. All those excessive things said tonight. I felt Johnny had put his finger on what was happening and had called in ancient lore so we could "maybe learn something" as Clayton would say.

Johnny smiled at the White guy next to me. "Yah, that twin, he regret he even open his mouth."

The White guy blushed a scarlet even deeper than his already beet-red skin.

Uncle Coyote, antsy and blustering, got up and thanked the women for such good food, muttering, "Time to go . . . long drive . . . where are those boys of mine? . . . here, let's shake hands." He said a few *Skélux* words to Johnny and his brothers that came out sounding as Anglo as my own pronunciation. When he touched hands with me, he mumbled, "Come and see me . . . some time, maybe sweathouse . . . down that way, Omak . . . yeah! . . . you talk Indian good . . . Why kin hooey!

His White nephews were already up and waiting for him at the door as he made his rounds to shake every hand. Then after they left, Jim stood and yawned hugely, announcing, "Well, guess I'll round up my White groupie and head down the road, too!" The laughter was stifled until people saw me breaking up, then they cut loose. At the door Jim turned and said, "If Coyote was my power, I don't think I'd advertise it!"

Kootch looked up at him all innocent-eyed and said, "You suppose he shits on the ground and talks to his turds?"

15

Late winter in the Okanogan. Snowmobiles roar across bare lake ice to holes where bored orchardists gather to fish for ling, their conversational voices almost intelligible from miles away in the empty silence at the base of Chopaka cliffs. Cross-country skiers emerge burn-faced from long treks over hills I haven't been able to get up into for a month. Snow so deep a pair of wirecutters dropped accidentally out the side of the tractor cab is left for spring thaw to recover.

Days so balmy in the warm breath of *Stla'wálalt,* South Wind, you know the snow is dying. But lasts because there's just so much of it. Homicidal tensions are relieved in the nearby town of Conconully by the annual Outhouse Race—outhouses on skids containing a seated occupant pushed by screaming contestants stumbling down the sun-greased snowpack of Main Street toward the finish line. Cars crawl by on the plowed highway packed full of Indians holding plastic containers of food on their laps, on their way to Winter Dances and feasts where the powers of nature are seen working in the lives of people.

And it's an easy day feeding cattle with Stuart because his son Boot, anxious to show how strong and fit he is, forks off most of the hay like a sweaty young machine in the glare of snow melting in the gaze of a hot sun.

I heard Clayton was back, visiting at the Woods place, so with the sun still shining over Chopaka Mountain I drove down to see him. As we sat visiting in the front room, empty except for us, Grandma came inching down the hallway with the help of a metal walker, dressed in a thick wool robe and fluffy pink slippers. When she got even with where Clayton and I faced each other, she stopped and spoke to him in Indian so slowly and clearly I realized I could catch her drift.

She was thanking him for asking for prayers for her recovery at the Winter Dances he'd been attending in Canada. Clayton joked that she was doing pretty good driving around in her new "car," referring to the walker. Since the Salish word for automobile, *p'wíhwin,* means "soft feet," Grandma slyly acted like she misunderstood, telling him she was shuffling along in her fluffy slippers as fast as she could. We roared at her pun. She turned to me.

"You got that, eh?" Then wagging her finger vaguely in my direction, she said, "Better watch what I say around you."

She moved slowly toward her favorite chair, then inched around in a circle and stiffly lowered herself to sit. Charlene brought us cups of coffee brewed the way Indians like it—so thin you can drink it all day long. It was obvious that Grandma making other people laugh was taken as a sign that the important part of her recovery had been accomplished. When Charlene began bringing Grandma up to date on news, Clayton and I resumed our own conversation. I told him about the sudden flood of memories about falcon encounters in my life.

He listened to my stories attentively, then scratched his head, trying to remember the word for falcon in Okanogan. He glanced at Grandma, and we sat quietly for awhile, listening to the women talk. Sensing the quiet from our side of the room, they fell silent.

As if talking to himself, Clayton wondered aloud in Salish what that bird might be called, that one flies so fast, like a hawk, but wings pointed and takes birds right out of the air.

"*Tl'tlákw,*" Grandma said, giving me an amused smile.

"Oh yah, that the one, *tl'tlákw.*" Then he went on talking to me about the solitary habits of falcons, how usually you only get a glimpse of them, and how they'd become so scarce in recent years.

"Where that all come to you?"

I told him the memories came back, one by one, as I was walking along below Lucky Hill and then along the road homeward.

"But you say you stop when it hit you, this bird might be what you got. And them bluejays makin' a racket. Then you go on rememberin' more. Where that? Where you stop?"

I thought carefully, looked at the place in my memory where I stopped. "Right there where all those big boulders are, at the base of the cliff, just above the creek where it turns into Fletcher's orchard."

"*Aaaa*, I thought maybe so. That place pretty dangerous, since way back. That big rock, tall, like a small house, sit there beside the old trail to the mountains that way. Narrow place where the big rocks, the creek, and now the road squeeze close together, like. That place *xa'xá*. Lotta pictures on the rocks. Indian doctor place.

"Maybe we take a drive. Go look at that place."

Later Clayton drove me down the bare highway in his car, creeping over the wet places beginning to freeze as the sun set behind the mountains. The county road was poorly plowed but he didn't hesitate to turn onto it and keep going, giving it the gas every time the tires started to bog down and spin. Fishtailing around turns and right past the place I had described, he drove up a rise and made a quick U-turn where the snow plows had made a wide place. Facing back the way we had come, he parked close to a snowbank as tall as his car, leaving the engine running and the heater blowing.

We were looking right down on the base of the cliff where huge mounds in the snow were hardly visible among fir trees in the dusky light. To the left and beyond, the orchard trees stood like bare claws in rows. I pointed out my route and where I stopped before getting to the road, a spot close to the snow-covered boulders.

Talking about the days when he was a boy and there was only a wagon road through here, we sat in the heated car looking out at the snowy world in slowly gathering twilight. He pointed across the creek with his chin to a small, flat bench almost obscured by the brush of leafless cottonwood trees, telling me that was the old *takalímxu*, or camping-place. He remembered a Model A Ford, the first car he ever saw, put-putting up the valley on the road, which was then just two deep tracks in the ground. One of Charlene's ancestors had painted his powers on the singularly tall boulder beside the road.

"That would be maybe, Grandma's uncle, I think. Maybe you ask Jim or his mom sometime, they show you where it is. Hard to see when I just young. Not look at it for years. They paint it with that red they get up in B.C., different places. *Tulameen* come from the earth, like a greasy rock. Paint everything with it in the old days, like to be the special color. So it don't last too very long, I guess, then it fade on the rock face. Maybe can't see it no more.

"So this get my mind goin', to think back, how only one man I know of have a gift from that *tl'tlákw*, that falcon. He the brother of that one who paint his powers on that rock, put up like a billboard there beside the trail where it pass that place of danger, his doctorin' powers for the traveler to see. I think maybe his brother put up somethin' about what he got, too, somewhere in those rocks. Maybe ask Grandma about it.

"Anyway, he was gifted with that second sight out in the hills, that second sight of the land. Like where everything is, what it's doin'. Where the animals are and where the berry bushes is ripe. He see what there even before he get there, that sorta thing. What he got make it easy for him to get plenty to eat, always find whatever he want.

"You hear him talk, you can tell he have a picture in his mind of the land, of everything all around. People want to find somethin', they come to him, give him somethin', so he use his power to find what they want. What he have different from some other hunting gift. Like with Cougar, to be able to hit whatever animal you shoot at. Or like deer tick, the deer just come lookin' for the man that have that power. Different kind of hunting powers. But that one got somethin' from falcon, he different kind of hunting power, more like a scout, see everything and he just pick what he want. Anyway, that what he get from that falcon.

"You kinda like that. You lookin' around all the time, remember everything you see real clear. Out in the hills, I figure out long ago you lookin' at the world with eyes like we try to train the young kids to see with. Like to teach 'em to see what there in the corner of their eyes when they lookin' straight ahead. To train themself to see what goin' on at the very edge of what they can see. Can't be much of a hunter, much of a berry-picker or a fisherman if you can't see like that. And maybe they miss seein' the *shumíx* when they out there to meet 'em, when we send 'em on a mission.

"Lotta things going on out on the edges around where we see. Like when you watchin' with eyes trained like that, you dancin' at the Winter Dance, you get a glimpse of them *shumíx* dancin' with us, like that. You gotta get a glimpse of them when they show themself. That how we talk to the young people, tell 'em maybe they get only one little chance. Them *shumíx* maybe just a shimmer, so quick. Just a glimpse, but if they train themself, that glimpse open up, you got 'em, they happy you got the eyes to see 'em. So they talk to 'em, tell 'em what gift they got, give 'em a song, their own song.

"That maybe how you see somethin' of what goin' on inside the sweatlodge, in the dark. That where a man who have those eyes to see get a glimpse of a lotta things. And you got that. Seein' like that is more than lookin'. Out there in the hills, in the timber, the animals feel to be touched by eyes like that. Like that deer you kill for me, standin' there just like to know what you're sayin' to him. Irresistible eyes, they say. They like that, everything out there like that, to be touched by eyes like that. The mountain, the cloud, the fir tree, the deer, the rain and the snow, they all tremble a little, when the eyes touch 'em. Shimmer a little. They have good for us when we do that. Make 'em feel good, so they like to help. Make things easier for us come-alive people."

Clayton fell silent as a fully loaded log truck crept past us, diesel engine idling along, chained logs groaning and swaying as the big tires went through iced-over potholes. The driver waved at us then took it slow down the hill. The truck disappeared around the snowy boulders with a plume of stinky smoke hanging in the still air. After a few minutes another came by, and I wondered where they might be logging in this kind of weather. Then I tried out the Salish word for falcon.

"*Tl'tlákw.* I wonder if that's what I got."

"Could be," Clayton said, watching the red brake lights of the log truck moving through the gloom. "I think that him all right. But maybe not. That falcon could be just the friend of who give you that gift. Happen like that sometimes. Like to hide behind his friend, his relative, so no Indian doctor can steal your power, make you sicken and maybe die.

"What you lookin' for is the person, that man or that woman who talk to you, give you what you got. The one that tell you what it is, what you can do. Maybe give you a song, maybe not. Lotta times hunting power don't give no song.

"You lookin' for the person that love the wind. The one say, 'Only wind is real to me.' The one appear just like human people, just like come-alive person. That how they come to you. You have memory of that—that what count. That kinda rememberin' is what I mean."

"I don't remember anything like that," I said.

"Never do. You not supposed to. That how it always go. Happen in their own sweet time. Maybe if you real sick, gonna die, he come and remind you, make you remember him. Or maybe the Indian doctor, come to doctor you, like Old Willie, see you got somethin' that want to come out. Maybe that what makin' you sick. So he say somethin', tell what he see, remind you, so all that come back to you, and you remember what power you been given. You do what that *shumíx* tell you to do, and you get well.

"But you not sick. Maybe different for the White man, maybe not. Some *Suyápi* I see, like to live the Indian way all their life, married to the Native man, the Native woman. Come out at the Winter

Dance, just like anybody do. Just like that woman I see last week *k'alt'álkw* (across the line), up in B.C., tremble all over, start to cry like a baby, have that look in her eye, that look like she seein' real far away, things we don't see. Then her song just come out, she start singin' and they have to help her to hold on. So cute to see her blonde head out there at the pole, like to have the pigtails waggin'.

"But my way of thinkin', to not live the Indian way, the White man gotta find his way. Not be sick, not go to Winter Dance, maybe some kinda power just like for the *Suyápi* to be Native. Some different way. Johnny Stemilt tell me you maybe think this way, too."

"Yeah," I said. "My heart's in there somewhere with what you said. I don't see where it's goin', but that's how it feels right to me."

"Same world, same animal powers, same earth and sky to give the gift to the human," he said, waving his hand slowly over the dashboard toward the vague mountainous shapes enveloped in darkness outside his car. "But different way given to different people. *Skélux* got one way. Yakima people given another way. Out in Montana, another way come with a pipe. On the coast, different way. The White man, like you, love our mother, have those eyes to see, maybe all those powers take pity on you, give your people your own way to be the Native.

"I not tell you before, but long time ago, I be only about fifteen, sixteen, my own father, before he die, tell me somethin'. One White man come to where my father have the sweatlodge on the Similkameen River, his desire to go inside and pray with us. First time I ever see anything like that. We see that other kinda White man sweat with us, dance, but that another kind. Not *Suyápi*, what we call *Sáma*, don't talk English good, talk another language."

"French?"

"Yeah, that kinda White man, but more like the Native. Have that heart like the Indian. They always doin' our way. But not the *Suyápi*, the English talkers. This one *Suyápi*, he like the sweathouse, he come back lotta times, he say he like that way. And it so hard in those days, even to have the sweatbath because the Whites say we only worship the Devil that way. Always puttin' a stop to things, so my father hide his sweathouse in the deep draw hidden by timber so the Whites don't know. So after while, this White man comin', comin', comin' to sweat with us. And my want to know, why does my father let this White man come and pray with us? He tell me: 'Maybe if we let them pray with us our way, they stop treatin' us so bad. They stop treatin' the earth so bad.'

"So I think about those words. All my life I wonderin' how that might come to be. And I talk with the others, Native people come from far away, to see how we have the different way. And we talk, sometimes all night long, how we have our different way given to us. But then we say, 'Yah, that like us, what you have there, we have that, too.' Because down deep, all the same. Not like the Whites, argue and fight about different way to pray to Jesus. We talk about our different ways given by the Chief of the powers, and we see what's the same. Say, 'Yeah, we believe that, too.' Some things all the same, like to be the Native way.

"Like how that spirit person give one gift to one man, another kinda gift to another man. Say like nighthawk, we call 'em *p'a's*, he give one man that protection from never get hit by lightning. That just his, for him in life to be protected from ever bein' struck. You out there, you see what I mean, how that nighthawk fly around so fast, dart back and forth, gone so fast you can't see 'em, then there they are again, other place in the sky. And in a thunderstorm, lightnin' hit all around, all the birds hidin', not one is flyin', except that *p'a's*, still zigzaggin' all over the place, never get hit. He don't care about that Thunderbird beatin' his wings, spittin' fire from his eyes. He busy stuffin' his guts with bugs, don't have to fear that lightning strikin' all around. You hear 'em fartin' in the sky, like they laughin' at Thunderbird. Maybe you see that?"

I told him I had. Especially above the Similkameen in the heat of

summer where nighthawks are so thick feasting on the rise of insects that a town on the Washington side along the river had been named
for them. I'd seen them continue to soar and swoop and let out their
grinding, groaning booms unfazed by a lightning storm sweeping over,
when all other birds had come to earth or disappeared into hiding.

"But now, to another man, nighthawk give a doctorin' power, he
give the gift to doctor the person struck by lightning. That somethin'
else, see, he can use his power to help others. But that a pretty rough
power to have. So greedy, so jealous. Gotta watch out for the doctor
with that one. You laugh when he fart, he maybe take what you got.

"See, hard to say what the gift gonna be. But some things, they
kinda all the same. Like maybe two men have a gift from the same
kinda *shumíx*. You see 'em both, they like to be same kind of person.
Get along easy. Like to have the same thoughts. Know what happenin'
with that other person.

"Like maybe they got different gift, different song from badger.
But you know these two men, they both got that strong heart, that
generous heart. They always givin' things to people. Or like bluejay,
he just like a stumblin' fool, a real loser. A man have that, you see
him like he don't care about hisself, stick anything in his mouth, he
out there in the snow with no clothes on. But then he just laugh,
always laugh, and it paralyze you, can't think of nothin'. What power
you got is gone, and that bluejay man, he done just what you thought
you could do. He just like that, laugh, and he do somethin' to you, so
you wonder what happened.

"Some *shumíx* give real strong power, no matter what they give.
Like the man with wolf, he have that real strong family way. Like to
be the leading family, the pack takin' care of its own. Or with eagle,
that dark one, *ml'kanúps*, so proud, the man know he can lead the
people, stand there with that fierce pride in his eye. Or pack rat, that
man have the gift to gather wealth together. He always out there
tradin' and gamblin' and puttin' deals together.

"Some powers real dangerous. They so *xa'xá* they pretty hard even for the one who have a gift from them. You see a man have somethin' from grizzly, *kiláuna*. You see he have that chip on his shoulder all the time. Quick to anger, to take offense. Or like the man have *suk's'skúm*, thunder, the one that hits. Or *su'u'wíkist*, he harm you with just a glance. Don't like to notice his eyes lookin' around for you, like lightning finding you on a bare hill top.

"Or like rattlesnake, what we call *xa'xa'úlaux*. That mean somethin' like real dangerous place on the ground. Real dangerous earth power there, and the man or the woman who have that, they always a real strong doctor. Somebody who can fix 'em up even when it's a bad case, no hope, they gonna die. The one with a power from rattlesnake, she cure 'em, just like that. But you around 'em, you feel where they standin' not a place you want to stand. They let you know not to bother 'em.

"Some powers, they never used for to doctor. Not strong enough, but good for the person to stay healthy, cure hisself. Keep 'em alive, go through life lucky. Never need to call in a doctor. Maybe power to do somethin'. Like maybe to have rabbit, *sp'palína*, be the fast runner, win all the races, but then that person be a little nervous, high strung. Or like some women have, *spítlem*, bitterroot give 'em somethin', always the first one up in the morning.

"In the Native way, we have our *chaptíkx* that tell us all these things. And we see the proof with our own eyes, as we go through life, to study what is there in the world. How the animals have these powers. How our people have these powers. And can't do nothin' but what they tell you when they give the gift, or later when you get to know them again. Only what they say you can do, that what you can do. No other.

"Maybe this help you, maybe not. Have to see for yourself. Find your own Native way. But this how it is all the different ways. It whatever they want to give you, and no other.

"Like I said before, one more thing, to send you on a mission. Come the warm days, I do that for you. Then we see what happen, what you got gonna make hisself known to you."

I asked him where that might happen, if he had a place in mind for where I would be sent on a mission. He laughed, put his car in gear, turned on the lights, and started the drive back. It was completely dark now, and ice exploded as the tires rolled through refrozen potholes.

"You like that blind boy always callin' out, *'La'kín! La'kín! La'kín!* (Where? Where? Where?—from one of the sacred stories). Okay, *Skélux,* Come-Alive Person. We go up to Chopaka. Start there and go back in that country, back behind.

"That Chopaka Mountain, we say *chu'pák'x,* means like 'sticking up above everything else.' That a man, like all the rest. Person, but a man that one, very big man, powerful, *xa'xá.* Watch over this whole country, watch over us, talk to us. Now that man, that other Chopaka, tell somebody his name. Just he have that name, to call him for help. Mean somethin' like standin' back and watchin'. Keep his eyes open because all kinds of things happen, like to fight, to come the hard blizzard, or even like when the Whites come and dig mines all around here. Or like now, he say they come to plant the apple trees on all the flat places. He know all what gonna happen. But he like the elder brother that don't get all excited, got that cool head. Aloof, like. He always there. Just always there, the one standin' the tallest.

"And that country back there, behind. What your people made a law to keep untouched. You know that country?"

"Yeah, sure. They call it the Pasayten Wilderness."

"We go that way. Or maybe just you. I wait for you. That country so *xa'xá* even the White man can feel it. Make a law to not tear it up like he tear up everywhere else. In the old days, that country make all the best Indian doctors."

16

Winter left the lowlands fast. In one day muddy snow became bare ground. A hard, gray world emerged, frayed and flattened by months of snow cover, the long, bowl-sided valleys ratty and worn in soft springlike weather, surrounded by mountains still glaring white where late winter lingered. Fingers of green tender things sprouted from the dirt and began to flower as *temxúlaux*, mother earth, woke from a dream.

The cattle were sick of hay and we were sick of feeding them. Running short of haystacks and hoping to speed up the season, Stuart set fires in the dry fields, burning off entire pastures in hours to stimulate the growth of grass. Overnight the blackened fields began to green up.

I was waking from a dream, too, footloose, wandering the hills, breathing and pumping blood, pausing to nibble on the first leaves of spring, the first tastes of green growing things. The bitter pulp of buttercups, the peppery lace of wild celery, the lettuce-tasting waterleaf. Leaves, flowers and stems, down the hatch, tasting of dirt.

And fasting one day at a time and staying awake all night out in the hills. Walking on moonless nights staring at the invisible ground, watching the slow, stately movement of constellations overhead, dancing beside a fire on the ground when sleep tried to take me by stealth in the last weary hour before dawn. Training myself to feel my way over the dark earth and trust that inner conviction that comes when a body knows what's there even when the eyes can't see it.

Climbing up the steep face of the mountain behind my trailer, I found a boulder-strewn flat about halfway up, just as the sun set on the south shoulder of Chopaka. Juniper trees are solitary and scarce in the Okanogan, so finding one there on the flat brought me to a halt. Bushy and impenetrable, thick with bluish berries, a Rocky Mountain juniper, a sacred tree all alone on this little bit of level ground on steep slopes. Fist-sized rocks of smooth white quartz resting on dull brown bedrock showed that other seekers like me had sat beside the gnarled sprawl of juniper, gazing out over the haze of lake air at Chopaka. I sat with my back against a fractured boulder shaped perfectly to my spine, feeling some certain presence near me, watching the last yellow glimmer of spring sun backlighting the shadowy, snow-covered peak sticking up above the endless sea of western mountains still locked in winter. I decided to sit with eyes open, just watching, waiting, observing, until all light was gone from the sky.

It took a long time. Set back from the edge, I didn't see the orchard and ranch lights go on below. Never closing my eyes, scanning the horizon, watching the western sky fade by imperceptible degrees, I became still, thoughtless, as unmoving as the boulder I rested against. The long northern twilight began to twinkle with almost invisible star points in a vague cloudy drift. An hour or more passed but still to my eyes adjusting to less and less light, the true dark everywhere else in the sky contrasted with a faint suffusion on the horizon in front of me. Shadowy movements swirled and jostled at the periphery of my vision, but I stayed locked onto the fading glow above the mountains.

Then something stirred inside me. Night everywhere now. A deep breath and a body only slowly yielding from stiffness, eyes blinked and freed from staring into the void. Leaning forward on awakening legs, rocking slowly on crossed feet, breathing deeply now, I jerk up into a standing position. There's a rustle in the juniper to my left, something big that makes my heart pound, something moving in the rounded shadow against a starry sky only ten feet away. I stare hard, trying to see what I'm hearing.

Then everything happens so fast and so silently, I react on pure instinct. A lighter mass appears, grows in size, becomes something flying towards me from the juniper, something wide and fast coming towards my eyes. Only time to jerk my head down into hunched shoulders as feathers brush across the top of my bare head. A glimpse of eyes staring into mine belonging to a huge bird with a four-foot wingspan. I duck and turn to see a great horned owl visible against starlight, great pumping silent wings taking it away into the night.

Heart thumping, adrenaline making me run in place, touched by the feel of the owl brushing the top of my head, my body suddenly breaks away at a dead run.

Leaping boulders, unthinking, running full tilt with my eyes glued to the ground a few feet in front, I run as if possessed. I run as if I knew what I was doing, because I can't really see what's in front of me. I fly so fast it's something else finding its way along to the end of the flat and along gradually descending ledges. Just a body aware, running so fast the world goes by in a blur. Leaping brushy areas, jagged rocks, vague dark somethings that my body rejects touching down on. Full speed around the curving face of mountain and down screes and slides and across grassy swales through the slap of tall sagebrush bushes. Heedless, flat out, onto the level pastures of a bench a mile away, I rush up to an opening between two dark brushy shapes. A gateway into further open pastures. But I skid to a stop. Something makes me stop. Panting, knowing in my gut that there's something dangerous, something threatening, right there invisibly in front of me. Something right there between the two dark brushy clumps I was about to run between. My mind laughs at my body stopping here. There's nothing there, see? I reach out my hand, feel into the nothingness in front of me. My god, it's a five-strand barbed wire fence!

Climb the fence and go on. Elated, laughing now, so clear that my heart knew what my mind did not. Words beginning to find their way through the seamless veil of sense experience, little mutterings commenting on what's going by like somebody else up there in the mind. "Boy howdy . . . That was close . . . Where are we going?"

Short, faintly recognizable phrases recreating a world like the litter of rusting farm implements I pass as I slow to a walk across sloping pasture land, once farmed but now abandoned to the sage and ryegrass and stubble of weeds. Drawn by the dark, unseeable places now, my body wanting more, into a ravine, soft steep slopes that my body leaps down with the joy of confident abandon. The smell of awakening willows, the rush of a creek swollen by snowmelt. Turn and follow it up into the dense dark of forest. Picking the way with no way of knowing, yet I know how, my legs move, my feet choose where to step.

Up and up. Hours and hours. Rotten foot-deep snow at an open piney divide. The get up and run of unseen deer, startled into flight by somebody sleepwalking, blundering too close, hooves clicking on stumbled rocks. Down into another steep draw between two mountains. The recognizable white clay underparts glowing by starlight beneath pines lining the creek downward—I know where I am, know where I'm going, but the names don't come, the pictures don't come to mind. Miles of silence and wind and little waterfalls plunging into invisibly deep pools. And then I realize I can see the world I'm moving through. Gusts of wind tearing through the pines, the vague gray of dawn, how light makes everything solid again. Weary muscles and joints slowing a solitary man descending the granite carvings of water and ice. By the light of day I'm me again.

And I've walked in a circle again. Beyond the trees ahead I see the orchard, the pickers' shacks, my trailer. The last hollow of granite shelters a circling pool of snow-smelling water, and I stare long at the reflection of gathering yellow clouds on the limpid surface.

One last thing before returning to the world of people and affairs. I undress, pile my clothes in my coat, wade naked into the icy pool. Down on all fours, then drop to the gravelly bottom. Up and down in the two feet of water, plunging and spouting like a seal, then up and out before death can take me. Stagger up a chalky bank to stand shivering in the wind. And then the faint rumble of thunder, a darkness in the sky coming from behind the mountain, and it begins to snow. A blinding, hissing flurry that turns to pellets and falls with a hushed roar through the pines. Guess I won't drip-dry after all. I pull clothes on over icy wet body. That deep chill like an ache in the bones, an ache at the heart of things. But god, I'm so alive! Standing out there where I know I belong, not at the mercy of nature, not conquering it. Equal to it.

Dressed and walking, I ease my way into the opening above orchards, and see the lake in veiled hanging showers. Moving through bare apple trees, steps taken toward home. Morning light pale on the very sticking point of Chopaka. The snow stops as quickly as it started. Slushy mud by my old familiar pickup truck. The smell of wet growing things, wet burnt grass. The sound of cattle mooing on the flats below. Calling to me. Yeah, time to break my fast and go to work.

Looking north in my mind's eye for so long, all winter long, it's a shock to find myself facing south in the spring. And it's a spring like no other I remember—wet and green and lush. How our mother gives forth life in such abundance! In the lowest, sheltered, sun-warmed places along the lake, along the river and the sloughs, millions of gnatlike flies hover in rippling clouds above the pussy willows. Blackbirds fly through with bills open. Ranch kids play naked in the frigid water, running in and out of the yellowish snowmelt with cherry-red legs. They lie in the sun on sandy banks thick with green grass, overhung with osier dogwoods in bloom and lined with budding poplars smelling like balsam.

Before the spring flood gets going, Charlene stands on the levee-like flat by the slough where she lives, directing the daughters of other mothers as they clean the banks below of litter exposed after a long winter. Decomposing paper diapers, beer bottles, plastic bags molded around drift logs snagged and temporarily stranded in muddy shallows. The debris of Canadian civilization washed down into her ancestral solitude at the foot of Chopaka.

On those bare-looking hillsides the girls pick wildflowers, with cheatgrass already going to seed and prickly pear cactus looking fat and purple in the cracks of rocks. Their little hands feel the woolly marvel of *shmucáhwin* leaves like wrinkled green arrowheads a foot long, and pick handfuls of sagebrush in mint-green tender leafiness only seen at this time of year. Through windblown hair they watch the preening and posturing of long-tailed magpies, so loudmouth noisy as they build rickety stick nests in dense thickets of serviceberry, chokecherry, hackberry, and sumac.

Below outcrops of dark volcanic rock and the glacier- smoothed granite boulders perched atop them, in an opening between vanilla-scented trunks of ponderosa pine whose wind-tossed greenery gives off clouds of yellow pollen, Jim Woods and his brother-in-law drag willow branches and clear a place for a new sweatlodge. A clearing ringed around by wild rose in pink bud, roses to protect against ghosts, to keep at bay the ancestors who come to the sound of singing voices, of sobbing prayers, and can't help themselves, wanting so bad to draw away into their own world the loved ones left behind. Jim's mom and sister are immune to the poison ivy rubbing their arms as they strip the bark off willow limbs with paring knives and skilled fingernails, making piles of bark ties for later, and shredding bunches of the inner bark for medicine to dry at home.

People just show up, making the work easier and faster, always doing things together, laughing at Roger Antoine's pointed jokes about how men who drink are afraid of the sweatlodge. Even Jim's brother-in-law, looking a little green around the gills from the night before, laughs ruefully as he builds up a thirst for the hair of the dog, sweating like nobody else in the warm sun. Men fist sharpened willow ends into the soft earth and bend flexible limbs in hoops to meet those bent over from the other side. Their shoulders brush the crooked, ragged, hanging branches of bitterbrush lined with perfumed, sulphur-yellow blossoms, their legs rubbing rabbitbrush oozing foamy flecks of sap.

Yarrow standing up stiffly, all fuzzy white-green on the flat tops, is ready to bloom. *Shía* berries, green and hard, hide among vivid green leaves on wine-red stems. Elderberry bushes are in full bloom, stemmy and flat-clustered creamy white. Their fragrance is like a drug to the swarming bees. Big old poplar trunks at the water's edge are tinted a fluorescent yellow-orange from lichens waxing in the damp. Indian balsam grows in mustard-yellow clumps, its fat medicinal root hidden in the deep earth, tops waving in the dry air on light green hills against a pure blue sky. Then a gust of wind, the south wind of renewed warmth and life, scouring gently through the valley, and the chill wet sweet smell of river takes over.

And up in the hills, up where I wander with my rifle making meat to help feed us all, fir trees and sagebrush and open grassy hollows, boulders of quartz and mica, cool cutbanks of fern and moss. Coyote puppies staring at me from above the dirt mouth of their den, diving clumsily for cover at the sharp bark from momma who darts away and circles, hoping to draw me away from her nursing babies. Protected, forgotten foldbacks in the mountainous landscape where the glaciers rounded and smoothed the surroundings but filled these narrow, hidden slots with deep till, little valleys parallel to the slope of mountain. I find a well-traveled game trail in waist-high grass where deer bed down, and nearby, a place for a man with spring fever to lie out in the sun. Just watching the deer watching me, ears and tails twitching, all of us in an altered state of consciousness, a thickened, slowed sense of being alive and doing well without even trying.

Stuart and the Montana bosses appear on horseback, lined out along the trail and likely to pass me unnoticed, out for a ride and laughing in pleasure at the bounding deer scattering from their beds. But Stuart's seasoned cowboy eyes find me stretched out under scrubby maples, under chartreuse flower sprays hanging from the tips of glossy red stems.

Then he's towering above me on his overweight palomino, one boot over the saddle horn, licking a rollie in the shade of his hat, grinning at me as his lathered horse shifts to the creak of leather. The long white horse face snuffling this man lying in the tall grass, liquid brown eyes under ears cocked forward, tonguing the bit and wistfully mouthing the blades of sweet grass with sensitive lips. The others ride on, unaware that Stuart has found their other employee out here as a silent hunter, roaming their oil-money domain with a .22 rifle and a handful of bullets. Someone their foreman calls Mr. Natural or Mr. Organic as he laughs out a cloud of smoke at the sight of my furred and feathered catch peeking from the leather game bag on the ground. Then Stuart spurs his farting, barn-soured gelding into an unwilling trot to catch up with the bosses, and I'm up on foot again, heading the other way, looking for a patch of wild onion I remember. Some earthy seasoning to go with the rabbit and grouse and chukar partridge in my pouch.

Up here the serviceberries are still masses of white blooms and the wild apricots hang with pink-white blossoms so thick only the largest limbs are visible. It may be too early for the onions. Or even more important, I have to cool my jets about finding them, about being too sure of myself that I know where they are, being too cocky that I'll have fresh onions with dinner tonight. Like Clayton said, warning me about things like this, it was up to our mother, up to the plants and animals to be there and give themselves to us. He had learned what his elders said was true, that the plants, the animals, the sweatlodge-sized rocks, the fish all can hear us when we talk like we're so sure of ourselves. Clayton the boy was so confident he remembered some particular stands of ironwood brush with long, thick, straight stems perfect for making a fresh batch of digging sticks. He took his dad up to the spot above Palmer Lake and was stunned to find all the stems crooked, bent, forked.

"This how they teach us to have respect," he said his father told him.

That patch of onions may be there, or they may not. I first found them years before and dug up the sweet, garlicky bulbs each spring afterward at the same spot below a granite seep in a sandy draw. But the spring before this one, Stuart's wife had said, "Wouldn't it be good to have wild onions with steak tonight?" And I had said, "I know where a big bunch grows every year. I'll go get some for you." Unfortunately when I got there, I found only one or two spindly plants. So this time I approached the draw with a humble request that if you onions want to give me a gift of your bodies, I will be thankful and treat you good and not take too many.

A fat yellow marmot lay asleep on top of the rock outcrop above the seep, basking in the sun between gorging on green after its long hibernation underground. I sat in a sandy garden of onions, flower buds just peeling open, millions of them, nodding in the breeze, grass-like green parts standing taller than I'd ever seen them. I began to dig, marveling at how these tiny points of consciousness in the dark earth grow up into the light and wind, and send down pale hairlike feelers into the gritty muck down deep. How the marmot asleep on warm rock and bumblebees droning past and an invisible cock pheasant calling chi-cooooook! and every creature in this world is such a mystery, having its own form and way of growing and living. And how is it, anyway, that my people think there's no such thing as nature spirits—or think they know all about nature spirits?—when in either case they know next to nothing about nature?

On the old *Skélux* calendar they call this *spítlem'tn*, time to dig bitterroot. Charlene and Grandma and the girls were out there digging, visiting the same bare ridgetops, the same thin-soiled, rocky flats studded with pine and cinquefoil that Grandma had learned from her grandmother where *spítlem* liked to grow. Jim and I chauffeured, chaperoned and watched for bears that now roamed the hills hungry and half-awake and grumpy. When women are busy with something this important, men just stay out of the way and try to be helpful. Jim had made lightweight steel digging bars out of thin rebar. Unlike Grandma's ironwood *pícha*, these had flattened spade tips and little side bars welded in place for the women to push the tip in with their feet like a shovel.

With tilts of her head or juts of her chin, Grandma would wordlessly show us which roads to take. They wound around the highlands connecting stock tanks to isolated ranch houses to ridgetop pastures too early for cattle to be grazing yet. Most bitterroot sites were on public land used only by ranchers with permits to graze livestock. But some choice ancestral sites were on private land, and some of the owners had angrily driven off Indian women in the past. These untouched sites Grandma would look at wistfully as we drove past, telling us the White ranchers didn't understand the food plants like bitterroot gave themselves as food for people at the time of creation, and they thrive better when people gather and use them. Other owners had longstanding agreements with the Woods family to allow them to dig roots as long as they closed the gates and left things otherwise as they found them.

Grandma would climb out and look around, never straying far from her walker, seeking out and talking to the pretty clusters of pink and white flowers with a distinctive orange ring in the center. Each plant was only found as a clump of flowers on the bare ground, the rosette of thick leaves already shriveled and hidden underneath. The Sunny Okanogan Elder Care Center was home to many seventy-year-old grandmas staring at soap operas that same afternoon, but Grandma Woods was out in the hills directing her family in a vital food quest, studying how the roots came up to the pry of the younger women's bars, telling us it was late in the season, we had to stay at it every day, the ground was drying up rapidly. Then while the others dug roots she would sit on a blanket, rolling the roots between flat hands and deftly stripping off the dark, bitter outer skin. Piles of white, twisted, carrot-like roots cleaned and ready to freeze or dry or cook up that night went into covered plastic buckets.

At one place we found a brand-new plank cabin built in the middle of a bitterroot garden. This was private land but Grandma had always been welcomed by the rancher who owned it, and since nobody was around, the women fell to digging. We heard some strange-sounding gunfire from the other side of the hill, and I told Jim I thought it sounded like a muzzle-loader, a black- powder rifle of some kind. He went to investigate and came back with a sick, angry look on his face. When a crowd of White longhairs came swiftly following Jim to where we were, I saw what bothered him.

It wasn't so much the two men dressed in fringed leathers like bearded Davy Crocketts, long rifles resting in the crook of their arms, powder horns dangling. It was the three women, dressed like the Indian squaws of movies, hair in braids and velvet blouses half covered with yards of trade beads and turquoise. One woman strode up in the lead, wearing a soft white deerskin dress in Plains Indian yoke style, beaded moccasins and silver bracelets, her flushed, freckled face clearly upset, wiping stray wisps of red-blonde hair out of her face. Downwind from them I could smell the reek of marijuana and incense.

The blonde Pocahontas looked in horror at so many of her flowers dug up—and taking the Woods family for Mexican farmworkers, yelled, "Propriedad privada! Privada! Véte! Véte!" Shooing them away like cattle towards our truck and car, she turned on me. I was just standing there, smiling.

"Calm down, crazy woman."

"You speak English?"

I told her the Waters family had permission from old man Rutherford to dig bitterroot on his land. She sneered that Rutherford had sold her this piece of land years ago and she and her Old West hobbyist friends had come out from New Jersey last summer to build this cabin so they could live on the land in the old ways—and besides, who ever heard of Mexicans with a name like Waters?

"They're not Mexicans, they're Indians. Okanogan band. This was all their land before it was stolen from them and carved up into ranches."

"Indians?" She looks stricken. By now the whole family is loaded up in our vehicles and Jim has started his hot, racy Barracuda engine.

"What were they digging?" she moans. "Are those flowers some sacred medicinal plant?"

"No, just food, but I guess that's sacred and medicinal, isn't it?"

"Oh, tell them it's okay, I'm sorry to have been so rude." Jim is already backing around and his sister is stony-faced with her boy at her side in the cab of my pickup.

"I don't think they want to dig here anymore. Tell you what—I'll come up and visit in a few days." She blushes and smiles. My fatal attraction to plump, freckled, redheaded milkmaid types kicks in despite the fact she's a trust-fund baby who bought the land with daddy's money. And lives in a make-believe world where eastern college girls can go out west and buy their way into being Indians. But she's gazing past me wistfully at Jim's Salish good looks, ponytail blowing in the wind as he muscles the Barracuda around and drives out the twin dirt tracks in tall grass.

"Oh well. Maybe I'll bring him with me."

"Would you? What's your sign? Come anytime. Bye!"

At the next place the timber is thick all the way up one side of a long ridge on public land. Not taking any chances after the experience with the *kayús Suyápi*, Grandma has brought us up to the remote, high mountain coolness where the bitterroot is barely budded out and thick, fleshy leaves are still green upon the damp ground.

Jim's sister, wearing a shocking pink sweatshirt you could see a mile away, anxiously kept her little boy Brandon from wandering too far from her side as she dug roots in the soft, gravely ground. She asked me to stay close and bring along my rifle as she moved along the ridge filling a pack basket on her back, so deathly afraid of bears that she paused constantly to scan the nearby edge of forest. Brandon had other things on his mind. Staring at me standing around with my rifle in the crook of my arm, and remembering the bearded longhairs in fringed leathers carrying rifles at the last place, he piped up: "When you were a White man, did you dress like that?"

The curious turn of his mind made me and his mother smother laughs. But then a sound like a breaking limb in the nearby timber startled her and she whirled to stare into the trees. I laughingly assured her no bear would come in range of my rifle since they always stayed away from me, never letting me hunt them.

"*Aaaa*, the great White hunter can't hunt no bears?"

"Well, I try. But it's no good. Long time ago I humiliated a crippled bear. Ever since, even if I see 'em, they never let me get close."

"Maybe that's a story you like to tell?"

While she dug roots with her head down and I stayed close as lookout, I told her and the boy about the time a decade before when I was living in a cabin with my woman who liked to butcher game. It was on the Illecilliwaet River in the Selkirk Range of British Columbia, a one-room cabin in melting snow where we lived while working in a cedar shake mill. We'd walk along the marshes in the snowy spring, watching for problem bears the rangers would catch in nearby national parks and dump off in our vicinity. One that limped had been scavenging around in the muck of the marsh, digging up cattail roots. If we came upon her too close, she'd woof! in alarm and climb moaning up the nearest poplar tree to perch until we were gone.

One day some friends were visiting so we all decided to hike up to some hot springs a mile away through forest. At an open spot on the way we could see the crippled bear down in the marsh, rooting for food as usual, so far away she was just a black dot moving among the first green clumps in flattened gray marsh vegetation. After my girlfriend pointed out the bear and told about waking up at night to the sound of her scavenging around for the food she smelled in our cabin, I said, "Watch this. I bet I can make that bear climb a tree!" Then I shouted with hands cupped around my mouth, something like, "Hey, bear! What're you doing? There's people here, watching you! You better climb a tree!"

And as we watched, the bear, startled and moaning, climbed a nearby tree and sat in the limbs looking around with poor eyes for whoever was tormenting her. We laughed and went on. Later in the afternoon when we came back from soaking in the hot springs, the bear was still up in the tree, and all I could think was how pathetic she was.

But after years of hunting bears to no avail, it began to dawn on me what I'd done. Anything else I hunted—deer, elk, raccoons, beaver, rabbits, bighorn sheep, badgers, marmots, squirrels, turkeys, grouse, or even animals I didn't hunt but could have had easy shots at like coyotes, cougars, grizzlies, moose, bobcats and mountain goats—it was always easy. But not black bears. Not *skum'hwíst*. No matter how close I got, and bears were thick as fleas on a dog in some places, they never let me get in range to shoot them. I'd track them, find their dens, find where they scuffed up the forest duff for beds to sleep on, and find their distinctive hairs snagged on tree bark where they scratched themselves. I'd hear them in dense underbrush and glimpse them hotfooting it away from me.

I'd even see them standing by the side of a mountain road, looking at me as I drove by, only to melt away into the trees if I stopped to dig out my rifle. Once I watched a young male on his long wander of early summer come down off Palmer Mountain and cross the green pastures of the Sinlahekin Valley, heading for a deep draw that led up to where I waited on one flank of Chopaka for Stuart to arrive with fencing tools to repair a section of fence broken by bulls. The bear came up the draw toward me waiting in ambush, but then he disappeared. After a long wait, I came out of hiding and looked all around, only to see him far above me, disappearing into heavy timber.

"So you don't have a thing to worry about, as long as I'm here with my rifle," I told her. The clunk of steel against rock stopped and Jim's sister turned, big-boned and sweaty in jeans and a yellow bandanna tied like a scarf around her cropped black hair. In the stiff ridgetop breeze her full pack basket smelled of wet earth and the unique, pungent odor of bitterroots.

"That's too bad, what you did," she said. Brandon was sticking close, listening silently to my bear stories, picking black dirt from his fingernails after helping his mother shake the clumps of soil from the dug-up roots. "I like bear meat. It's the best. Maybe I like it too much. Bears are the animals most like us, like people. They're maybe just barely animals, eh? They get so mad when we take the food they like to eat. But maybe someday they'll change their mind about you, ain't it?"

"Maybe. Every time I see one now, I tell 'em how sorry I am. How bad I feel that I did that to 'em. But that's the way it goes. I can't take it back. Live and learn. It's up to them—it's their life and there's nothing I can do about it."

17

The next day we were up on a high ridge again at sunrise, the women digging steadily, moving from flat to flat where the *spítlem* grew in isolated clusters, always leaving some, never taking too many. Driving up there in the half light of dawn we passed the huge boulders at the base of Lucky Hill where Clayton had told me Grandma's uncle had painted his doctoring powers. Jim's mom and one of the older girls were riding with me in my pickup as I followed Jim's Barracuda up the winding mountain roads, so I talked to Charlene about what Clayton had said and wondered aloud if maybe when we came back down later in the day she or Grandma could show me the rock pictures. She listened but said nothing.

As the morning wore on, warmer and warmer in the cloudless sunny exposure of open ridges without a breath of wind, Grandma took off her car coat and moved around stiffly in a dark blue dress, a scarf embroidered with Native designs tied so low on her forehead her eyes were barely visible below it. All this physical exertion, the long rides on bumpy roads, the getting up and down from her blanket, peeling roots . . . it was obvious her mended hip was hurting.

In the heat of midday we sat in the shade of a lone ponderosa pine leaning uphill from just below the rocky drop-off. The view in every direction was beautiful. A few clouds darkened the still snowy western mountains and we could see snow on all the solitary peaks in other directions. The valleys were hazy and green. We ate sandwiches and cold grouse and fresh bitterroot cooked in a kind of pudding. It was the laziest kind of warm afternoon and nobody was anxious to get back to work.

We saw the children playing a ways off stop in a bunch and point at something on the ground, the oldest girl pushing the others back from whatever it was. Jim and I went to investigate. It was a horny toad, about five inches long, camouflaged invisibly against the ground, looking like just another reddish-brown speckled rock—until it moved. The oldest girl, thinking to head off disaster from the ignorant White man going down on all fours for a closer look, said, "Don't bother him. If you don't treat horny toads just right, they'll make winter come back." She looked around the sky as if expecting gathering storm clouds.

"*Anewí k'shwinúmpt,*" I said to the tiny creature staring back at me. Brandon leaned against my shoulder, gazing at the horny toad as fascinated as I was. Wide and flat against the ground, with a short pointed tail and a fringe of swept-back horns behind its lizard-looking head, the little thing moved slowly into the shade of a tuft of grass, its mottled orange and black colors fading to a gray-green matching the new surroundings. In seconds it was almost invisible again.

"Yeah, they're really powerful," Jim said, watching from off to one side. "They're like Indian doctors, real strong healing power." He turned and stepped away, then called to the women still sitting in the shade, "Horny toad!"

I heard Charlene and Grandma talking in Salish, then Charlene called back, "Grandma wants to see if he'll blow for her!"

Jim came and asked if I had any tobacco. I went to my pickup and came back with a bent cigarette from the glove compartment and some matches. The horny toad had moved again, and was now wiggling over bitterroot blossoms, his backside slowly shading towards a speckled orangeish-pink.

Going around in front, Jim lit the cigarette and kneeled down to face it. He blew a cloud of smoke over it, and the armored lizard hunkered down motionless, closing its eyes. Jim apologized for bothering it, saying he knew the horny toad had great power to heal and telling it how bad he felt that his Grandma was still hurting from her broken hip.

"We won't treat you bad, grandfather," he said, continuing to blow smoke over the unmoving creature. "I know you'll help my grandma if you want to, that's why I give you this good smoke."

Then Jim picked up the horny toad in one hand, and it didn't struggle, its eyes opened and filmed over again as he carried it to the women, waving the cigarette smoke over it. Under the pine tree, Charlene took the toad gently into her hands as Grandma lay on her side and pulled her dress up to reveal angry blue bruises still blotching the loose skin of her upper thigh. Grandma hummed a Salish tune, and Charlene took up the wordless melody, singing in a soft but penetrating voice, weaving the horny toad's nose slowly back and forth in time over the injured place on Grandma. Jim and his sister began singing, too, so when I joined in and the girls tried to follow the melody, we were all sitting in a circle around Grandma, singing her song together, hoping for this horny toad's blessing for Grandma's sake. The cigarette burned down to a tiny stub, so Jim pinched off the ember and shredded the remains, sprinkling tobacco over the horny toad tilted face down in Charlene's hands, moving back and forth inches away from Grandma's bruises.

Swelling up and curling its horns upward, the lizard snorted in a sudden blast, blowing air so forcefully Grandma's dress flapped. Grandma moaned and trembled, and the others interrupted the song to cry "*aaaa*" and look at each other with big smiles. Charlene thanked the horny toad in Salish and when she turned and set it reverently on the ground, the unperturbed lizard promptly changed from the dark brown color of her hands to a bright rocky color, and ambled slowly away.

Grandma sat up, smoothing her dress down her legs, a dreamy smile softening her wrinkled face. She rubbed her hip and said to Charlene, "Yah, that feel a lot better." She looked out towards the disappearing horny toad and said, "*Wai, shox'merrím, limlemt!* (Goodbye, doctor, thank you!)" Then she stood up, noticeably spryer than before, and walked around talking in the brisk voice of authority we knew so well, directing us in preparation for the next round of digging.

Later in the afternoon I was off alone with Charlene on a spur of the ridge where she was digging widely scattered bitterroots with an ease and speed I found amazing to watch. She began to tell me about Indian doctors, about people who had been healed or hurt by them, and about Old Willie, who she said was the only one the Waters family really trusted because he was a relative. An Indian doctor who was related could usually be depended upon not to use his or her powers to steal a spirit partner or cause illness or injuries in the family. And such a doctor could be called in to work on a family member victimized by an unrelated doctor who was motivated by bad thoughts, jealousy or rivalry, or was hired to use his powers for those reasons. It was a rich half-hour of frank revelation that touched me and showed me she was thinking about my desire to see the Indian doctor pictures painted on the big rocks we passed that morning. But now I was even more mystified that Jim seemed so afraid of Old Willie.

"That's because some powers do things on their own. Real hard to handle, even for the Indian doctor. Like real good power to cure, but unpredictable. Gotta have her own way, take offense real easy, quick to anger. Don't like noisy people, or people who stand out. Jealous of others, eh?

"Old Willie got one like that. He have others, good ones, many of 'em. I don't know just how many. But that one, pretty mean muckymuck, pretty hard to handle. Maybe some kinda grizzly bear give him that. But anyway, that power did that to my son, made those marks on his face, scarred him bad.

"Oh, that Jim was noisy, such a talker. He wasn't afraid of anything when he became the teenager. And so good lookin'—that what done it. Old Willie never wanted to harm him, he wasn't even aware of it. This was back when he didn't have very good control of his power. Now maybe that can't happen, but you never know.

"Anyway, so Old Willie felt bad about what his power did to my son. He was real bent over, couldn't stand up straight, and he had all these marks on his body, like welts, like claw scratches on his back, like a grizzly clawed him. This happen when they sleepin' in the same room. Woke up and he was cryin', said something attack him in the night.

"Old Willie felt so bad, he sponsored him in the sweatlodge retreat, hopin' to cure him and help him gain spirit so he could better protect himself in life. That went good. You can see there's only a trace left on Jim's skin.

"But that one that hurt him, that grizzly bear, I think that's the one by the way Old Willie dance that power in the Winter Dance. All you can do is guess, but we pretty sure that's the one who gave him that power. I think maybe my son can still see that grizzly bear, feel him around whenever he's around Old Willie."

On the drive back down in the late afternoon, Jim pulled off the road ahead of me near the house-sized boulder. Across the road from the creek rushing by in full flood, swamping the alders and willows along the bank, the huge boulders glowed white in low sunshine, so different from the gloom of winter.

Standing like sentinels in the fir forest, tops covered with mats of lichens and small flowering violets, curving sides glittering with crystalline bareness, the rocks seemed even bigger as we got out and walked up among them. Fletcher's orchard could barely be seen beyond the screen of cottonwoods, but the scent of apple blossoms filled the air as we gathered around Grandma leaning on her walker in front of one face of the largest boulder.

"*Wai, kch'kícht,*" she said in the casual greetings of Natives everywhere. "Well, I'm come here. And you still standin' here, like when I just little. *Líiiiiim-tenun'tm!*"

At eye level, on a dished granite surface, I could see the weathered red ocher designs she was looking at, speckled with pinpoints of lichen. Other, fainter pictures could be seen all around the boulder, and on bare parts of rocks all around. What she gazed at was a large, irregular circle painted through the head of a human figure at the bottom. Inside the circle were a huge birdlike figure with a zigzag tail striking outside the circle, a doe deer in profile, and unrecognizable figures in a field of crosses that looked like stars. Painted arrowhead shapes pointed outward from the circled visionary story, and one arrowhead pointing inward was surrounded by a turn-aside symbol with hash marks showing the times this Indian doctor fought and won against the attacks of other doctors. Beside the human figure at the bottom there were six hash marks in a row, the number of powers he used in his doctoring. Below that was a bear paw, and below that a narrow vertical line with two dots at each end.

Charlene talked about how this was family knowledge, that the things told in the family were to keep the family strong, to teach the children as they grew up, to keep the family going through all the generations. Grandma sat down on the thick duff of fir needles and one of the girls climbed her walker like a jungle gym to perch wordlessly on top. We sat and waited to hear what story she would tell about this rock picture painted by a family man from the past.

"You tell, Charlene," she said, untying her scarf and letting her little great-grandson sit on her lap and finger her white braids. "The young ones, and *Sáma* here, they not hear me usin' the old language. They not hear how we have our powers unless you tell it."

Charlene straightened up and began to speak. With the sun casting a reddish glow on her face, and the sound of passing cars from the other side of the boulder, we watched Charlene's gesturing hands and listened.

"Years ago, before civilization, we had certain people that was gifted to heal and cure the sick. In this day and age we cannot be walking down the street and all of a sudden feel that we want to be doctors, and pow! we can be doctors. No. In the Indian way we are born to be a doctor. Born to be a great hunter, a basketmaker, a horse trainer, or whatever.

"And the family is the people that do the groundwork. They train their youth to respect their elders, to be helpful to their parents. We mark the day we see the child that is so quiet and aware, and we wonder, who is that child's family?

"By the young parents bringin' up their child in the true Native way, one day some elder will see that little boy and like him. This is what happened to one couple who have a child, a little boy, and they bring him up right. After he was born he was put in a baby board. After the baby board he learned to speak Indian, and they teach him to respect his elders.

"One moonless night the young couple were sittin' at the fire, and they were tellin' stories and laughin'. Camped right across the creek over there. Happy people. It was dark with stars out.

"The next instant they noticed the tall elder appear before them and warm his hands at the fire. He made his wish known that he want to pass his gift to the child, that one day the child may be of service to his people.

"The parents give their blessing. The old gentleman, he call the boy over. The boy was small, only seven or eight years old, and the moment he hear his name called, he ran to the elder's side, sat on his little heels and said, 'Your wish is my command.'

"The old man, he like that. He say, 'If you are not afraid, I want to send you on a mission tonight.' He name that mountain that watch over us. We can't see him from here, but not far beyond that hill there."

"Chopaka!" several young voices said in unison.

"He told this little boy, 'You go there and stay the night. Come the new day you can come home.' So the little boy turn to his parents and said, 'I am sent by my elder on a mission. I must leave this moment. And I am not afraid of the dark, I am not afraid of dead people in the dark.' The parents said, 'You may go.'

"The boy started walkin' away from the fireplace into the dark, moonless night," Charlene said in a low voice, gesturing up the valley of Cecile Creek in the shadow of sunset. "Just like all children, he keeps a glancin' back toward the fire below. He wonder if his relatives might have a change of heart to be sendin' him all alone into the dark.

"He keeps headin' toward that mountain and keeps lookin' back. That fire looks smaller and smaller. It looks so far away, and then he don't see it no more. Way up in the timber he stop and listen. He hear a lot of noise comin' from that mountain, of happy people playin' and yellin'. That little boy felt good that he was not the only one out there in the darkness. So in his hurry to find these people that are havin' so much fun, he start to run. Sometimes he fall in the brush and hurt himself. At last he come to the place where these people were havin' so much fun.

"But he found that nobody was there. Just dark and alone. Some lost place, far from home, out there in the dark, in the timber. Little clearing, like. And there was a little rock in the middle, so he sat down on that rock.

"He look around wonderin' where all those people disappear to, and he see like a movement. Just out of the corner of his eye, and he turn to see, and standin' there was a lovely woman. She had long hair hangin' down her back. She lookin' at that boy, and she say, 'Welcome! We knew that you would come here and we been waitin' for you. When you grow up to be an adult, this will be your power: You will have that power to heal and cure the sick.'

"She so lovely to look at, and she speak with a real lovely voice. After she give instruction to the little boy, she said, 'This will be your song:

("'Walking along there clicking on the rocks,
Just clicking on the rocks . . . ')

"She told him, 'When you grow up and you help your own people, you will shut your eyes and get a vision of what happen to that sick person. You will tell that sick one, "Here is what happened. This is why you're sick now."'

"After the lovely woman give instruction to the little boy, she turn from him. She move like to go behind him, and he turn quick and see she just now the deer. She turn into a doe deer, so lovely, long ears, long legs, leap away and he hear her walkin' away in the dark, just clickin' on the rocks.

"Then he alone, starin' into the darkness. He see a grassy area nearby, matted down like a nice mattress, a deer bed, so he lay down on that. He's tired. He fell asleep.

"Next moment he felt warm heat on his body, he wakes, he opened his eyes and it's daylight. He jumped to his feet and ran home, he could see the way. When he reach home, his parents did not question him because they could tell he gained his spirit, his powers, and they know one day when he grows up he will be a help to his people.

"As time goes on this boy grows up. He's a teenager and he gentles his first horse, he kills his first deer, he spears his first salmon."

Grandma, zipping up her car coat in the chill of dusk, flapped the scarf in her hand in a gesture of impatience.

"So, yeah, he grows into a man," Charlene continued, speeding the story along faster. "He marries, he have a family of his own, now. As time went on, one day this man felt sick. He just rest and don't eat. He stay in bed two days, three days, four days. He started gettin' thin. His parents and his wife had a little talk and they decide they should get an Indian doctor to come and help the man.

"So this woman doctor come and worked on him. She gets the vision that years and years ago, when he was a child, an elder gave a gift to him. And she started tellin' every little thing that happen to him: Where he heard that noise of people havin' fun, how he ran to find them, how he was all alone but then the most beautiful lady in the world speak to him and give him instruction. And how this lovely person turn into a doe deer that leap away into the darkness.

"This sick man layin' there said that it happened so long ago that he felt maybe it was just a dream. He was so young when it happened. He admit what the doctor tell him was the truth.

"So the doctor advise him to give a dance, to have the people gather and have the Winter Dance. By doin' that, he is trainin' himself to one day be a doctor and help his people like she is doin' with him. And he's gettin' older, he's about in his late forties and early fifties when this came to him.

"So he gave that dance and they danced every winter for three, four, five winters. And he finally had that gift to cure the sick.

"So then one time down to Conconully one woman was dying," Charlene said, glancing at Grandma. Grandma *aaa*'d in approval. "She was in bed for so long, the people felt that soon she will die. They heard about this man that just became a new doctor, and they sent for him. A little party of people came over and asked him to come and help this sick woman. So he's a real doctor, now.

"He went over to doctor this lady. His wife went along with him and when they got there, she dressed him up to work. They had a rawhide over his shoulder down to his waist. On that he had four deer hoofs, that was the doe deer's hoofs. And to see him walkin' out there, doin' his dance to bring the power, those hoofs clickin' together, it bring to mind the doe deer walkin' around in the mountains.

"He put his hand to the sick woman's head, just almost to touch her forehead like this, and he get the picture in his mind of what happened. He told this sick lady that not long ago a group of women went to dig bitterroots, and while they were out there workin' in the tall grass, this lady felt a sudden movement in the grass. This scared her and she jumped away.

"She parted that grass with her *pícha* and she see a rattlesnake there, all coiled up, hissin' at her. That gets her so angry she took that snake's life, she beat that rattlesnake with her diggin' stick, she kill that snake.

"This new doctor tell her that there was a school of rattlesnakes nearby that saw her do this, and they went back and told their leader what happen. This chief of the rattlesnakes felt hurt. He start to have bad thoughts toward this woman, that she was just warned by that snake, but she take his life. She shouldn't have killed that rattlesnake. That is the reason why she's so sick now, because of those bad thoughts, which in time will kill her.

"The sick lady, she smile. She said that was true, what the doctor see, that's what happened. Now she felt sorry, she shouldn't have done that, but she was angry when she killed that snake."

At that point in telling an episode in her ancestor's doctoring career, she had to stop talking because a loaded logging truck came down the hill with its transmission brake flap-flap-flapping so loud we couldn't hear her. When it passed on down the valley, she finished by standing and saying:

"That doctor was so great that he took that snake's bad thoughts and washed them in pure water. Took 'em into his hands and washed 'em in like a bowl of water from the creek. He told that sick lady, 'Now I'll blow those thoughts back to that snake and set him free.' And that's what he did."

Grandma got up and leaned on her walker, gesturing to the rock picture with one hand, then started slowly down toward the road. Jim walked alongside her, not helping her but staying close, letting her grab his arm on the steep part. The oldest of the girls looked up at Charlene and asked, "Did that lady get well?"

"Oh, yes," Charlene said. "She live a long time after that."

18

It was late afternoon on a hot, hot day when I drove up from the Columbia River into the sandy hills bordered by endlessly rolling wheatfields with curving furrows contoured to the slopes. The end of a day of solitude looking for something in the basalt desert cliffs cut by the immense murmuring silence of the Big River going by. Dusty dryness of early summer, south of my usual haunts, so hazy with the great tropical wet rising from a river wide as a lake. Dark smudges on the horizon where massive tractors dragging gangs of disc blades turned over wide swaths of bare dirt, and fine dust rose up in clouds browning the edges of a baby blue sky.

Clayton had pointed out these hills once when we were driving by this area. Cowboys called this stretch of highway "The Sand Dogs," an area of dune sand held in place by scattered pines, bitterbrush thickets and huge clumps of Indian balsam whose tree-like scented roots sank away for yards with very little taper. This was glacier outwash sand that had been blowing for a thousand years up over the sloping edges of a basalt gorge from the banks of the green river below. The Sand Dogs were marked in my memory by the odd rock formations standing up like solidified black haystacks spaced randomly across the blowing barrens. These were some of the old people-eaters, Clayton said, frozen where they stood by Coyote decreeing for all time that they stay put. They were unable to chase down humans anymore, but this was still a dangerous place. I could feel its deep pull every time I drove by and looked up there.

My mother had tracked me down. She arrived by bus in the little apple-shed town of Tonasket, slowly walking the sidewalks leaning on a cane asking for directions and transportation out to the remote ranching valley where her long-lost son had finally settled down. I'd been driving to town myself when I passed Stuart in his pipe-rack pickup going the other way, waved to him flagging me down and backed up window-to-window to find him looking at me with an amused grin.

"I guess you know this lady," he said, already fast friends with the distinguished-looking woman in travel-worn catalog bush attire sitting with hands clasped on the cane standing up between her knees. My own mother with wet eyes to finally see me again, see me strong and healthy and burned by sun and wind and long cold winters.

Extracting a promise from me to bring her to supper at his place that night, Stuart loaded her and her suitcase into my truck, and I drove off, everything in my life abruptly changed. She was more fragile than I remembered her, recovering like Grandma from a fall that had broken her hip when she was irrigating her little peach and citrus orchard in the hills of Southern California. The sound of her familiar voice called up a world that had come to seem like another lifetime, the story of someone else's family and growing up. The hard thing that had always stood like a stump between me and the people I came from melted away in the determined, respectful way she spoke to me of life gone on without my presence. What had been in the way anyway? Something dangerous to them, something clinging to me that smelled of gun oil and uniforms and crowded bodies screaming and chanting and carrying signs. Something I couldn't quite recall but looked like a man running in the shadows, poisoning the lives of anyone he cared about if he let them get too close.

She told me my father was so ill he couldn't make the trip with her. She spoke of my cousin in prison in Arizona, my uncle dead after a barroom brawl over a woman, my sister married and her daughter already riding horses, a niece I'd never seen. I found that I cared about these people. My mother's heartfelt desire to remind me who I was and give me the opportunity to belong again if I wished stripped away my defenses. Her hand touched mine on the truck seat, and I

remembered that this was the woman who had suffered to give me life. Whatever I had done—and at that moment I remembered the FBI agent crashing into her house, stiff-arming her out of the way to get to me rising up from the dinner table—whatever I had brought down on their heads, nothing could change the fact that she had given me life. And had sought me out, still trying to breathe life into me.

Blinded by tears, I pulled off the road and wept for the first time since the day I landed in the Okanogan. My mother sat silently, crying herself. We stared straight ahead sniffing, wiping our eyes, unable to speak to each other.

"It's so beautiful here," she finally said. I'd pulled off by a marshy lake under a white bluff, and across the road orchard sprinklers ratcheted slowly around in circles, wetting the rich green shadows under apple trees. "I can see why you love it here. Your father didn't want me to come. He said to leave you alone, not bother you if you don't want to come back. But when he goes on one of his binges, I hear him out in the garage, like he's talking to you about going hunting. Men!"

She sighed. "I came to see you to make sure you're really still alive. A mother's feeling for her children never changes. Your father would have come when he realized I was going regardless, but he's just too sick. He won't tell me what the doctor said, but I can see it in his eyes. It's cancer. I don't think he'll be with us much longer.

"But now I've seen you and you don't have to play host for me. Stuart seems like a fine man to work for, but I know this might be awkward for you. This wasn't your idea, this was just your old mom popping in on you unexpected. The southbound bus goes by Tonasket again in an hour. I really can't stay long, anyway . . ."

But I kept her with me for two more days, feasted at Stuart's and visited with Grandma and Charlene who told my mother stories over coffee and Indian ice cream about this son who she'd seldom seen in fifteen years. And at night I'd listen to her breathing from the bed I made for her near the woodstove until she'd wake up to the sound of grinding wood, my pack rat chewing her way back into my kitchen.

And I wondered what I would do. Whether I could be any good to my parents. One thing was for sure. It was time to stop thinking about myself. They needed me, if only to know that I was okay after all, that I was in my right mind again, that I had a life worth living. It was the least I could do. And I found myself praying in the dark, voicing the pain in my heart that came burning through my chest like a hot breath, pleading with the great silent ones out there who ruled this waking world of day and night and wind and storm and moving bodies on the land. To help those I loved, to take pity on us, to heal my limping mother and take away my father's cancer and touch my cousin's heart beating in some prison cell.

The cry went out from my body like lightning striking my trailer and rain pounding down and hail smothering the lurking fearful shapes always there at arm's length in the shadows. There was nothing I owned, nothing I could sacrifice for those I loved but this body, this life, this breath. So I knew, finally and certainly, that I had been given some purposeful gift in life, and now I was on the brink of rediscovering it, retrieving it, embracing it. All the events leading up to this moment of Clayton about to send me on a mission added up. I had to be of some use to my own people. I would go into this quest as a sacrifice for my relatives. I would go into the hills crying for the sake of my mother.

The trailer had shuddered in the blast of a thunderous roar. It really was a lightning storm out there, and hail pounded the tin roof with a deafening clamor. I got up and opened the front door, standing just inside the deluge, heart pounding at the blinding flashes of lightning and unearthly bumping of mountains that made me feel small and fragile and exposed. But there was no question in my mind that my prayer was being answered, that the Thunderbirds were seeking out and scouring away and cleansing the wet dark world of any lingering demons. Crashing and booming with all the power of the universe, the hail turning to a biblical rain that flooded past the muddy front stoop, it rained down to give life to all of us and felt like all the blessing I needed to go forward in life.

"It's really coming down," my mother's voice said, sounding awed and oddly peaceful behind me.

"Yeah, it's really coming down."

And then I had driven her all the way to Wenatchee, the nearest town of any size where I could put her on a plane back home. I used up all my money but a little to buy gas to get back to Chopaka. When we hugged and cried one last time, she said, "I think something good is coming for you, Tom. I can feel it. Whatever it is you have here, hang onto it." And the realization hit me that even in her own physical pain, in her grief over the imprisonment of a nephew who had been like a son, and the impending loss of her husband, my father, she was thinking of me and trying to give me some hope. It was sobering. I hoped I could live up to her example.

On the drive back in late morning sunshine, my eyes had been drawn to the haystack rocks and the sandy wastelands where Coyote had tricked the *en'ahlna'skéluxtin*, the people-eating monsters of ancient times, and made them stand in stone forever. Even driving by in a pickup truck you could feel their animosity to humans. I was in a fey mood, not comfortable with this new self, this new family man who had come to speak in my voice and look at the world through my eyes.

Alone for the first time in days, I parked, got out, and went walkabout into the basalt cliffs overlooking the river so in flood only the tops of fringing willows wagged above the current. It was half a mile across here, where the Big River began to slow into a dammed-up reservoir, one of many that had been built to harness power for electricity, irrigation, and flood control. The deep green-blue water whispered in the cliff vault silence, telling me of always going by, always heading somewhere else. And I had been standing still so long, letting the good catch up to me, that my mother had caught up to me.

Moving, moving this body, driving myself up and over the rough volcanic hardrock layers, each bed of basalt set back a little from the one below it, cut by coulees and bare except for clumps of grass and cactus and brush. Sweating in the stifling heat, letting my body go free as sentient muscle and bone picking its way knowingly over the rocky earth it came from. Like a young boy thoughtlessly throwing his body into ceaseless, repetitive physical strain, immersed only in the doing of it, I bouldered and slickrocked and cliffmounted blindly for hours, only vaguely looking for something.

In other times like this, made to feel the real, somehow pried open like an unwilling clam, reminded of some wound that had never healed over, I remembered heading for a bar to look for trouble, a beer-haze revel of punching and grunting and rolling on a broken-glass floor. It did the trick of letting me forget for a time . . . But now I was a man someone needed, someone who had suffered and sacrificed for me. And that man who would kill or be killed, who took control with a vengeance, that man was biding his time and looking for trouble as I moved in a blur like a troubled animal searching the rocky reaches above the Columbia.

Who was I? Was I the boy who picked lilacs on the way home from school because he knew they were his mother's favorite flower? Or the man who leveled his rifle against another man's chest, telling him indifferently that he could back off or die, it was his choice? Was I the one his parents depended on during long road trips to study the maps and find the best way to where we were going? Or was I the night stalker who led a party of draft dodgers and deserters through driving rain across the border into Canada, threading the maze of shoreline rocks and barbed wire lit by spotlights right under the noses of border patrol officers sitting in a parked car drinking coffee? Was I the one who stood up to my father and made him stop beating us kids when he was drunk? Or the one so enraged by American military policemen in civilian clothes illegally dragging off a drunken deserter buddy in front of a Vancouver pub that only a cocked pistol in my face kept me from beating one of them to death with my bare hands?

Scuffing against the bare bones of Mother Earth for hours finally calmed me. I came out to one side of the giant wave of sand curving up and over the wall of riverside mountain. A high, rocky vantage point in hot wind, a place to stop and stare and wonder. I knew I was both those persons that clashed and struggled for room inside me. There had never before been a reason for them to make peace and work together. Now there was. And I saw them as different men meeting for the first time and needing to join together in some difficult enterprise, aware that they needed each other. They were ineffective or destructive without the innocent heart of one to temper the fearless fury of the other.

From this breezy, elevated vantage, beyond the dread black humps of haystack rocks, I could see the sand hills dotted with familiar scrubby trees. These were the dreamer hills that Clayton said were the retreat of power men and power women in ages gone by. So I wasn't looking for trouble after all. I was looking for something to make me whole. Something that came to mind in the form of a scrubby tree. A tree that protected and purified and remained unviolated. A juniper tree, the sacred cedar, whose smoke drove away and kept at bay the evil ones, the *kast xa'xá*, the ones who were drawn to violence and death and bad thoughts. From up there I could see a winding dirt road that approached the dreamer hills through the rolling wheatfields that covered the whole plateau above the cliffs. So I picked my way down the long, rugged, black descent to the river and my pickup truck below, holding in my mind the desire to find some juniper in those hills, some sacred smudge to smoke my body with and take home to keep me open and solid as I readied myself for going on a mission.

And that's how I found myself driving into sandy hills in the blinding sun of late afternoon, sweaty and sticky with dust, mindful of the dread feel of dull black rocky knobs getting closer. Then there was no more road and I got out to face south into the still, undulating waste of hot sand before me. I was ready to do anything to change what had been and be whatever it was a man was supposed to be in this life. Live it as it is. Accept it. Do something with it, before my time comes to be snuffed out like the deer I killed. Look for the threads of purpose in the weave of events. And I'd been doing that, and this is where it had gotten me. I had to go on. See where this path led me. Do it as awake and ready for anything as I could.

I began walking into the sandy expanse, conscious of the brooding haystack rocks I passed on my right, rounded hulking shapes that I could only squint at with the sun so blindingly bright on the horizon behind them. There was a creepy presence of unknown, unseen eyes that had held nothing but malice for all things human since the beginning of time. I could feel them insinuating their thoughts into my mind, hear their voices moaning on the wind that blew over them.

The hair on the back of my neck stood up. I experienced every step forward vividly, like the time I walked down the row of policemen in gas masks, the tactical squad called to my state college to quell a demonstration against the Vietnam War and liberate the administration building taken over by protesters. As he had then, the dark man inside me came forward, exulting in the taste of danger, so aware of the fragility of being alive.

Brush sparrows began flitting from bush to bush ahead of me, white wing bars flashing, leading me on. On the horizon ahead a dark spot on a certain hill caught my attention. Something drew me in that direction. The hills became dunes, with deep unexpected hollows I had to trudge through, losing sight of the dark spot on the horizon until I came over another crest. I continued on, the sparrows gone, the sun setting into a brown, hazy layer beyond the invisible river to my right like sunset in smog. When the sun sank out of sight a cool breeze sprang up that felt delicious on my overheated body. In growing twilight I waded on through the dragging sand, closer to the dark shape on the hill that now looked like a v-shaped scrub cedar. I could see other juniper shapes beyond, a scattering of sacred trees dotting the heart of the sand hills, a rare concentration of so many that I knew why dreamers came here—such encircling protection and power so close to danger. The nightmare feel of the haystack rocks faded as I approached the trees that defend humans.

Dusk shadowed the hollows but the last rounded hilltop was still in the light at the end of day, and from twenty feet away the old, gnarled, half-dead juniper, the object of my search, held my attention. A bird the size of a crow sprang from the branches and flew up, stopping me in my tracks. Heart pounding, I watched a hawklike bird circle with choppy wingbeats, a master of flight effortlessly looking me over a few clicks out. Then with a tlaaa! tlaaa! tlak'w! the falcon broke off and flew away low over the dune tops to disappear into the gloom. There were no words—only a knowing, a certainty of a gesture made to me, a yes! from the mysterious world at the moment of twilight. I took the last steps in a daze, then found myself leaning into the sour, cedar-chest-smelling branches of the juniper, feeling the scaly scratch of twigs on my face.

The fragrance woke me up. It would be night soon and I didn't want to get stranded in a place like that. Stuart had let me off for a few days to be with my mother, but I was expected early the next morning to irrigate hayfields. Besides, the haystack rocks still loomed to the west in gathering dark, and I knew people didn't come here to dream unless they had something, unless they were awake to the gift and using the power that would protect them. For me, that meant waiting for another time.

I spoke to the old tree, twisted and half-dead on the exposure of the hill, barely surviving the ceaseless windblown sand of centuries. I apologized and thanked him for letting me take some of his body for a good use. I knew he was male because junipers are either male or female, separate trees producing either pollen or berries. This one had no berries and I could feel the withered tips of male ends where pollen had been released earlier in the spring.

I broke off dead branches and built a fire. By its flickering light I broke off more wood and made a bundle, which I tied tightly together with my leather belt. Then I smothered the flames with green boughs and stood in the billowing smoke, letting it cover my whole body, letting the powerful smoke of *púh'nilhp* make me solid and of one mind and heart. Spreadleg over the coals, breathing smoke, I stayed put for a long time. Then I shouldered my burden and trudged slowly northward through the night. Protected by the reek of juniper smoke, I passed unnoticed, unmolested by the haystack rocks, back to my truck and the long drive home.

As the familiar shape of my pickup came into view in the starry darkness, I heard the first unearthly call of a poorwill, Shoo-MEEuh! Shoo-MEEuh! Shoo-MEEuh! It was the first one I'd heard that year, and I stopped to listen. Between long silences I heard the whistling phrase repeated for long minutes to my left. Then another bird called from a distance to my right. Then others in all directions, rising and falling as invisible birds wandered the sandy ground of brush and grass and stubbled fields hunting insects that came forth in the cool of night. Their call was haunting, unbearably heartfelt and sad, yet somehow stirring me to seek out something in the dark of night. It was the sign I was waiting for, the return of the *shumíx* birds Clayton said would announce the time for sending me on a mission.

Swinging my juniper wood into the back bed of the truck, I got in, started the engine and turned on the lights. Tiny bird forms scuttled along the ground in brushy shadows in the glare of headlights. Red eyes gleamed as they looked at the lights, then looked away. I drove slowly down the twisting road to avoid hitting the numberless kangaroo mice bounding across in front of me. When I got back down to the paved highway, I could smell the invisible river, the thick humid sweetness, and as I turned north and flew along the canyon highway in buggy darkness, I thought yes! I'm ready to seek out something in the dark of night.

19

Days later, I stirred from sleep hearing the wind blowing hard outside, shaking my trailer like a ship at sea. Making me smile. The tremendous blow outside brought an unmistakable message. It was time and I was ready. Nothing had been said, but I knew Clayton would come for me.

I lay in bed listening to the creak and shudder of plywood and tin, my fragile shell of a home being battered by a gusting, ceaseless outside force. The world was breathing hard, and I loved it. Soon I was up, sitting on my front step watching the sunlight grow and feeling the full strength of the wind.

It's a gale-force easterly, dry and warm, smelling of mountain forest and summer flowers. A mountain wind twisting and turning, coming from different directions, pausing, then battering everything in its path. But it steadily trends from east to west as I watch, listen, feel. How this little corner of the earth is always there for me when I wake up in the morning, how it now moves in the terrific wind gusting down the mountain out back, making the big pine out front toss and sway, tearing a swath through the orchard tree tops like an ocean wave, blowing on across the lake toward Chopaka.

The peak is crisp and hardrock gray, nearly free of snow in the first glimmer of direct sunlight, the lake dark and oily and lined with racing whitecaps. The apple orchard is a deep irrigated green, acres of shadowed, leafy motion, tall orchard grass bending, leaning, like everything else standing above ground, toward Chopaka and the dark mountains beyond. Everything pushed in the direction I'm going to be going.

Underneath the mindless euphoria of sitting out in the wind

there's a brooding sense of unfinished business. A life in a world I only dimly recall is pressing on me to make amends, make peace, renew the bonds of family, face the music. A page has turned, and it's all blank ahead. I'm going forth to live up to my mother's love, to make her sacrifice for me worthwhile. So I'm ready to go where the wind blows. If not confident, at least willing. For now, there is nothing to do but wait.

I'd trained Stuart's son Boot to change the sprinklers in fields of young alfalfa, and Larry Dubois was back, working alongside Stuart for a few weeks repairing fences and hauling salt blocks up to mountain pastures. I had no idea then that this was the beginning of the end of my association with the ranch that had made everything possible for me in my early years in the Okanogan. The wages weren't much, but the trailer was free, and like now, it wasn't hard to get off and do other things. So I could linger in the morning storm of dry wind, sprawled on the pine-board step like an old hunting dog, uncaring, well-fed, lazy, ready for anything, watching for something to happen.

A voice in my head says, "Here he comes," and then I hear a car coming by on the highway below. Slowing down and turning up my road. The familiar sputter of Clayton's old Ford station wagon, tires crunching on gravel, dust thrown up that is scoured away in twisting threads by the wind. He parks under the thrashing limbs of the lone ponderosa, off to one side of where people usually park near my pickup. I can see him sitting there at the wheel, door thrown open, not getting out, just looking around vaguely as dried-out bundles of pine needles fall at an angle from the tree, making little brushing noises as they strike his car.

When a thing happens as I foresaw, as I knew it would, there's such a solidity to life at that moment. Such a sense of rightness, of being more alive than usual. Of being exactly where I'm supposed to be.

Like me, Clayton is studying the world in the blast of wind, the stark details of hillsides, racing wisps of cloud, and wildflowers everywhere, moving points of color that catch our eyes. His head turns to watch the dust lifted and driven across the bare roadway between his car and my truck. Then he looks in my direction for a long time, unmoving, lost in thought. I can hear the faint hiss of his car's radiator and see the steamy trickle of wet onto the ground.

The long minutes stretch into half an hour of doing nothing. No wave of the hand, no voice calling out, nothing more than being present, being aware. Eventually I see him stir. He climbs out and leans against the far fender of his car, back to me, his short, gray hair flitting in the wind. Long minutes picking his fingernails, then his nose. The wise old Indian power man studies his finger, then wipes it on the car door, making me laugh at how when it's all said and done, we're all just human animals, living ordinary lives, doing ordinary things.

It makes me think of the words spoken by an elder, a poetically inclined, white-haired gentleman who spoke up at a feast I attended weeks before. Everybody crowded around tables, eating and drinking and visiting in the community hall. The elderlies would simply stand up and speak in clear voices, sharing their thoughts with everybody present, usually in Salish, and sometimes saying the same thing afterward just as beautifully in English: spontaneous, heartfelt and traditional speeches in the high-pitched, sung style so favored by the *Skélux.*

"We will be proud of who we are, as we did not ask to be born the man or the woman, we did not ask to be born the Indian or the White. Therefore, we accept ourselves, who we are, and what we have this moment. A handful of seeds, tossed on this earth, as now we see on the hillsides, the flowers, nod their heads when the wind blows. All colors, and not one flower is better than the next flower. We are like those beautiful flowers on this land."

I'm sitting on my front step and Clayton Tommy is leaning on his car, arms folded over his barrel chest, looking at the world. His eyes hold in the direction of Chopaka, so I look up and see what he's watching: A dark pancake of cloud beyond the summit, a flat, hovering smudge so different from the windblown white wisps scudding by overhead. Then as I watch, another flat rounded layer forms just above the first, and then another, and another. A rare cloud formation I suppose meteorologists have a fancy name for, it looks like loosely stacked tortillas hanging above and beyond the sacred peak, deep inky black between each layer, the outer edges crisp and fluffy white. Sometimes so sharply outlined by the rising sun that it looks solid, then it fades into vagueness, shifting to form yet another pattern of layers. The only thing I know about this cloud formation is that it appears when high winds blast against steep mountains.

Nothing can be so utterly, unspeakably beautiful as clouds when they form into shapes never seen before and never to be seen exactly the same again. And the stacked clouds hang only over the country behind Chopaka, the country I'm about to be sent on a mission into. Nowhere else in the sky is there anything like this dense hovering presence.

I get up and go inside for my light field jacket. The fan of falcon tail feathers hanging from a nail sways slightly to the windblown shift of the trailer. It occurs to me that Clayton is not going to say anything about the wind or the cloud. Little certainties pile up. As I have come to see for myself how the world speaks, moves in signs informing anybody who pays attention, he has said less and less about it. Doing things in concert based on those signs has become normal.

Back outside, buffeted by fierce gusts, I shut the door firmly, not knowing when I'll be back. When I walk to Clayton's car the hood is up and he's kneeling just inside the orchard, holding a sprinkler from turning, directing the stream of water into a plastic bleach bottle. He fills several bottles and comes back as I release the radiator cap. We stand there together, saying nothing in the glug-glug of filling the leaky radiator. His eyes say everything, liquid brown and alert, squinting to the blow of dust, taking everything in. Studying me without meeting my gaze as he slowly screws on the cap. Then only the slightest wave of his hand as he rounds his open door, gesturing for me to close the hood, load the bottles, get in.

But at the highway, instead of turning left toward the road that went up Chopaka, he turned right, and in a little while we pulled in at the Woods place. He drove past the doublewide sitting quietly closed up like nobody was awake yet, and through the overgrown pasture along the Similkameen River, still barely emerging from night shadows, then turned into the cove of rose bushes and pine trees where the new sweatlodge was built. And there was Jim, sitting in a folding aluminum chair by a rock-heating fire that roared sideways in the sweep of wind.

I could see that the rocks had been ready for some time and that he'd been adding wood as he waited for us. He stood and cleaned the rocks with a pitchfork as Clayton and I undressed in the lee of opened car doors. At the raised canvas doorflap, I recognized the torn green wagon tarp that had barely survived my sweatlodge retreat being used to cover the willow framework. Jim grinned at me, popping a handful of fresh *shía* berries into his mouth one by one like peanuts.

"Be sure and come back, dude," he said.

Clayton shooed me inside with his bluejay fan, then stood talking to Jim in Salish. At Jim's "*Aaaa,*" the old man kneeled and crawled in, joints creaking, to sit in his place beside the pit. From outside Jim cleaned out the pit with his bare hands, tossing the dry leaves and debris into the wind, then scattered loose sage and cedar into the hole. As glowing orange rocks began to roll in off the end of his pitchfork, the lodge filled with scented smoke, and as they piled up it grew hotter and hotter inside.

It was the first time since my self-training that we'd been alone together in a *kwílsten*. Clayton finally spoke to me, asking about my experiences fasting and staying awake all night out in the hills. We talked casually and humorously about how things went for me. But he didn't like the story I told him about the great horned owl brushing the top of my head. Shaking his head slowly, he muttered something in Salish to Jim kneeled outside, done bringing us the rocks, who responded "*Loot! Loot!*" with his head hanging, wagging side to side.

"But then, this have to be a mixed sign," Clayton said softly, measuring his words. "Since that owl fly from a juniper tree to touch you with that message of death. Some good to come with a death foretold."

It was a stunning interpretation. Something I'd never dreamed of since I hadn't made the connection between the Native stories of owls as messengers of human death and my own run-ins with owls. Instantly my thoughts turned to my father, and my mother catching up to me.

Jim handed in Clayton's waterproof basket full of river water and closed the mildewy canvas from the outside, plunging us into hot, stuffy darkness. There were only about ten rocks clicking and shimmering in shifting patterns at our feet, but the heat seemed to center on my face and head, burning my scalp even without any water splashed. Clayton took his time arranging the canvas, tucking and twisting here and there where faint daylight showed. Finally satisfied that we were in complete darkness, he sighed and began praying in Okanogan. At each naming of a natural power he sprinkled water with his hand, and bursts of boiling steam rushed up, each one hotter than the one before. He finished with *Sxwútl'i uhl Chu'pák'x*, Mountain Goat and Chopaka, pouring directly from the basket into a deep, awful raging from the rock pit, suddenly so hot I rocked back and forth in pain. We suffered the intense burn in silence, feeling it only slowly moderating as time passed.

Instead of singing, Clayton began speaking in the dark. He talked slowly about owls, about how sometimes they were what they seemed, big birds hunting silently in the night *(senína)*, but how sometimes they were messengers from the land of the dead, or the spirit of a dead person, or the guise of an evil-thoughted power person seeking out a living victim *(spá'tla)*.

My own experiences with owls up until the horned owl brushed my head had not prepared me for this. Owls had been, like falcons, just another creature out there in nature. I thought about the time one spring afternoon when I was climbing up a lava rock cliff in southern Oregon. I pulled myself up to a ledge and found myself at eye level with a barn owl stepping menacingly toward my face. With my hands and feet clinging precariously to clefts in the rock, my face was vulnerable and the owl seemed huge only two feet away. Hissing, wings held outstretched, big saucerlike pattern around the eyes staring at me, the owl came slowly towards me, claws scratching bare rock. I glimpsed the nest behind her, the fluffy cluster of newly hatched owls she was protecting, and I knew I was in trouble if I didn't move fast. Ducking below the ledge just as she went for me with her wickedly sharp beak, I bouldered with a burst of speed down and sideways and up another route. When I paused to look back, I saw the owl leaning out from her hidden home, gazing silently at me moving away, head pivoting on her shoulders to keep her focus on me until her face was turned all the way backward.

But as I listened to Clayton's voice in the dark, to his careful words broken by long pauses because it was so painful to breathe the blistering steam, I began to see that there was a seldom-talked-about lore about owls communicating to humans the kind of news nobody wants to hear. Like everything else, it was a practical lore, rich with the insight of generations of experience, grounded in actual events, and guided by the circumstances of an owl encounter to make accurate predictions and interpretations. A warning never came without other corroborating events—accidents, illnesses, bad luck or news from afar that made you fear the worst. And owls could be persistent, hooting every night in a tree outside your house, or following you wherever you go, even in the city, to make sure you get the message. Clayton told of persons he had known whose serious illness or death had been announced by owls.

In the disembodied, burning darkness I realized I hadn't told him or anyone what my mother told me about my father having cancer. I brooded, sensing in his muted words, his persistent monotone talking about owls as messengers of death that he was pushing me, seeking in his usual indirect way for me to make some connection, to make my run-in with the great horned owl personal. "So there's nothing I can do about it?" I blurted out, sad and angry and feeling defeated in my prayers for my father.

"*Aaaa . . .*" was all he said. I heard more water splashed on the rocks, felt it get even hotter. Clayton flapped his feather fan invisibly in the burning steam between us, saying nothing.

"It's my father," I said, my voice a sob. "He has cancer. My mother, when she came and found me, she told me he probably doesn't have long to live. I don't know . . . well, I guess I do—this good thing that she came all that way to find me. To have a mother again. But my dad—what can I do? I talked to him on the phone. He acts like nothing's wrong, like it's not even happening."

"*Aaaa*, this what I wonder about," Clayton said in the dark near me. "Yah, they come and they warn us. They see what comin'. How things goin' that way. Maybe die, maybe not. Depends. If the one they warn about keep goin' in the way they goin', not able to turn aside, then yes, their time is comin'. But can be change if it's not too late. That one that gonna die, he have to look at that, want to live. Seek for the other way to go in life.

"This how it go. We pay for what we do in life while we still here in the world. Not later, not like the Christians say, in the hereafter. No. They not lookin' at how it is, not see what right in front of their nose, plain to see. The heart attack, the fall that break the bone, the long time in bed. Not just some accident, some thing that just happen.

"Like the Indian sick with bitterness at what the White man done to us, suffer every day from the diabetes. Die that horrible death as his body stop workin' little by little and he just want to leave this world that have no sweetness for him. Or the White man eating away inside, nursin' that hurt, that resentment, that secret hate that come out in the way he talk like he gonna fight, he gonna beat that cancer! Letting those bad thoughts fester inside until it grow like a bad medicine, like the *en'ahlna'skéluxtin* eatin' him, eat his body from the inside.

"Maybe too late. Think what's the use? But we still breathin', we can look into it. Want to live, *en'hwl'hwl'tíls*. To have that want, to turn and look and ponder. Can't see if you don't look. Go to one who can see those kinda things, the Indian doctor who have that gift. Who say the words, who have that picture in their mind. How this came to be. What happen in life that bring on this time of going out of the world. Can be done. What that owl warn about, that what is to come, if that one don't do nothing about it."

"*Aaaa*," I said, absorbing the wisdom of his words.

"Old Willie, he talk about how our prayers cure our loved ones. Those powers, they hear us cryin' in the sweatlodge, cryin' for to heal the ones we so afraid gonna die. He say they do that for us, they go and do that, just what we ask. But many times his helpers come back, tell him that one don't accept that prayer. The one that do, that see what wrong and want to let that go, want to live, pray for hisself, cry for the want to live, then they can do that for the relative who pray for him. Cure anything.

"But see, if they not accept the cry of the relative, then those powers can do nothing. Can't help 'em. No matter what we do in life, if it not too late for our body, those powers can make our body to be good all over again. They have the power, not us. I seen that. Like to be dyin', but then all gone and get healthy again.

"That how it go. That one that gonna die have to see that. Want to live. Not pretend that what others do can really hurt 'em. Accept the prayers of loved ones. Want that for hisself. Not fight, no, let go of what killin' 'em, what been growin' so bad in their mind, their heart, for so long that now it take their life.

"*Wai i hwi.*"

He broke into song, a ridiculous Bluejay song with a grunting push-up, followed by lines mocking people's insincerity and secret desires, shaming words that sounded like Bluejay could see it all and had no pity for human weakness.

> ("You down there,
> You ate good food when we went hungry,
> Now you lay holding your guts.
> I'm laughing in the tree limbs,
> Laughing in the tree limbs. . . .")

Clayton kwash-kwashed his bluejay call, flapping the feather fan in time, and I joined in, laughing out the melody that aped the feel of more serious power songs, but trailed away in a gibberish that took the sting out of everything Clayton had said. We sang other songs, beautiful and familiar sweatlodge songs that had been handed down for generations, some of them the gift of spirits whose words we repeated that spoke of coming to where we were, to see us suffering and hear our cries and act on our prayers. We sang in the pain and hope of living, lifting our voices in unison as humans have since coming alive on this earth, until we were only in this moment, this dark burning heat, this thing of the heart that strips away everything else.

Clayton scratched on the inside of the canvas for Jim to open up, and there was the sudden rush of cool outside air, the smell of roses and the sound of birds. Such a relief to cool off. Such an entrancingly beautiful world out there. The bedraggled look of two men, shiny wet, lost for a few minutes in the glare of ordinary light. The sense of having been somewhere far away, because the ordinary appearance of things looks so unlikely.

Then he had Jim close it up again and we went on in the furious splutter of Sweatlodge speaking in a fiery voice, bathing us in a scalding breath. More songs, and the house lights come up, the familiar white glow, figures dancing in the void to the beat of driving rhythms. Clayton snapping his fan like a bird flying in the darkness, driving superheated air against my skin, enveloping me in a shroud of flame that draws me back from staring into the vague shapes of another world. Stay here and pay attention! Breathing each breath, feeling each beat of my heart, so willing and accepting and humbled that I hardly feel the heat any more. Awake to my own purification. Something great and brooding lifts away from me. I remember I'm going alone into the mountains behind Chopaka. I cry out, "*Kwun'kwanmíiiint! Kwu akskin'xítem!* (Take pity on me! Help me!)"

"*Aaaa!*" Clayton agrees, his voice hoarse and impassioned.

In the quiet that follows, the heat fades. I notice the stirring of ordinary things, the sound of a distant truck shifting gears, the steps of Jim moving around the fire outside, the slow murmur of the river. Clayton lifts the flap and Jim comes quickly, throws the canvas up, uncovering half the lodge framework.

We drift slowly to the river, bodies steaming in the wind. My hands touch the poison ivy we walk through, fingering the leaves I've been afraid to touch all my life. I'm indifferent to anything but the narrow world of experience in front of me. The banks of the river are muddy, my feet sink deep in the muck as I wade into the slow turning of cold water. That still feeling comes over me once again, how good and simple life is, floating in the current of a river. Turning slowly, breathing in life, watching clouds of gnats hovering in columns in the lee of shoreline cottonwoods rustling violently in the wind.

Climbing out, walking wet into the wind, I'm back where there's no thinking about anything; that welcome altered state where there's only observing, moving, absorbing. Moving as in a dream. Separate and different. The wind nudges, startles, swirls around my naked body, saying something. Oh, I see . . . The trick is to stay in my own mind, not go off as into a blackout. Look at the fire burnt down to coals swept by the wind, at the sweatlodge still steaming, at the fragile pink flutter of wild rose blossoms.

And here there's a memory of sorts, too. Of things seen, felt, done while I was here at other times. Things so clearly moving to a different purpose. Presences watching invisibly in everything around me. This moment will probably be lost, too, I think, sighing. The amnesia of everyday life. But when I'm here like this, I understand that everything that ever happened or will happen in this waking dream is compressed into an ever-present Now. A power to simply live, exist, breathe. I expect it to fade in the return of thoughts, of seeing Clayton dressing and Jim loading boxes and baskets of serviceberries from his car to Clayton's, of coming back to the flow of events and my place in them. But it doesn't fade. Jim drives away. Nothing is said to break the spell as I slowly pull on clothes so unfamiliar it's like enclosing myself in some kind of alien space suit. So unlikely, yet a ritual so deeply ingrained my hands and body slide and fit the cloth into place without my knowing how.

An understanding of things Clayton does comes right into my reverie. Smudging the inside of his car with cedar, strewing rose petals on the seat where I'm to sit to keep the ordinary, pitiful world at bay and protect me from dangerous ones that now have access to me while he drives me to the power of the waiting mountain. A morning sweat is utterly unlike an evening sweat, I see now. In the evening, after a day of ordinary life, the gradual opening up to where Sweatlodge is, crying for help in ordinary life's doings, so much to be pulled out, purified, that there's a sociable, scatterbrained, rueful return to life with people, food to eat, bed to go to. But a morning sweat is so close to dreams, to the silent wondering before ordinary things take hold. A sweat for taking action, for purifying what the day brings, for making me alive to the power that moves things. Making me and the day *xa'xá*. For taking hold of things like I am now. For going on a mission, sent by my elder, to what waits for me.

As we speed south along the highway, the world rushes past so fast that I only see a few things. The Sinlahekin Valley still in wind-blown shadow before the sun tops Palmer Mountain. The twitch of hairy ears that betrays a group of whitetail deer frozen in an opening of deep alder woods, staring at us passing by. The familiar one-handed way Clayton holds the wheel, steering around curves. The shafts of sunlight streaming through gaps in the hills, yellow, opaque, like gleaming solid bars. And sounds under the rush of wind, the clatter of a loose spring under the car, the distant moo of a cow.

Then there's a flash of movement to the left, at the very edge of my vision. I turn, but it's gone. I have only a fleeting memory of something vaguely seen. A large birdform in flight, shooting between pine trees. The falcon shape, the falcon wings beating so rapidly it's just a blur. So disturbing, just a glimpse way out on the periphery, and I feel something dropping, shifting downward inside my body. So jarring, I begin to brood on it, begin to feel it like a warning. Something bad. Something dangerous. But what? I begin to wish we could stop, could pull over so I could study this sickening feeling settling into my empty guts. But I say nothing, unable to break the silence, just stare straight ahead, unsettled, wary, expecting something bad.

Then a flock of bluejays flies across the road in front of us, kwash-kwashing in many strident voices, some almost hit by the windshield. Clayton recoils in surprise, hits the brake and pulls over onto the shoulder. My relief is instant. He turns off the engine and leans over the seat to dig in boxes behind us. Turns back with a mashed packet of Player's Canadian cigarettes. Finding one unbroken in the foil squares, he lights it up and blows smoke toward the fading bluejay racket uphill from where we're parked, black-headed blue forms fluttering from tree to tree. He smokes the entire cigarette with infinite slowness, not inhaling, merely blowing puffs of smoke out the window between mumblings in Salish. He gestures with the cigarette, offering smoke to features of the world around us, to things I can see and things I can't see. He pinches the stub, dropping pieces out the window, then starts the car and drives on, gradually easing up to fast again.

A mile down the road, near the intersection where we turn off to head up to Chopaka Mountain, an accident has just happened. Old man Rutherford was pulling a trailer full of hay bales in his antique International pickup truck too fast around the curve where the pavement drops down and turns sharply to skirt an irrigated field. When his trailer turned over, his truck skidded across the highway and took out twenty feet of barbed wire fence on our side. Rutherford's youngest daughter, Stuart's sister-in-law, had been following in her own pickup loaded high with hay, and she and the shaken old man are already dragging the scattered bales off the blacktop. Clayton slows to Rutherford's daughter strutting around in jeans and high-topped cowboy boots waving us around the debris of broken bales blowing in the wind, and the old man waves sheepishly to Clayton as we pass.

Up the gravel road that leads to Chopaka, Clayton said nothing. But I saw the placid look in his eye, the faint smile wrinkling his cheek. He was genuinely amused. He finally glanced at me several times, sensing I'd been shocked into everyday amnesia by the vividness of the wreck.

"That how it go," he said simply, smiling like the Cheshire cat.

What? Oh yeah—the falcon glimpsed, and then the flock of bluejays. Being warned. Acting on the warning. Use it or lose it. The cramped knot of foreboding in my guts, gone like it was never there. Replaced by a loose, spreading warmth in my chest. Something I remember detecting before at times like this, growing and making a home inside where my heart beats, growing in strength at each realization of how a power of the world was moving, informing me, clearing the way for me, offering itself for my use—if I heeded. Something hot and liquid, spreading away, like blood flowing from my heart. A sensation that now located where I acted from . . . or failed to. But I was learning. I wouldn't miss this one again.

Yeah, like going to school all over again. But this time instead of facts and argued-over theories and accepted rules that applied to everybody, it was what I personally experienced, what happened inside me, what happened outside to me, and what action this led me to that probably meant nothing to anybody else. All of which led to eminently practical results—like not getting into a car wreck, or evading capture when I escaped from the military stockade, or warning my friends when the Border Patrol was sneaking up on them. And there was Clayton Tommy, living it, modeling it, giving me the stories and the lore that awakened me to doing it myself.

The car overheated several times on the way up. Each time he stopped to let the radiator cool and add water from a bleach bottle, he sang his *shumíx en'kwaí'lm*, his power song, given to him by one of the forces of nature in childhood. Since nobody sang their song unless there was good reason to call in the power and use it, I could see he was keeping his car going up the steep grade on more than gasoline, spark plugs, and extra water. I couldn't help but feel humbled and grateful for all he was doing for me. But he acted like he was having the time of his life, like it was nothing but fun to be struggling slowly up the mountain in a car on the verge of dying. In that last steep mile, the old Ford barely put-putted along as fast as I could walk, Clayton grinning and patting the dashboard in encouragement, calling the car *Tlax'tlxáp* (Old Man). When we dropped over the edge of the bowl and down into the crowded lodgepole pines at Cold Spring camp, his car finally gained speed, and Clayton crowed, "*Nikhná, náxwt i in'kewáp!* (Goodness, my horse is running away!) His work done, to be let out to pasture, all of a sudden he in a hurry!"

The engine died and we rolled to a stop near where we used to camp when we hunted here in autumn. So lush and green in early summer, a chill, high-altitude wind making the lodgepole pines sway, and wildflower-fringed springlets of icy water bubbling out behind a split rail fence to keep cattle out. A low, severe roof of dark cloud overhead, but blue sky everywhere else, the morning sun climbing higher. The smell of wet charcoal and shrubby cinquefoil flowers in full bloom, looking like yellow roses. Whiskey jacks perched tamely on swaying branches to study us, silent gray jays wondering if there was going to be plunder for the taking in camp this time. That would be up to Clayton. This was my jumping-off place, the end of the road, where I would go on alone.

Clayton kindled a fire in the metal ring set on concrete provided by the state forestry department, tilted the cooking grate upward, and lined it with rocks to make a windbreak. I broke branches for his fire, working my way past a massive picnic table carved with initials surrounded by hearts and arrows, half hidden where somebody had dragged it under pines tossing in the wind. Clayton sat feeding a big fire, staring at the flames, leaving the camp set up for later. The back of his station wagon was so full of containers of *shia* berries, I knew his time waiting here for me would be busy with sorting and process-ing the new crop. Gray jays glided silently from the back window to nearby trees, already busy stealing and stashing the sweet-tasting loot. Through the window I fingered the mounds of berries so like blueberries, ranging in color from pale maroon to purple to near black. All stages of ripeness from the almost tasteless white innards of the maroon ones, to the tart, purplish, mealy perfection of the dark ones, to the black shriveled ones that tasted like raisins. It was tempting, but I just looked and smelled. Maybe I would break my fast with these fruits when I returned.

Clayton coughed, and I looked at him sitting impassively on the new grass by the fire. This was it. Separation. I went and sat across from him, to be close to the thoughtful old man who had become everything to me.

"Old Willie tell me somethin'," he said. "He have a dream one night not long ago. His power come to him and say, 'Look at that man over there, that White man who want to be the Native.' And he say he look and see you, but you just a little boy. You talkin' to a young man. He say he know who that young man is, who that *shumíx* is that offer you his gift. He tell me to tell you, he know you goin' to see that man out there where you goin'."

"*Aaaa*," I said, though it meant nothing to me. A young man? When I was a little boy? I was as blank as when he first suggested that I had some spirit encounter when I was young, way back when we wandered along Omak Lake.

"Don't matter how long it take, *Skélux*, could even be your time is over for livin' on this earth, maybe take you. Maybe that man comin' to get you. Some boy or some girl, all alone out in the timber, in the darkness, they face the same thing. No way to know for sure, all up to them out there. So—you as ready as you gonna be. Their want to know that you are serious. Not just pretendin', not out for a picnic in the hills.

"This the way we show 'em we want their help in life. To go to a place like those mountains there," he said, pointing with his chin toward the bare peaks to the west. "Way far away, all alone, wander in that quiet. Suffer for it. Not eat, not drink. Only when we all alone, sufferin', way out there where nobody go, that the way they take pity on us. See us make that sacrifice, wait for us to come to 'em. Show themself, talk to us, maybe learn somethin', come back with somethin'.

"That how it been since the beginning of time. This, what you do, not something new. This the oldest way for all people, yours and mine and all different kind of people. Ever since we come alive on this earth, this what we do to gain the help we need, the power to live like the real man, the real woman."

When he paused, I looked up to see him looking me in the eye.

"Maybe you think after all these years, after all I say to you, you maybe think I just kiddin' around. That this old man just foolin' you, just foolin' hisself. Just tellin' fairy tales, and maybe he know better."

Never had he stared me in the eye like that. I dropped my eyes to the popping flames, uncomfortably feeling his scrutiny. He said nothing, like he was waiting for an answer. I knew he wasn't kidding around. But I knew what he was getting at—the almost irresistible mass delusion driving the world I came from, where people think the world is only nuts and bolts, biology and reason, the agreed-upon deadness of natural resources and jobs and dollar bills he called "frogskins." And how that made my people and younger acculturated Indians think nature spirits and a spiritual government ruling the world was mystical mumbo-jumbo. Or came to Native religious practice confusing it with the ingrained ideas of a Christian god, or claiming it as the privilege of ethnic identity. Or assumed it was equivalent to Eastern philosophical practices, or supportive of their New Age beliefs.

I couldn't be sure I wasn't stuck in there somewhere myself, but I didn't think so. It was a tragedy of our times that our own Anglo sacred stories of living in a world of nature spirits had been so devalued and ridiculed that the term "fairy tales" was now how something was dismissed as childlike pretending. As fooling yourself, instead of keeping alive the true nature of life on earth. But I wanted more than anything else to be a real man, a man worthy of the blessings of earth and sky. So here I was, ready to risk everything on the conviction that the natural world was aware of me and ready to help me. If that meant that I would die in the trying up here in the wilderness, so be it. I had thrown away my life many times for much less worthy purposes.

I really had nothing more to say to Clayton. I was ready to be sent on a mission—there was nothing else for me to do. It was the next and only thing I faced at that moment, something I had to do before I could do anything else.

"I'm too old and ready to pass out of this world to be foolin' myself," Clayton finally said in a low voice. "Loved ones I grew up with, live life with, so many gone out of this world. Go ahead of me. And they say things before they go. They so close when their time come, they already half over there where they goin'. They see both—

this here, and that over there, what waitin' for us all." Again he lifted his chin to the western mountains. "They see those that went before them, the relatives come to welcome them.

"The ones that go like that, like my mother wastin' away in her bed from the TB, so pitiful to hear her coughin' all night long, they call to me, their want for me to listen to what words they have to say. And what they say, don't wait to look for the spiritual. Don't wait to live the spiritual. The spiritual is there, in all the things we do, in all that we see and hear and feel. Just full of it, if we look for it. If we have the eyes to see and the ears to hear. Always there, waitin' for us to take our place in it.

"This, from the last breath of those leavin' me," he said, his eyes looking far away. He sighed. "This, all of this, their last breath to tell me, we not kiddin' around.

"So you hear my voice as I talk this English talk, this White man's words, to take the time and ponder what you hear me say. I now send you where they goin' for the thousands of years, to do the same thing, and my want as you go, as you wander alone out there, you ponder my words. If the Native not foolin' hisself after all, then pity the poor White man. Pity the poor earth that give him life, that he treat so bad like he don't even belong here."

He dug in the fire with a stick, stirring and churning the burning pieces of wood with strong feeling.

"I see those videos the kids bring home. I look and I see in another way. All these movies about go up in the space ship, go to the moon, go to the stars. Maybe the White man, he the alien from outer space. Maybe he forget where he come from, been on earth so long, but now have that craving to go home. Never tell the truth about what he doin' to the earth and to the people who belong to the earth as her children. Just usin' everything up for hisself, wasting it, not thinkin' about it, not feeling it. Like to be always lookin' somewhere else than where he is standin'. Thinkin' about somethin' other than what his body is doin'.

"But then my nephew bring home one day the White man that love this earth like we do. That feel her touch, that see she is aware of us. That make me wonder. That give me hope. Maybe these strangers from some other world that take and squeeze and turn everything into something dead, maybe they have a change of heart. We will see. That what we been doin' all along, ever since your people came and took over things—waitin' and seein'.

"We all the same, *Skélux*. We all people. We all got the same inside. But just the few Whites like you to be the natural person, to think with the heart, to be real with others, to know who you are. Be down to earth. With the Whites, this so dormant. I think maybe too many generations they believe in a selfish god. Or maybe no god, no nothin', unless it's frogskins."

The wind rose to a gust that scoured sparks and burning embers away into the wetland flowers. Clayton was quiet for a long time as we stared at the fire burning fiercely in the metal ring. Finally he got to his feet and went to his car. He came back carrying his bluejay feather fan and a plastic freezer bag full of dried flat cedar.

"My want that you come back to us, that you be blessed by that one that give you the gift in life. That you come down from the mountains the power man, the man that got somethin'. The man that have the gift that others can see.

"*Wai i hwi.*"

He had me stand to the west of the fire, downwind, as he dumped half the bag into the flames. I was enveloped in the rich, cedary smudge, unable to see anything in the whiteout, feeling the brush of feathers and listening to his measured words in Salish offering me to the forces of nature. When the cedar burned away and flames swept up into my face again, I stepped back, gasping for breath. Clayton sat back down, hung his head and fingered the bluejay fan on his crossed legs. I turned and walked away into the timber.

20

From the moment I walked away from Clayton's fire, I held only one constant thought in my mind that I knew instinctively was the bedrock of being native in this world—that the natural world I wandered in was alive and aware of me. Nature held the power, had the greater knowledge, knew my thoughts, saw my actions, and demanded of me a respectful, heartfelt willingness to give up everything that supposedly held me up in life and let go into that outer void that seemed like death. Demanded it in an ancient agreement that if I did my part, then nature was compelled to yield up to me some part of itself that I could use to live more effectively . . . unless it was time for Mother Nature to take me back. Only if I was consciously, truly pitiful would those persons living to my eyes as trees, as animals, as winds, as mountains, take pity on me and reach out to me.

Looking back, I could see that I had been living this intuition even before I first laid eyes on Chopaka years before, when Jim Woods and I stopped at the border fence. And it had grown and gained strength and been fostered by my Okanogan friends until now I saw the true difficulty in it for a White man, or any person raised in the modern fiction of humans as the ultimate power on earth—it was not about pleasing me, not about exalting me. In fact, it was not about me at all, not the usual me I was familiar with. It was about whether or not I was willing to take my place in the true order of things. See myself in something like my proper size. Either the world was alive and aware—or it was not. It was that simple. In order to be where the forces of nature knew and did things, in order to hear them speak, I had to be where the natural world lived consciously, not where we modern people had come to live consciously, so remote from any but ourselves.

Without reverence for the source of my being able to live day after day, I would be living in denial of the facts. Persons just as alive as me had died to feed me all my life. Whether a plant, a seed, a nut, an animal muscle, a cup of water, or a breathful of air, it was exactly *there* that life had its most basic meaning. The idea that the earth and all nature supported me, fed me, fed us all, without being aware of what was going on was simply incredible to me. That trees and animals and rain and fields of plants grown for food were simply dead things, inert and without feeling, there to be manipulated for the use of the only creature supposedly capable of conscious life—that was the falsehood, the pretending, the delusion that was destroying life on earth for us all.

Without paying attention first in life to what nourished me, nurtured me, gave me all I really had, I would be living a lie. By purposely denying myself the essentials of life that come from nature, and going, suffering, into nature alone, I was sending a message that I gave homage to the source of my life, of all life, for the purpose of deepening that relatedness. Of making that bond more conscious, more clear, more the focus of my thoughts and feelings. Only then and there will the forces of nature reveal other sources of life for us. Powers that go beyond the pitiful rational limitations of our ordinary human makeup, a makeup designed for no more than basic survival.

Somewhere along the line I got an image in my mind—how in ancient times whole mythologies and cultures had been created out of the starving, suffering consciousnesses of humans wandering in a breathing world of nature almost devoid of their own presence. Focused where I was focused—on the sources of life. And what would come of it for me? There was no way to know. I was not the source. But by offering myself to the living source, maybe I would find who I was looking for—the one who had given me that little extra in life, that sensed power that Clayton had been awakening in me, that went beyond the everyday and had made me lucky—seen me unscathed through so many illnesses and injuries and unlikely escapades. And made hunting and wandering in the hills so easy.

This thing of the world being alive and aware—it was no abstract idea I held in my thoughts, no proposition to be tested. I was too far into the living of it for that. The pose of the White man who is simply curious and expects that if it's true, a blindingly bright revelation will come and find him, an eagle will come screaming to his quiet meditative seat on a hill and make him be convinced—what a laugh! If he's already the ultimate holder of the power of deciding what's true and what's not, what's real and what's not, then even if a force of nature took pity on him and made a gesture to him, he wouldn't see it for what it was. How could he? He is too used to thinking that everything out there is for his use and at his command. That it exists only to further his own life, to be the raw materials of his comfort and security, to be the source of his pleasure and edification and self-aggrandizement. As Clayton said to me more than once, "Them *shumíx*, they go right by the man like that, don't even see 'em. Like they not even there." Well, of course. If you see nature as dead, inert, incapable of conscious awareness, then that's how nature must see you.

No, it was not an abstract idea, it was something I had felt in my bones all my life, but only now was it in the foreground of everything else. A man could give lip service to how the natural world is alive and aware, and still not do anything in his life that demonstrated he lived by it. Or was willing to die by it, which was something I was reconciled to as I left the world of humans behind and headed for the summit of Chopaka Mountain. Sweating and fasting and staying awake all night had prepared me, given me a taste of what it would be like, had hardened me. But there's nothing quite like the privation and exposure of high mountains, moving on two legs over rugged country without eating, without even one drink of water from all the streams I waded, for days and days, to bring a person face to face with how weak and fragile we really are. And how dependent our minds are on the illusion of continuing, of living on.

At first I wandered in country that was at least familiar—our autumn hunting grounds—and I had the benefit of being so fit and well-fed and alert and willing that I took in everything like a scout on recon. If these were my last days on earth, then I was going to be who I was to the hilt.

Every time I return to the high country it takes me by surprise how different things are from the lower elevations. There's a biting clarity in the sunlight that sharpens the edges and colors of every-thing, and makes the lowlands seem dull and lifeless by comparison. Every tree, every rock, every flower and bird and cloud has a discrete, singular presence that speaks of unfiltered, blazing sunshine, harsh winds, brutal winters.

Up here there's little sign of human presence, almost none of the symptoms of human destructiveness so obvious in the lowlands, even in the remote valley I live in. Knapweed-infested pastures where cattle have trampled the life out of the ground, lake shallows choked by infestations of Eurasian water milfoil, orchards reeking of chemicals sprayed so often they're devoid of insects, miles and miles of weedy, washed-out stumplands where most of the trees are gone to make buildings and houses in cities. Air Force fighter-bombers screaming over a few hundred feet above hayfields because there are so few people to complain. Paved roads and cat trails, fences and fields, sewage and smoking dumps, all absent up here where the forms and forces that make it all possible are still going about their ancient ways, largely unaltered by the White man's madness.

Within a mile of Clayton's camp I came out at timberline on the backside of the sacred mountain and moved slowly up the steepening ascent. The dense black and white monotony of lodgepole pine forest gave way to open stands of spruce and alpine fir carpeted underneath

with shooting stars and fairy slippers, mats of glossy green kinnikinnick and gin-scented ground juniper, tangles of thorny gooseberries with transparent green drupes hanging with shriveled trumpets. Springs bubbling over mossy rocks through gardens of wildflowers, the fleshy kind that live in waterlogged ground near the roof of the world—marsh marigolds and spring beauties, yarrow and paintbrush, twisted stalks and lilies of all kinds, roseroots and monkeyflowers, bluebells and penstemons and phacelias. All crushed so easily underfoot. Cattle trails and tracks and droppings even up here. Scores of trees chewed bare about four feet above ground where porcupines stood on packed winter snow eating the inner bark. Shadowed, boggy ponds ringed by spruce trees with roots alive in water. Spruce grouse standing motionless as if invisible, stepping tamely aside only when my line of walk would come too close. Young, bushy spruces torn apart by bucks scraping itchy velvet from new antlers.

Up the open rocky slopes, the gray hardrock screes of Chopaka, I come to the last trees of all, whitebark pines standing alone, some burned by a long-ago fire to a bare, black glitter. The exposed bare rocks, loose and angular, are scabby with lichens, hiding the odd quartz rocks glowing rose-orange in the shadows. Charcoal black and fluorescent green lichens crust the boulders, crust all the rocks, except where individual trees burned down to scour the rocks bare around them. I climb into the center of a cluster of bleached-white pine skeletons, and find half exposed in the weathered charcoal a fist-sized smooth, round rock of white quartz. Another questing stone, I muse, and am answered by the arrival of a flock of gray jays on the wind, their tame, mewing calls coming from bits of feathery flutter clinging to bare branches above and around me.

I continue up the dry slopes of sulphur flower, spirea, and aster, until I come out on the flat areas just under the very summit and wander the rank and swampy-smelling areas like coarse, wet pavement, threading a maze of jutting boulders and low, mounded patches of elfin forest. Alpine firs and whitebark pines sprawl in long, wind-blown tangles no taller than me. Some stand in the lee of boulders, vertical, tapered trunks only six feet tall, with limbs streaming away in only one direction. Others are completely prostrate on the rocky ground, a twisted trunk, snaking among flattened mats of boughs, that twenty feet away finally rises up a foot or two with tender new candles braving the wind. In still, sheltered places scented with balsam are deer beds on mattresses of wildflowers, grass, moss and rare plants I've never seen before.

I work my way around the mounded piles of rocks standing up above all else, the very topmost peaks, one higher than the other, bare of anything but a fierce east wind huffing in the crevices. We who know who has the power in the world don't stand on the very top. Off to the east side I pick my way with thoughts about the arrogance of mountain climbers scrambled by the rarefied air. Down a long sloping bareness, I lean into a cold wall of wind, and as it opens out, the view is incredible. An endless sea of mountains in every direction except the southeast, beyond Moses Mountain, where the haze of the Columbia Basin disappears into flat nothingness. I come to where the mountain falls away into the abyss of the Similkameen Valley and stand at the top of avalanche chutes that go all the way down, six thousand feet, to the flat valley floor below, where the river snakes around in looping slowness. Hardly able to squint into the wind and see my familiar world in miniature below—the sagebrush flat where Jim and I crossed the border fence, the Woods family doublewide by the bend in the river, the lake silvered by racing winds, the green squares of orchard, the rounded, resting-animal shapes of the lower mountains, the road by my speck of a trailer—seen in the silence of hiking short-breathed at high altitude. The drag to a halt, ears finally popping open into the ceaseless roar of wind. The tug of home and hearth so far away, glimpsed now in blank lassitude, in oxygen-starved shallow breathing as I lean against a rock so as not to be blown over. Thoughts float by.

One comes by that looks oddly appealing. I'd heard about a local community action group down in the county seat, a social services program that was looking for a rural outreach worker, somebody to serve the northern part of the county that is spread out below me. They wanted somebody to bring government programs to people with not enough to eat, poor transportation to medical services, trouble paying high utility costs. I had never thought about such things. But maybe if I went and did that, I could be of some use to my people. Use my years of college, my ease in talking to all kinds of people. Maybe re-enter the world I disappeared from so long ago that I could only see it from a distance, the way I was looking at my valley home below. It seemed unlikely, yet I could see myself doing it.

Then I saw the mountain goats looking at me. Closer than I'd ever been to them before, six or seven stand in a strung-out group on the other side of a ravine from me. They seem unafraid of coming close to me, as if they knew what I was doing up here. Dull white shaggy animals, hump-shouldered, stock-still, with black backward-curving horns, beards blowing in the wind. The adults, motionless, stare at me, and the restless kids break into sure-footed play on the vertical wall of rock, their little bodies mostly leg and hoof, leaping six-foot gaps carelessly, bounding over the perched skeletons of prostrate trees for the fun of it. I look into the black eyes of adults gazing levelly at me and I hear Clayton's words the day I met him, talking about Chopaka and the goats going across cliffs, like walking on thin air: "Them goats speak for that mountain, tell us how we gonna live. Always watchin' out for us."

A feeling of gratitude washes over me, and I blurt out to the silent bearded faces studying me: "Yes, *aaaa*, thank you, *limlemt*, *sxwútl'i*. I'll go look into that, when I'm done up here. Maybe you know better what I can do. I'll look into that work . . ." Stilted maybe, but straight from the heart.

The mountain goats turn aside, move slowly with the wind toward the summit behind me. Their smell suddenly strong on the wind, I'm reminded how their meat is too musky-tasting for Whites to care for it though I've heard it called "Indian doctor food" by more than one Okanogan. Living up here in the most precarious, rugged heights, they hear the mountain's thoughts, passing them on. Big-bodied, sure-footed wraiths in the timberline clouds, in the fiercest winds, going about life, finding food, raising young, wandering in families. Doing the same things we do, but in such a powerful place under such perilous conditions, no wonder they know the power way to live. One slip and it's a mile to the bottom there.

When they go out of sight, I heave up and go on. Around to the north of the summit, then west. The wind behind me now, pushing me down the rounded, grassy ridges leading away from Chopaka. Down to where the air is less thin, the ground rolling and less steep, the high ground leading northwest, following open ridges lower than Chopaka but still higher than all the country roundabout. The sun of afternoon finally fading into the gloom hanging overhead, the low roof of cloud still there, but spreading and dissipating as the wind loses force. Light loses its sharpness, rounded summits seem to fade further away, becoming indistinct in the shadowless distance. Tramp, tramp, tramp, the steady mile-eating pace of a man on two legs, going off into the unknown.

But then I come to the freshly repaired barbed wire fence that marks the international boundary. Looks like winter snows really do a number on this cow barrier. A well-trod path paralleling the fence on both sides—made by U.S. cows on this side, Canadian cows on that side. What a laugh, this imaginary straight line foisted arbitrarily across the rugged high country. Then it hits me, and I laugh out loud— how ironic! The border runner who has crossed this line so many times, charged up like a commando going behind enemy lines, and here I am instead going peacefully parallel to it, following it into that wilderness ahead on a solitary quest.

Soon day comes to an end, and the fence is more on the ground than strung from post to post. I cross the remains of the fence many times until I don't see it anymore. I go into timber in country I've never been in before, though I've seen the peaks from a distance. The boundary here is only a twenty-foot-wide swath cleared in a straight line through forest. Somewhere beyond a high divide, I realize it's so dark I can hardly see anything.

Through the dark, dark timber, I am barely making headway, feeling with each step for the ground, walking aimlessly now, vaguely downhill, wherever my feet lead me. Such an utter, moonless dark in the heavy conifer forest, only the faintest glimmer of stars showing through the murk of sky, the wooded stillness without a breath of wind. And the same pinpoints of light seen in the sweatlodge flicker at the edge of my wide-eyed, unblinking, almost-blind vision. Spirit lights, motes streaking by, flashes of deep blue, startling red, garish yellow. Only when I stop and sit against the wide trunk of a tree do I cease trying to find my way, and turn inward. A familiar smell seeps from the rough bark of the tree that supports me, the smoky tang of Douglas fir. One of my old friends.

It may be the short nights of northern summer, but it's a long night for me, trying to stay awake in the endless drift of dark. Nothing to do but watch, listen, ponder. This could be my last night on earth. Long hours of dreamy wakefulness, marking every sound, every shift in the endless flow of nothingness that exists out in the bush without our knowing, until we're out there in the middle of it, witnessing it. Ready always for something, somebody to reveal themself. So cold in the wee hours in my light field jacket that I breathe deep to still the shivering, but at least there's no way I'm going to fall asleep. A rough night passed with groggy attentiveness to every whisper or creak, and even colder in the dim gray visibility of first light. How the sky brightens but doesn't penetrate to the forest floor, a pale suffusion of something to come—false dawn.

And then the real dawn of day surges up, bringing everything into focus, and I look around, make out the great shaggy trunks of ancient fir trees around me. Come to realize I've spent the night in an old-growth grove of firs, sitting in a cove of gnarled roots exposed above the duff, my back leaning against a great elderly of the mountains. Soaring above me, huge limbs reach out to touch those of other trees, hanging thick with the wispy beards of Coyote-hair lichen, the moss that the Okanogans cook into black pudding. High up, most of the trees fork into two trunks, looking like giant tuning forks reaching into the sky. The topmost boughs begin to sharpen into pink light as the first rays of sun touch the world above me.

Squirrels and birds begin their morning songs and the stir of breeze filters down into the forest. To hear the wind moving, rustling a distant tree, though the one I'm under is not moving . . . will this be the last time I notice that? Stretching cramped legs and a sore spine, body twisting and tearing up the musty fir-needle duff, rolling around in the dust of the earth that drifts up into shafts of morning light. Gathering strength for another day in the church of dirt. Time to go on.

It's so hard to put into words what happens when we're out there starving, thirsty, sleep-deprived and having lost the thread of everyday life. How do you write about something so far from the ordinary experience of life, so far from where words live so easily that we use them to share a sense of being in the same world together, and describe how things came alive that only I saw? Words fail not just because language doesn't cut it, doesn't even come close to evoking the sense of being so lucid and yet without thoughts, of having lost a grasp of the familiar flow of time and space. Not just because words can only hint at what it's like to be lost in direct experience below the threshold of thinking, and only the crocodile brain knows what's going on. But more because when the veil lifts and things come through directly from the conscious world around us, it's more real than the second-handedness of words can approach.

Out there, far from the familiar certainties of home and work and everyday experiences, there's a silence so vast it swallows the sound of our own minds thinking. Out there, something happens to us that's so vivid and so intimately personal, only with someone who's been there himself do we find it possible, feel free to share a little of what we saw, of what we lived at the very edge of death. And with someone like that, very few words are necessary to call it up and go back there together . . .

"When they left me there, the mosquitoes were so bad my sweat was bloody. I was so . . . desperate. I wouldn't give up."

"It got so slow, maybe one breath every step. Just that breath kept me alive."

"I forgot about food. Water took longer. God, I was so dry my gums shrank back, I could feel the roots of my teeth with my tongue."

"They told me I had to stand there in the snow the whole time. After a couple of days my hips hurt so bad, like two rocks rubbing together. There was this little bulge of rock, right there to one side like this, so I'd lean against it and get some relief."

"I was looking someplace . . . someplace I remembered looking way back, when I was a kid. Like, it's always there, but I stopped looking there so long ago, I'd forgotten about it."

"Well, it was just like what's there, the land how I see it, where it meets the sky, but it came alive and crawled."

"And there's this guy looking at me."

"So horrifying, that I'm looking at what's under the earth there. And I realize my heart's not beating, I'm not breathing. I'm gonna die, or I'm already dead, but it's okay, cause I saw how everything moves down there."

"It rained the whole time. Wet through, just huddled on the ground in my blanket. Thunder so violent, like the war, booming, but so beautiful."

"What did he say? You know how they talk, like not words but you know what they're telling you. Something I can never forget, but never say."

"I didn't think I'd cry like this to talk about it. It was like . . . so crushing. It was like when the fighters went over and the napalm went off . . . and it burned the sweat off my body, crinkled my clothes. But I was still living. That grateful, I guess."

"It's in here, now, right here in my chest."

"I'll think, God! life is so good. I'll cry about nothing. And pow! like roaring in my ears, and there she is. Way off, but coming. And I'm right back there."

"And sometimes I'll feel an itch on the insides of my thighs. Right where you squeeze a horse to ride. And I gotta get up, go walk, be out there alone, dance around. Because he's around, wants to show me something."

"After I been there like that, nothing's too hard in life anymore."

"Who ever heard of that? Three of 'em came out of the trees and walked right up to me. Like they knew I wasn't goin' nowhere and they wanted to see why. So I just cried about grandma to 'em."

"When I came down, got back, I seen why they let me in on that. Showed me that stuff. Things lined up."

"Now I gotta do things different. That's what they said. No guns, no metal around me. That way I'm fine. Took me back to that time I had the pistol barrel in my mouth, gonna end it all. Same taste of metal. And they just say to me, okay, you can come away with us now, or you can stay alive and do what we tell you."

"They see something when I can't. Like Darlene, she says to me, 'How did you know Dad was going to lose his leg?' It was up there, they just showed it to me."

"I come down and it all looks the same. But it's never been like before. I can see something like moving behind everything."

"So I put it off, makin' that thing I saw him carryin'. But when the wife said we're through, took the kids and went to Seattle, I quit work and moped around. So I went around, scrounged up all the feathers and beads and stayed up all night makin' it just like I remembered. I was just going to bed at sunrise when she drives up, says she changed her mind."

"My grandma told me we all went around with like this blindfold over our eyes. We couldn't see it for how it really is. Out there I got a peek around that blindfold and saw that she was right. Oh, I just cried. I never really believed all that stuff she told me when she was alive. But everything she told me was true."

"I never heard so many voices coming from so many directions, but they all told the same story."

And the silent eyes of the guys who went there but didn't get anything, listening to our talk, staring into the fire. The ones who sipped the rain water puddled in their blanket, or slept, or sought out the shade when the sun was too hot, or chewed leaves or berries when the hunger was too unbearable. And the even more pathetic ones, the guys who went out there for the sole purpose of having a visionary experience, who sat there for days and nights waiting for it to happen, who toughed it out to the bitter end, only to come back and say something like, "Nothing happened. All that time, and nothing out of the ordinary happened." These were the guys who always got a good night's sleep, even out in the bush, curled up on the ground. You snooze, you lose.

Because without sleep something comes to a stop inside. I'm just there in my body, but I struggle to keep walking, keep looking, keep crying for something. Days and nights, dark timber or bright rocky summits, hot sun or cold wind, walking vaguely westward or sitting and staring at the world around me. My body becomes something unfamiliar, a sack of bones and meat, skin like parchment, so dry I can't even smell myself. At some point I cease to remember directions and go toward whatever attracts me. Always I'm looking for someone, questioning the enormous leaning spruce tree, the rushing stream, the herd of bighorn sheep turned to stare, the muck-smelling surprise of a beaver dam, the sky always arching overhead . . . asking if they know who I'm looking for.

Voice cracking, can I even sing the songs? They wheeze out of me, and I sing so the world can hear me, can hear me, can hear me . . . What was that? Something answering me? A throaty something bumping along the tops of mountains. Something long and dark on the horizon over there. A slate black wall coming to blot out the sun, coming towards where I stand on this bare hilltop. Flashes of lightning so fast I can hardly see, curling and twisting around inside dark clouds. Here comes the powerful one that hits, *suk's'skúm*. My knees buckle in the fear of lightning, and I sit, unwilling to move away, seek shelter, but unable to stand up to such a deadly power.

The thunder grows louder and louder, the sky splitting open in the invisible battering voice that sweeps over the land and over me. The squall line approaches so fast, like vaulted billowing interior worlds, tufted edges, deep dark holes, flattened streamers, flashing electric eyes that spit from the vague blot-out above to the tunneled blackness below, where the land disappears into the sweep of a wet curtain. Something muttering and hammering in the distance, falling down toward me, then thundering right through me. The air comes to a halt, hovers, but I hear wind in the distance. The first outliers of storm race over above me, scudding blots of inky fog twisting over themselves in the furious push to somewhere.

I cry out, "Take pity on me!" just as the wall of wind blasts me. I'm stung by bits of hail mixed with dusty raindrops, the curtain sweeps over me. A blinding flash of enraged light, a hissing vacuum in my ears, my hair stands on end, and there's an invisible slap on my thigh, like someone's open hand striking me. *Su'u'wíkist* claims the hilltop where I sit, stabbing so close there's no sound. I'm in your hands, great one. I'm shaking in my boots at your power to kill me.

I'm just this little body here on the earth. It's up to you. See me—I'm ready for whatever you decide to do with me.

Knowing I could be struck by the lightning bolts as thick as tree trunks standing for split seconds all around me like strobe-lighted columns of atomic force, I go still inside. Death is right there, and there's nothing I can do about it. Everything sizzles in a blinding, soundless brightness, like a nuclear warhead going off, and I feel every ounce of me draining out in a rush. Then there's nothing.

Then something winks back on, and I'm back in my body, only I'm lying on my side, pounded by the full force of a monsoon rain, like lying under a waterfall. My cheek rests in the flow of muddy water, and I smell a smell I've never smelled before—sulfurous, burning, acrid. But I'm alive, and I see the flashes, hear the thunder behind me, the great one moving away, moving on. My thighs feel paralyzed, and the place where I felt a slap now burns with a pain like someone hit me there with a hammer. My jeans are smoking. I'm unaccountably laughing, sobbing, so startled to still be here on earth. When I stretch, move, try to sit up, my thigh muscles go into spasms, so I just lie there, wallowing in the rain and mud, squeezing and massaging the knotted, cramping meat with my hands. As the rain slows and the thunder recedes into distant muttering, the feel of little crowded animals squirming around in my thighs fades.

I sit up, soaked through, my legs weak and sore, to marvel at the world scoured and cleansed and purified by the passage of the storm. The ground steams in the first return of sunlight. The rain stops and a breeze moves the drifting fog over the hilltop, opening and clarifying a sweet-smelling world so wet and fresh and beautiful. And far to the east where the back of Chopaka is lit up by pastel sunlight, a rainbow gleams like wet light, the ruff of the earth serpent revealed for all to see and wonder at. The earth so touched by the thunder power's purifying passage that for a few moments the deep power of our mother glows on the surface, arches up and hangs looking at the sun.

"Who are you?" I say to the windblown tree whose fragrant, piney boughs I walk into and let brush me with long green needles. Standing by itself on this ridge, apart from small groves of stunted trees here and there, not much taller than I am, but with long, sweeping limbs reaching out and up into the sunlight of midday. Thick bundles of needles, ranked in bunches at the end of flexible branches like worn-out brooms, waving in the wind. The short, leaning, twisted trunk covered with bark so silvery-white and smooth, yet having a maroon cast around furrowed edges . . . and my mind rises up out of the void of silent knowing, into the business of conscious thought, prompted by my desire to put the pieces of the puzzle before me together. Oh yeah, whitebark pine, that's what we call you—the rare one who lives only up here on rocky, stormy summits. We have to gather your cones and break them open to eat your nuts. Because your cones don't open, ever, you just drop your cones still closed tightly. Until slowly your cones decay, weather away, rot open, and your little ones are free on the earth.

I finger a cone, remembering the raised points on the scales. Study the long glossy green needles, smell the familiar sweet scent, find the faint white line along the length of each needle. Yes, this is you. But who are you? How is it you live like this in the world?

I sink back down to where things just are. I look at where the tree comes up out of the ground. I see him/her buried to the waist, only the upper body above ground, arms stretched out to the life-giving sun. Lower body hidden deep, knees barely showing here and there as twisted roots exposed over rocks, locked and holding on and drawing life from the earth. Right there at your waist, at the ground line, that's where your navel would be, if you had one. That's where you were born, where your seed broke open and you grew down and up.

I sense the living presence of the pine tree I'm touching. So much older than me, and your kind so much older than humans. So deep

and silent and never moving from this exact spot for an entire lifetime. Like a child asleep and not noticeably breathing . . . is the child
alive? Parents know the certainty that passes within them, that tells
them yes. And why should this ancient power of the earth speak to
me? I'm one of those creatures who cut down their upper bodies, kill
them and slice up their flesh as boards, use them thoughtlessly in
the building of millions of houses.

I can feel someone looking at me. Someone hidden staring at me,
and I go deeper, deep into that place where my eyes touch the world
at the periphery of vision. *Wík'wst . . . La'kín! La'kín!* Yes, something is watching me, some equal presence regarding me. Touching
me with its attention. Scanning the vagueness, I'm drawn to look at
a deep shadow beneath wind-pruned lodgepole pines. My eyes hold
on the dark place so impenetrable because the sun overhead is so
bright. I shade my eyes with my hand, and the shadowed place begins to reveal shapes and details.

Then I realize I've locked eyes with someone there in the shadows. Dark, liquid, unblinking eyes. The amorphous shapes and patterns arrange themselves into a strong male body at rest, an enormous rack of antlers in velvet, the summer-rufous hair, the moist
black nose. One of the great fathers of the mule deer, resting in the
shade during the heat of noon, and he's been there, watching me from
twenty feet away, ever since I walked up into the branches of the
whitebark pine.

But it's hard to stare into his eyes. It's like the grappling of invisible power beams, and like there's something behind his eyes, reaching across into me, behind my own eyes, examining who I am. Yes,
it's me, the one who kills your children and eats them. The words
form and my mouth moves in a whisper, "*Aaaa*, thank you . . . for
your many gifts of food. This is me . . . the one who gives you a good
death. I guess you know . . . I'm not eating. Not looking for deer to
kill. Do you know who I'm looking for?"

The buck visibly relaxes, breaks his gaze, turns his regal head aside. Ears flutter to the buzz of flies crowding close, the same flies swarming around my face. He rises up to his feet, turns and slowly walks away, such power and muscled grace, velvety antlers turning this way and that, casual and unhurried, and before he's out of sight, something tugs at me. I follow him. . . .

Something like biting gnats, no-see-ums or mites have burrowed into my ears, making me scratch them at bloody, swollen places. I don't think about it—I've done this before out in the hills—I simply pick yarrow greens, mash them to a grainy pulp between rocks, add some of my precious spit, and apply little poultices to each raw sore on my ears. The itch goes away and I forget the dabs of yarrow. Later I wonder, what are these stiff, dry, scabby things on my ears?

Sometime in the night I can't take another step. I sit down on the game trail I'm following and rest my back against a boulder the trail skirts. Pull my collar up and bury my hands in pockets against the chill settling heavily here in a wet creek bottom. It's so late in the night that the handle of the Big Dipper has gone from vertical to almost horizontal. The trail threads through dense streamside thickets and trees that like water. The wet cold of summer night in the mountains sinking to the bottomlands like this, forming a dew, making my slow breaths visible.

Lapse. Staring blankly, listening, feeling. I look up and the constellations of autumn are rising in the eastern sky. Can't be too long before dawn comes. Lapse. So cold and still at this almost dead time of the night. I'm here. Where are you? Lapse. Something moving, coming down the trail towards me. Some animal in the dark, following the trail, slowly, about the size of a big house cat. My heart pounds faster as it comes closer, all my senses strain to make it out. Slows at finding me blocking the trail, sniffs, inches closer, sniffing. Inches from my shoes a vague form sniffing, sniffing, then snorting. Snorting loudly like it detests the smell of me. Moves off in the thicket of shrubbery, rustling the leaves as it makes a wide berth around me and comes back to the trail on the other side of me. Back on the trail it walks on away, a barely discernible waddling, rocking gait. By faint starlight I make out white stripes, a bushy tail held high. Skunk! I laugh for the first time in days, a dry shaking of my insides that bubbles up through my lungs and dissipates in breathy pleasure.

Lapse. Something hits my face. I barely notice. Then something hits my face again, and a stick falls into my lap. I come up from the deep vivid awareness of dark to the odd sense that someone's throwing sticks at me. Somehow I don't care. The crocodile brain isn't really a crocodile brain. It's more like a bigfoot brain. It's a place where there's only the wordless, instinctive doing of life. And I could see how I could stay here, I could live like this, I could go bigfoot. But something clamors where I'm not listening. Something like my mother calling me faintly when I was a child. Something I'm not supposed to ignore.

Then there's a sharp whistle that shatters the silence, a very human *threet!* from the bushes in front of me. My heart is thudding in my chest, but I'm strangely tranquil, as if a gunshot had gone off next to my ear and I'm in shock. All the bigfoot stories flood back to me—the way people are suddenly drowsy, lulled asleep yet still aware, grow stiff and unable to move, but still see what's going on around them. I knew that if I didn't surface up into words and get up and get moving, I was going to be face to face with something big and hairy that was going to want to throw me over its shoulder and carry me away. I struggle to my feet, stammering, "No . . . thank you, *schwanaí'tux*, that's okay . . ." My chest is cold with raw fear. I dig in my pockets for something, anything. My fingers close around a worn pack of matches, the only thing I've brought (just in case, right?) "Here . . . you can have these matches!" I say, and place the last vestige of my own doubt and will to control things on the ground where I was sitting. Turn and walk away up the trail, panting, heart pounding. I'm physically incapable of breaking into a run, but I stride along like an elderly mallwalker for half a mile until I get this image of myself fleeing for my life but trying not to look like it. Another laugh bubbles up out of me.

I find myself in places of incredible beauty and power. So slack and empty inside, so far beyond the thought of food or water anymore, moving so slowly that I seem to float in slow motion. Finding that I've been sitting for longer and longer times whenever I slumped down, coming out of reveries so deep that they hold no memory. Wondering what I'm doing out here, then remembering. Feeling where I am, whether it feels good and right to my body, or bad and wrong. Drawn by this sense to something roaring. Something that roars and feels good and right. A scraped and scoured granite hardrock country glittering with quartz and mica, that feels like love. So easy to love you, mother. A dull, seamless roaring and rushing draws me to a brink, an edge of smooth, rounded granite sheared away in a vertical drop-off. It's down there, in that narrow defile of timber, hidden, but there, I can hear it. So hard to ease down scree slopes and bouldery steeps with logs covered with soggy moss. So weak and inattentive, my body not working the way I remember it used to. But finally the open bottom of wet rocks and cold mist, so vague in overcast daylight, a small clear river falling, jugging, hissing, pounding down through a slot and rushing out at a plunge pool. Ears popping with the force shaking the earth so close at hand. Slumped and lost in the pulsing roar drowning out all else.

I've lost all sense of scale. I don't know how big the waterfall really is, or how close the little dipper bird is, standing there on the slippery rock. But he's looking at me, knows I'm here, as he does his little dipping motion. He seems big to me, white eye ring, no tail hardly. Slate black. Water ouzel. Ouzel? Where did that name come from? I don't know your name in Salish. They won't talk about you, say your name. You must have some great power, something to fear the consequences of trifling with you.

The dipper throws himself into the rush of water—he's a dark blur moving quickly along the pebbly bottom, finding good things to eat, disappearing for awhile; then, flying up out of the water far upstream, he stands on another rock. Does his squat thrusts on slippery rock, his dance of power. In again, walking on the bottom upstream, always upstream, then out and dipping in the roaring silence. Into the plunge pool, gone a long time, then flies right out of the explosive, raging froth at the bottom of the falls, to perch, dipping, in the spray at the side of the falling river of water. Then the thing so hard to believe: He flies out into the mist, turns, dives directly into the middle of the falls. Up near the top where the water comes over the edge still clear to the rock underneath, not yet vaporizing into a white blur, I see the vague, tiny, underwater zigzagging of the dipper, like switchbacking up a mountain trail. He forages his way right up to the river curl, then bursts out at the top for one last squatting dance on a rock before flying out of sight upstream.

Oh, the master of the raging mountain streams, the teacher of the lore of diving in ice cold water, the underwater power that flies in the air and dances on slippery rocks. That does impossible things down under there. How many times have I seen the shivering Okanogan kids come out of the river and dip up and down like that on the bank, then throw themselves back in? Things learned, taken to heart below the veil of words, how the powers of the world move in so many ways . . .

Up high where the wind blows, avoiding the wet lowlands at night now, staying up where the ceaseless invisible force pushes against my body, where I'm so alone in such vastness that I weep at how nothing is mine but this now of being aware. Yet it's so much I can hardly bear it, so vast and so full I would leave this world now so easily . . . But breaths keep coming, the heart thuds *pu'ús, pu'ús, pu'ús*. Yet another sunset and the wind is a voice moving over the land, huffing and roaring, falling and drifting, swirling around to speak on this side, then on that side. Big birds hang in a row in the updraft over a long, steep ridge, wings held outstretched, noses into the wind, drifting sideways, rocking in the strong gusts. Two big hawks, a vulture, several ravens, spaced out, playing like kids in a lineup, jostling and changing positions. At the end of the ridge each one dives, flaps hard, works around to the head of the line, and keeps the soaring line of birds going sideways in place. Doing nothing but enjoying the power that lifts and carries them, playing in the wind they were born to love and live by. All differences forgotten in the joy of the moment.

It comes to me, how many times I've dreamed I was doing what they are doing, soaring, arms wide, high in the sky with the earth moving by below. Seeing everything on earth as it looks from up there. Looking at what everybody's doing. I know that feeling. How there's a power that lifts and carries you, lets you turn and dive and rise and glide. Flying in dreams I knew instinctively that it was a little bit of me and a whole lot of an invisible, moving power around me that made it happen.

These lapses are disturbing. All I remember is the wind blasting against me as I sit, back resting against a lightning-shattered stub of tree, with still a few limbs alive, sweet-smelling boughs waving in the blow. But now it's night. Stars obscured by clouds. I haven't taken a breath in so long, I suck in the living air, the life-giving wind, feeling like that's all I am—a big lung that breathes.

Only the wind is real. And why is that? Who told me this secret? All I remember is that it was something whispered in my ear that I said out loud. Here, where I feel my life draining away, where I'm so weak and only a thin thread remains, breath is precious. Only the wind is keeping me alive.

So rough this night. So cold, so dry, so alone. I don't even remember what sleep is like. What am I doing here? Oh yeah, struggle to stand up in the dark wind, lean against the broken tree, among the shattered splinters of wood a foot thick and as long as I am lying around on the slope. Raise my hands up high. See me here, hear my voice, take pity on me. I have a mother who suffered for me. I have a father who is dying. This is me. You gave me life. Help me. I want to live.

Sitting there through the night with nothing but the raw emotion of clinging to life. Breathing. A sack of bones on a hillside. Why am I here? Clayton's voice comes back, telling me something about my childhood. Something back then when I was a boy. Do I remember when I was a boy? The images float by of the vaguely windy, hilly land where the prairie met the wooded bluffs that dropped down the muddy river. It's not like remembering the past, it's like reliving it, being there again, floating away to the house with two gabled windows sticking out of a steep shingled roof, walking in the fragrant alfalfa fields.

Mom and dad arguing behind a closed bedroom door. I'm throwing rocks at passing cars, trying to hit the hubcaps. The sky is yellowish-green and it's hot and humid, the silence broken only by my mother calling frantically for me to come inside. Then huddling with sweaty, pressed bodies all around me in the corner of the basement, listening to the tornado roaring like a freight train outside, toppling trees into the street.

In all my adult life, I've never been back here like this. How could someone so free, so innocent, so full of piss and vinegar grow up and come to this place of desolation, this sense of having no reason for going on in life, this clinging to a thread of hope that there might be something more than the running away to stay free that brought me to the Okanogan and this suffering alone in the cold night of the mountains?

More memories to relive. I go into them, walk around in them, feel their familiarity, feel their power in making me who I really am. Seeing those people who were just there to me as a child, now seen through adult eyes for the things they said that ring true, for the ways they behaved that I aped, for the way they treated me as how I came to feel about myself.

The mother who tucked us into bed at night, two brothers to a bed, wetting our cheeks with her kisses. The father who shared his love of tinkering with car engines with me, but who went into a rage when I came home late one night and hit me so hard my head crashed through a window. The grandmother who gave me paints and paper, who taught me how to draw and taught me not to fool myself about how good I was. The teacher who I loved like a second mother for her gentle voice and deep brown eyes. The uncle who dropped whatever he was doing to take me fishing, once even losing a job to take me fishing, who later died in a barroom brawl over a woman. The older boy, a man really, who I met one morning, an oddball like the older retarded guy we kids followed around . . . and the retarded guy talked so funny! Didn't care about anything, would pull his pants down and crap off a log into the creek just for the fun of it, stuff that made our parents worry we'd act like him. But this other oddball, the guy I met one morning, he's different, some kind of wizard or magician, maybe. He's standing there in the first rays of the sun on the grass, where the robins were hunting worms. He was so obviously glad to see me, he wanted to show me something, and as a robin flew by he simply reached out and caught it with one hand. He set the robin on its feet on his other hand held out flat, and I saw the way the robin's feet clung to his fingers. It stood there ruffling its feathers as I watched, awed, then it flew off. The guy smiled and told me it was easy, there was nothing to it.

Wait a minute. What was that again? He reached out and caught a bird flying by with his bare hand? I don't remember ever remembering this before . . . what's this memory doing here? And yet it's as clear and real as any of the other memories of my childhood that I've been reliving. He was so full of life, so compellingly attractive. So clearly trying to share something important with me. He told me things I don't remember, things about how you catch birds so easily. He was somebody so utterly familiar and meaningful to me, yet I never saw him again.

Something is clamoring inside me, but I ignore it, look around at the world, see it's almost sunrise, there's no wind. Take a deep breath and shake the cobwebs out of my head. So if this is something that really happened, why doesn't it fit into the flow of memories? Where are the things before and the things after? When and where did it happen? Okay—it was summer, at sunrise, and I recall the exact spot not far from my home. Yes, that was a place I walked by often, but what was I doing wandering around alone at sunrise? Suddenly I remembered the summer when I was about nine or ten. My mother telling me when I was grown up that I'd been so moody, going around alone, sleepwalking, appearing by her bed in the dark babbling, and sometimes she'd get up in the morning to find me already up and gone outside. Yes, I remembered those silent dawns before anybody stirred, and finding myself staring at the robins walking and stopping, cocking their heads, digging for worms with their beaks. And wondering how I came to be there. Back when life was a seamless flow of experiences. . . .

And the clamoring inside me suddenly bursts forth, grabbing my attention just as the sun does, rising in front of me a little to my left. So far away over the mountainous world of the Okanogan, but blindingly bright and bathing me in a yellow light. The wind is gone, it's utterly still, and I know this is the memory I've been looking for. That was the man who gave me a gift in childhood. The memory had existed in the ordinary events of my life, not as something amazing or visionary. It was just something I experienced, someone I met, and only now as an adult do I see it for what it was.

I realize that at the moment the man reached out and caught the robin, I was facing in this same direction, and the sun was rising in the same place, a little to my left. I'm bathed in the memory of him, how fascinating and powerful he seemed to my youthful eyes, how he felt like an older brother or an uncle to me. How easily he caught the robin flying by so fast. The sound of his voice, so encouraging, so clearly conveying to me that I could do the same. So full of love and warmth, and yet, as I recall now, from here as a grown man, he had a glittering hardness, an otherworldly glow about him standing there in the first rays of the sun like this. He was not like anybody else in my life, before or since.

My heart is full and warm, and I'm touched and energized by what I now know. All the little things in my long life that whispered something to me have become connected with this moment in my childhood. How I flowered into an older boy so full of life, how I became lucky, how I got away with things. How my parents began to see me as smart and talented. How I found things people had lost, how I recovered so quickly from terrible injuries, how I lived on an inner fire that sent me off into the world. And even in the horrors of America in the 1960s and 70s, war overseas and war in the streets at home, I made my way unscathed with something watching out for me. Squad leader, stockade troublemaker, campus protest marshal, border runner. Gas station mechanic, logger, shake splitter and ranch hand. All the way to bush hermit and barfly, hunter and scout, and now lonely, isolated human being, remembering how I came alive in this world, and I'm still here. Seeing how falcons show themselves to me and things happen that give me new life. The man who sneaks around borders, crosses frontiers and dives out of the blue after what gives him life.

It is enough. I'm so grateful, so filled to the brim. No words can say how deeply this has touched me. Incomprehensible events in my life suddenly make intuitive sense. I know how he wants me to be, to behave, to act in the world. I know I have to live this out. I know there's more—more about that sunrise encounter that I only vaguely recall—talk, sounds, doings. But I can't go any farther with it now. More will be revealed. Besides, I have him right here, now, in my chest, in my heart.

I know I'm to carry this back, so I stand up, so full of power and grace it startles me. I speak to the world, the spiritual government that saw fit to give me this gift, give thanks through eyes flooded with tears. So dry I have no saliva, yet I give water in gratitude, wetting our mother with tears falling to the ground.

It's time to return. Aflame with the memory I walk away from the lightning-shattered tree. I walk steadily for hours without tiring, easily visualizing the lay of the land and how to cut across country in the shortest way back to Clayton's camp. Then I hear the most beautiful sound and smell the most fragrant smell. A small, clear spring in willows. A tiny pool just big enough for my hand, just before the water spreads tinkling down the rocky slope. I sit and lift the water to my mouth, the icy unfamiliar wet that comes directly from the earth. It tastes like nothing, but my hand won't stop bringing up more. Ah, ah, ah! I'm alive! I will live! More and more swallows, feeling the trickle down into emptiness inside me, a cold layer of something in my guts. Finally I stop. More than ever before, exhaustion crushes down on me. Water gurgles inside me. Yes, alive, alive. . . .

I awaken by the spring hours later, come out of an utter black nothingness that seems like a lapse of a few seconds. The first sleep in days, my eyes raw and gluey. Everything so crisp and alive to my eyes again. I drink, drink, drink. Get up and go on. Following the high ground, the ridges, the easy trails. Hunger gnawing in my guts so stimulated by drinking water.

I'm standing under an aspen tree, staring unaccountably at a brownish-gray feather a few inches long lying on the grass. What? It's just a robin feather . . . then the memory floods back. I pick up the feather, hold it in my hand as I walk on. By this I will remember. By you leaving this here for me to see, to carry along and look at, I won't forget.

I sleep on a deer bed, wake up holding the feather. It's only a few more miles now. There's the back of Chopaka so close, there's the huge sweep of lodgepole forest where great fires burned in the 1920s, there's cows grazing the lush grass, there's the hazy valley lands so far below. I'm tottering now, stumbling with not much more gas left, but it's all downhill now, and if I stay on this four-wheel track, it'll take me right to the camp by the spring.

21

The taste of hot black tea and sweet mealy serviceberries—that's what I remember the most about coming back to civilization after my mission in the mountains.

I could see Clayton was expecting me. He wouldn't look at me—if you've ever been there when someone came down, you remember how their eyes can burn holes in things—but stood up from sitting by the fire ring as I walked up. He held in his hands the half bag of cedar and his bluejay fan, as if he hadn't moved for days since I walked away. Dumping the rest of the cedar onto the hot coals, he held me by the arm, leaned me into the thick smudge, then had me stand in the spreading drift of smoke while he brushed me off with his fan. Speaking to the powers of the world in Salish, his voice was a sleepy, quiet, soothing sound, but even so, it went through me like fingernails scraped across a blackboard just because I hadn't heard a human voice in so long. He finished with a high-pitched "*Wai i hwi*" as he patted my chest with his fan, sealing his work with a motion like pressing something into my heart and making sure it stayed there.

It was such a relief to sit on the ground as he built up the fire and poured tea and set down a bowl of the ripest, plumpest *shía* berries for me. It was embarrassingly difficult to form thoughts, much less actually say anything to him. I couldn't wipe the silly grin off my face, it was just so good to be in the presence of another human being again. It was the sweetest possible thing, this being with my own kind again, but a shyness kept my mouth shut. Clayton made it easy for me, never speaking directly to me. His camp was already struck and loaded into his car. He was ready to head down the mountain, but he sat impassively across the fire from me, carefully aware of me without intruding anything towards me.

I remember it was such a delight to eat again, crushing berries in my teeth, chewing with mouth muscles that hardly remembered how, swallowing, feeling them going down. Feeling something good and solid moving inside me again. And bitter tea so hot I had to sip slowly. Black tea steeped with some herb that smelled and tasted like wild anise. The fire so bright, so talkative, so intensely alive, burning the lodgepole pine branches so fiercely and quickly down to coals.

Another lapse into that dark void—not the last time—and I wake up on my back on the ground where I was sitting, the fire almost out. Clayton looks bored, glances over at me stirring to sit up. It's that last bittersweet moment of daylight, after sundown but the sky is still a cobalt blue. The cold evening air flows downhill, bringing a peaty, sprucey smell down from Chopaka. I stretch, wondering how my bed at home will feel after I've become so used to bare ground.

I go into the timber to relieve myself and when I come back the fire is out, soaking wet charcoal, and Clayton is sitting at the steering wheel of his car, warming up the engine. In and out of drowsy snatches of humming machinery and wind and glaring headlights, a long, winding, downhill drive back to another world. The heavy lowland air damp and full of strangely intense smells—cut hay and sagebrush and lake and pavement cooling in the dark of night.

Again we're at the Woods place on the River of White Swans, at the sweatlodge, and Clayton is standing around a big fire talking to other Indian men. I lean out my open car window and look up at the dark mass of Chopaka blocking out half the sky's stars. Up there where something, something . . . oh yeah, the man who showed me how to catch birds flying by, bare-handed, that odd young man from my childhood. I feel into my coat pockets, find the crumpled robin feather. The words "mission accomplished" run through my mind, making me laugh. Something is quickening inside me, words flood my mind, the social thing tugs at me, I want so bad to join the men around the fire, laugh, talk, be back in the world. But I know the lore. I won't cross that line back with my own kind until we're done in the sweatlodge.

Inside, alone, where Clayton put me at the far back, it was the rush of familiar, womblike comfort. The sweatlodge smell, like willow and sage and canvas and fir and musty earth. Men crawled in by the light of the fire, Clayton to my left by the pit, Old Willie so slow and fragile, sitting finally with a sigh to my right. Jim Woods handing things in, crawling in big as a sumo wrestler, pulling the canvas down so the only thing I could see was the orange inner glow of hot rocks.

I remember how no matter how much water Clayton splashed on the rocks and searing steam roared up, I wanted it hotter. I slapped my skin with my hands, blew superheated breath on myself, whipped myself with a fir branch, and still exulted in the burn, wishing it would just get really hot! In the steamy breath of Sweatlodge I heard my own voice return, blending with the other male voices, singing the old otherworldly songs that cried to us from so far away.

Then Jim crawled out to open up, and in the hissing, sputtering silence, I saw him out there sprawled and shiny wet by firelight, moaning softly. Old Willie said something in Salish, his voice so soft and slurred that all I could make out was something like "first hunter." Clayton *aaa*'d his words, sent Jim to the river for more water, and turned to me, his wet face by flamelight looking drawn and full of suffering at how hot he'd had to make it for me.

"Maybe now you have somethin' to say. This how they doin' it for the all time past, to go up there where the power is, and bring somethin' back. That maybe there some words for the people who wait. Because they give those gifts that the people may want to live."

Old Willie *aaa*'d in strong agreement.

Without thinking, the words came out of me. How I relived the scenes of my childhood. How I remembered an odd young man calling me over, standing in grass, in the first yellow light of sunrise. How he wanted to show me something, how he reached out and caught a robin flying by, how he held it out for me to see, and let it fly away. How he told me it was easy, how he told me things about catching birds I couldn't remember, and how I knew this was the one Clayton had told me had given me a gift in life.

The two old men *aaa*'d along with my telling. Jim returned and handed in Clayton's pitch basket full of cold water. At a word from Clayton, Jim closed the sweatlodge from the outside and steam burst again from the rocks. In the absolute darkness, Old Willie spoke at great length in his indecipherable, lisping Salish, his voice rising and falling in the chanting measures of telling a story, each phrase punctuated by a long pause that Clayton filled with his *aaa*'s. I was silent since I couldn't follow any of it. I was grateful when Clayton interpreted for me.

"He say he know that one. He see that one in his dream about you. Can't be say that one's name in the White man language, maybe punish him, take away his helpers. Then he die. Maybe when you learn more to talk the Indian language, he tell you more.

"That one who catch any kinda bird, any *skakáka*. That one real old, to be the one power good to find other powers. *Aaaa*, he that first hunter, got no song of his own, 'cause he know the songs of all the different birds. Up at sunrise, they all singin' to him like that, their different songs, what they offer to the come-alive people.

"See, like he say, *skakáka*, that's any kind of bird, any animal person who have feathers. In another way, we say *skakáka* to be the *shumíx*, any kind of power a person have. That time you just a boy, to be just *wusw'ásxa*, just the robin there in the grass, eat the worm, fly past. But any kind of bird. To catch any bird, any *skakáka*, that how he seen it work in the other man with that power. That how it work, what you got. That who that man is.

"What you seen that other time, we go upriver for *k'ulsht*, to train yourself for ten nights and days. To see them other persons over there, them other powers, how they like the animal, but also like the human person. You see it like that first hunter see it, he say. You see with his eyes, maybe.

"*Aaaa*, that the oldest one who hunt. First hunter. He give to the one he choose, the gift to be the good hunter. To catch game easy. Like in the old days, everybody look up to the providers. The one who have lotta meat, feed everybody. They be the leaders, like, because they the good providers. The parents want their daughters to marry the man who have that kinda gift, they know they live good, have all they need.

"But in another way, see, that first hunter give the gift to hunt for other power. Catch the songs easy. See, two ways to be the *shumíx*, two the same, but different. Like to catch easy whatever fly by."

Old Willie said something that sounded like English, and Clayton laughed, but I didn't understand. The older man turned and spoke right into my ear, his frail, sweaty hand cupped against my cheek, his words slow and carefully pronounced:

"Them days, man got that partner, to have a lotta wives, ain't it?"

I came slowly out of the deepest, most tenacious sleep into the gradual awareness that I was somewhere with people talking. It was like when I'd hunt on foot for days in the bitter cold of winter and finally be back warm at home—I'd sleep in utter oblivion around the clock and wake up, drifting in and out, ever-so-slowly surfacing just like this into the waking world. I was lying on somebody's couch. By its familiar smell, the recognizable adult female voices talking nearby and the murmur of the river outside an opened door, I knew I was in the Woods doublewide, on the front room couch. Was it last night that I came down from Chopaka?

Winking in and out of conscious awareness, I formed a picture of what I couldn't seem to open my eyes and see yet. The direct sunlight coming through the window so hot on my jeans told me it was afternoon. The children were playing a game just outside the opened door, the girls and one boy, Jim's nephew. He was playing a fish, and by the sound of scuffling on dirt, he was a wiggly one, not easy for the laughing girls to catch.

"This fish doesn't want to be caught!" the oldest girl's voice said, laughing. "He's a bad fish!" More giggles and shrieks as the girls tried to catch the struggling, flopping boy-fish. Then they must have caught him and carried him away, their voices receding out of earshot.

Still winking in and out, I hear Jim's sister, the boy-fish's mother, saying she played that game when she was a little girl, and how you never knew, some boys were good fish, easy to catch, and others were bad, and fought you all the way.

I got a picture of the four women sitting around the dining room table, sipping something from cups. Grandma, Charlene, the young mother, and Margaret Sisencha, Old Willie's sister. At least Charlene was busy with her beadwork from the familiar sound of a needle dipping into bead trays and the pulling tight of thread on loose material. I could smell the ever-present food-cooking smells coming from the kitchen.

"So did me and my friends," I heard Charlene's voice saying. "Clayton Tommy was always a good fish! But his brother was just terrible! Sometimes we never did catch him!" That would have been her deceased husband, never named directly, and the wistful warmth in her voice told me she had liked the bad fish better.

Grandma said she and her sisters played the game, too, taking the game back to the fourth generation present, but said it was different then because it was the children acting out what they witnessed the adults doing, the first fish ceremony at the time when the silvers were running in the creeks.

In summer the landlocked salmon or trout that lived in the lake by my own trailer would suddenly fill the creek that ran across the ranch hayfields with their flashing silver bodies, a day or two of vigorous spawning before they disappeared. One of the traditional *Skélux* foods, gathered in the old seasonal round, a sudden hoard of fish to trap and feast on and dry on wood racks. But nowadays only a few risk-takers like Jim Woods would sneak onto private ranch lands to hide in the bank willows and net a few so Grandma and other old timers could taste the fish again that they craved, that they said was so healing and was the best food to eat after fasting.

In the old days each important food had its "first one taken" ceremony, and for the silvers, the first fish caught was laid on huge arrowhead-shaped *shmucáhwin* leaves where it was prayed over, cooked in a special, respectful way, and everybody present ate a little of it before fishing commenced in earnest. Whether that first fish gave itself up easily to capture or struggled and fought was an important part of the gathering, carefully observed and much discussed as they fished and feasted and hung split fish bodies on the long stick racks in the dry sun. A struggling first fish might mean the silvers had been offended by something the people had done or failed to do, and an obviously willing fish could mean the silvers were happy to offer themselves and a season of plenty would follow.

"Yah, that how we played it, too," I heard Margaret's voice saying in her spirited, edgy way that I remembered even in my waking fog, which had silenced Larry Dubois way back when she told the story of Sweatlodge. "We had to figure out what we did wrong to make 'em so mad they fought us like that. Take care of it, so we wouldn't starve." Then her voice dropped to a softness I'd never heard from her. "My brother was always a good fish, too. In those days, the fish talked to us. Willie always said, 'My want that you live good!' Then we cut him up with our sticks like knives, you know, and he say, 'That feel good!'"

The giveaway of the self seals the pact with all that have a right to live in the world together. Such a power these women have, to hold and embody the Native way they were born into. And the children passing on to younger children an English-language version of the oldest way to play at living good in the world. Strange, sleep-fogged thoughts fading in the growling of my stomach, in the increasing interest my nose is taking in something delicious bubbling in a pot in the kitchen—one of the silvers.

"*Sáma* is awake and listening to us," Grandma said. "Go and see if that fish is done. He be up in a minute."

It was culture shock to be walking sidewalks and wearing town clothes again. Learning government jargon, memorizing federal program requirements, listening at staff meetings where seasoned social worker voices spoke of getting all our ducks in a row and being part of the solution instead of part of the problem. They didn't really have all the money they needed to fund my position, so half my time as north valley outreach worker was as a volunteer.

I was busy in a whole new life and there was hardly any time to stop and reflect. So many new people, meetings to attend, interviews with clients, forms to fill out. The kind of life I thought I'd left behind—but here I was, throwing myself into the thick of it, making something of it. I didn't realize how much Native talk had influenced me until I was called upon to talk up the community action "mission" at places like the chamber of commerce. With my own people it didn't work to use words like Clayton did—use language to direct the mind away from thinking and towards the nonverbal experience of things. I had to promote something not popular in the rural West—an ethic based on caring about and sharing with those not eating as much, not sheltered as well, not as healthy. They knew they were throwing the new kid to the lions, but I had fun with it anyway. In a rural county of mainly

Anglos still living out the old frontier mentality and preoccupied with cows, apples, alfalfa and logs, there was a lot of hostility to what I was doing.

"Heyyyyyyy, Hippie!" Stuart would yell from the window of his pickup when he came to town, his grin a mile wide. Hair grows long when you don't cut it.

"Heyyyyyyy, Redneck!" I'd yell back, and step up to his door with my leather briefcase in hand.

"You still throwin' away our hard-earned tax dollars to any bum with his hand out? Why don't you get a real job?"

"Like what? Feeding cows? Watching the grass go in and the shit come out?"

"Raisin' beef is an honorable calling! Anyway—I hate to see you like this, all duded up. And on foot! I heard your pickup gasped its last. Old Bob has a car for sale at the Chevron station. Cheap, but it runs. I suppose my tax dollars are keeping you in cash, hey?"

My new car was a late sixties white Ford Falcon station wagon that burned oil but got me around. Okanogan County was about the size of Connecticut, with thirty thousand people spread thin, and in those days there was only one stop light, thirty miles south in the biggest town, Omak. Distances were far, only the main roads were paved, and many communities I had to visit were on the other side of mountains. I needed a car, and it took everything I'd ever learned from my father to keep this one running.

"A Falcon, eh?" Jim mused. "Now *there's* a coincidence . . . or is it?"

I knew my car seemed familiar somehow, but it wasn't until I parked next to Clayton's full-size white Ford station wagon that it hit me. It was like a smaller version of his. Jim sat on his front porch looking from one car to the other in mock confusion. Then he looked inspired.

"I can see where this is going!" he said. "Ya know, Uncle

Clayton's woman, she has that daughter, Rose, the skinny one that won't give me the time of day, you know her? Well, I hear she's lookin' for a man, eh?"

The phone rang one morning, so early it was still dark outside the little frame cottage I'd rented at the edge of town. I'd never had a phone of my own before that, but it was something I had to have in my new job. It had taken a month for me to stop jumping every time it rang. I got out of bed and went to the kitchen listening to the sound of ringing to find the phone in the dark. Outside, headlights crossed at a distance, the apple shed workers crossing the bridge over the Okanogan River on the way to work.

"Hello."

"*Uch iklí* Clayton Tommy?" an unfamiliar, older male voice asked.

"*Loot alá* (Not here)," I answered.

Click. I smile in the dark, hang up the phone, entertained already so early in the morning. The old full bloods don't waste a word. I don't know who it was, but probably some old pal of Clayton's, somebody who knew to look for him at my house. Since he wasn't here, that's all there is to it.

What a difference from all the ritual Anglo blah-blah-blah I'd been going through in my calls to make appointments—the elaborate phrasings to explain everything, the careful words to make things work.

I remember sitting there, looking out the window, staring at the first blush of dawn on dark sagebrush hills. The curved sliver of an old moon about to disappear for awhile. The morning star rising so bright and steady. The smell of new paint in a strange house. I was up anyway, and I had to drive to the county seat for my one day a week in the office . . . might as well go for a walkabout out there. I'd be stuck all day in an office under fluorescent lights, my paperwork spread around me on an unused table. And I didn't have to leave for hours.

Out in the cool fragrance of summer dawn, I headed away from the lights of town and up beyond the last orchard, into the hills where waist-high dusty sagebrush felt so good brushing against my legs again. Along the way I remembered it was Clayton's birthday tomorrow, and I was invited out to the feast of traditional foods at the Woods place, the excuse of his birthday as good as any other to get together and eat, just like that first day I arrived in the Okanogan. In my shirt pocket is a folded envelope—plane tickets to fly down and visit my mother and father over the next long weekend off.

In no time I was up on the glacial benchland and behind the screen of hills where the only sounds were the first songs of day birds and the rush of a creek over rocks. Daylight grew and it was so warm already I knew it was going to be another blistering hot day. The creek was hidden in thick riparian undergrowth, a brushy tangle of alder, sumac, serviceberry and wild rose under the cottonwoods lining the bank. I had to get down on all fours and crawl into the wall of leaves to get to the stream of cold water tumbling down over slippery rocks. Quail called invisibly all around me, *síkaka, síkaka*. The alders leaned over from both banks, interlaced overhead, making a hidden tunnel I could barely sit up in.

I looked upcreek as the first brilliant light of the rising sun streamed through the leaves and lit up the water rushing toward me. For a long time I stared thoughtlessly at the misty glitter, the foamy pounding, the palpable solidity of wet air trapped and illuminated in the low, narrow, green leafy passage. Then movement at a distant turn, something flying down the tunnel towards me, so fast I barely register the blind bird eyes staring where it's going, past the obstruction of me, like I'm just another tree at a narrow place in the tunnel. Without thinking, I reached up and caught the bird flying by my shoulder.

It isn't anything like I might have imagined. I don't know how I did it—it felt like someone else doing it. The smack of a speeding fluffy robin against my palm, the impact that leaves downy feathers floating in the air, my fingers closed around fragile, outstretched wings and neck. The robin is limp, and I'm suddenly sorry I killed it for no reason. But then I cradle the almost weightless form in both hands and I can feel the tiny heart beating furiously.

The robin comes to, grabs my fingers with scaly toes and stands up, ruffling and grooming its feathers, looking around a little dazed. It preens on my outstretched hand, then lets loose with a few notes of song. I feel the sudden push and release as it springs up and flies away downstream.

Afterword

I tried to label this book a nonfiction novel, but few who've read it mistake it for fiction. I will say that I stayed as close to the truth of what happened to me as I could and still tell a good story, because this is life and death stuff and there's no good fooling ourselves about it. Because I lived and learned from Indians (yes, that's still what they call themselves in English in Indian Country), I couldn't help but tell their story, too, as it informed and affected me. But since I'm not here to speak for the Native people who helped me, I fictionalized the heck out of their side of the story, making everybody who appears in this book except for myself unrecognizable as actual persons. I also purposely moved most of the events to a different location to protect the privacy of everyone involved.

Going public with things shared privately for my ears only has not been easy. Some of those whose words or versions of sacred stories appear in this book died before I even thought of writing a book. The others agreed with me that telling how I came to know their lore was indispensable to understanding what happened to me. One elder, before he died, gave me specific permission and encouragement to tell all the stories he'd shared with me. His words kept me focused on telling the only story that's really mine—my own personal story.

"I knew you pass it on someday. That how it work."